# A YEAR WITH
# THOMAS MERTON

# A YEAR WITH
# THOMAS MERTON

*Daily Meditations from His Journals*

## Thomas Merton

Selected and edited by Jonathan Montaldo

HarperOne
*An Imprint of* HarperCollins*Publishers*

HarperOne

Library of Congress Cataloging-in-Publication Data
Merton, Thomas, 1915–1968.
A year with Thomas Merton : daily meditations from his journals /
Thomas Merton ; selected and edited by Jonathan Montaldo. — 1st ed.
p. cm
ISBN: 978-0-06-075472-3
1. Devotional calendars—Catholic Church. 2. Catholic Church—
Prayer books and devotions—English. I. Montaldo, Jonathan. II. Title.
BX2170.C56M485 2004
242'.2—dc22 2004054000

08 09 10 11 (RRDH) 10 9 8 7 6

# ACKNOWLEDGMENTS
# AND DEDICATION

Bellarmine University's Thomas Merton Center in Louisville, Kentucky, the major and official collection of Merton's legacy, preserves over a thousand of Merton's black ink drawings. *Dialogues with Silence: Prayers & Drawings* recently exhibited a hundred of these works. The Center also preserves nearly twelve hundred of Merton's photographs. I thank Dr. Paul M. Pearson of the Thomas Merton Center at Bellarmine and Kris Ashley of Harper San Francisco for their assistance in choosing and preparing the drawings and photographs that illustrate *A Year with Thomas Merton*. I am equally grateful to Anne McCormick, the New York–based trustee of the Merton Legacy Trust, for expertly steering this book toward publication.

The photographs and drawings that appear in this volume are by Thomas Merton and are used with the permission of the Merton Legacy Trust. All journal entries are from the seven volumes of Merton's journals published by HarperSanFrancisco. Each journal entry is referenced by its original date, the volume in which it appears (I–VII), and by page number.

Tommie O'Callaghan, a personal friend of Merton's in Louisville, Kentucky, and another Merton Legacy trustee, conceived the idea for this book and significantly aided its editing. She had been introduced to Merton by his friend and mentor Dan

Walsh, who had also been Tommie's university professor. Tommie was delighted but never overawed in Merton's company, and thus Merton was comfortable in giving her his confidences and close friendship. When in the city on doctor's visits, Merton would often repair to Tommie's home, sharing time and food with her and her husband, Frank, and their seven children. The O'Callaghans became Merton's Louisville family, and he often enlisted them to provide hospitality for his out-of-town visitors. When Merton formed the Merton Legacy Trust in 1967, which ensured the protection of his artistic legacy and would provide oversight for any publication of his work after his death, he chose Tommie as one of the three original trustees. Thus, since the Trust's creation, Tommie remains the only still active original trustee. For nearly half a century Tommie and Frank O'Callaghan have opened their home to countless Merton friends, researchers, and pilgrims to Gethsemani Abbey and Bellarmine University's Merton Center. *A Year with Thomas Merton* is thus dedicated with gratitude to Tommie and Frank O'Callaghan and their still-thriving collaboration in preserving and extending their friend's legacy of ecumenical hospitality.

# LEARNING LOVE'S LANGUAGE:
## THE SPEECH A DAY MAKES

*It is necessary for me to see the first point of light that begins to be dawn. It is necessary to be present alone at the resurrection of Day in solemn silence at which the sun appears, for at this moment all the affairs of cities, of governments, of war departments, are seen to be the bickering of mice. I receive from the Eastern woods, the tall oaks, the one word DAY. It is never the same. It is always in a totally new language.*

THOMAS MERTON
(*Journals*, MAY 1965)

On December 10, 1941, Thomas Merton arrived at the Trappist Abbey of Our Lady of Gethsemani and began his well-documented twenty-seven-year journey toward becoming a monk. Days before his departure for Kentucky, Merton had written a letter dated December 6 to his best friend, Robert Lax. He wrote Lax to say that he was renouncing any future he might have had in New York in favor of discovering a better country and learning its new language. At Gethsemani Merton hoped he could learn to speak in an idiom that more perfectly translated all his experiences into the language of God's mercy to him.

Merton was young when he entered the monastery, nearly two months short of his twenty-seventh birthday. Although his autobiography, *The Seven Storey Mountain,* would not make its epiphany until seven years later, in 1948, Merton had all along been cultivating the rich and tangled roots of his experiences toward God by writing about them. At sixteen Merton was writing personal journals. He had a gift for autobiography as he possessed a phenomenal visual memory. Years after the fact, for instance, he could describe all the landmarks in sequence and detail that had dotted the route of his daily bus ride from his aunt Maude's house to high school in England. His journals record an instance of a game he played (May 14, 1941), in which he described his general activities on the same day for the ten years prior to 1931! As he ruminated on the ever-growing archive of his journals, the young writer discovered hidden turning points that were guiding him toward the unfolding of his personal destiny. As a young man Merton knew he was a writer, but by writing journals he plotted a path toward realizing the unexpected vocation of becoming a monk.

The early autobiographical writing was Merton's way of gathering the strands of his youth's disparate experiences so as to map his way forward and out of his first three decades. *The Seven Storey Mountain,* written when he was thirty and had been in the monastery four years, was Merton's retrospective on the "book" of his early journals. His autobiography chronicled his orphaned childhood and a desperate adolescence that were radically transformed by a more merciful providence when he accepted baptism as a Roman Catholic at Corpus Christi Church in Manhattan when he was twenty-three years old.

Prominent among the premonastic experiences that Merton was translating into deeper meanings as he wrote journals was the loss of his mother, Ruth, to cancer when he was only six. Then he was orphaned and on his own after the death of his beloved artist father, Owen, when he was only sixteen, an event that might have commenced his writing journals. Although the most seriously sorry event was censored from the autobiography, in his early journals he excavated the deeper provocations for having made a mess of his freshman year at Cambridge University in England, when he partied too much and slept around—and fractured his jaunty adolescent self-image badly by fathering a child and escaping responsibility with the help of his mother's father. Where was the silver lining in the cloud for him as he fled England for America and Columbia University in New York City? Who and what experiences guided his conversion to Roman Catholicism and then moved him to want to become a priest, even as he continued to nurse literary ambitions of having his novels published by the best New York houses? What or who providentially cleared his safe passage across the Atlantic from England to deliver him to the best years of his youth at Columbia in New York and then finally guided him to a monastery in Kentucky, which became, according to his autobiography, *the house that would hide [him] in the secret of [God's] face?*

In that letter to his best friend, Robert Lax, only days before his departure for Gethsemani, Merton consciously made the metaphorical correlation between his wanting to become a monk of Gethsemani and his wanting to learn a new language.

*Maybe St. Lucy's Day I start out for Kentucky, full of prayer. (Next Saturday). . . . There is absolutely no language to say the things that are to say about this except the language of love: but there He will teach me to use that language like a child and a saint. Until which I cannot talk about Him, Who is all I want to talk about.*

*And in Him, while I sing in the big church, will be also: Lax, Gibney, Seymour, Slate, Rice, Gerdy, Knight, Huttlinger,*

*and Van Doren, and the Baroness, and Mary Jerdo, and my*
*brother and my uncle and my aunt and my father and mother*
*who died and Bramachari and the whole mystical body of*
*Christ, everybody: Roger, Gil, all people, Jinny, Lilly. All people.*
*The living and the dead. All days, all times, all ages, all worlds,*
*all mysteries, all miracles. . . .* (The Road to Joy, New York,
*1989, 163–64)*

These final paragraphs reveal a quality of Merton's inner work as a monk and writer that would endure until his death. God's destiny for Merton always manifested itself as a *word* spoken to him for his salvation in the context of his relationships with everything he deeply loved: persons, nature, books, ideas—the remembered beautiful things of his entire life. His "farewell letter" to Lax concludes by evoking the mystical body of his best friends. As the letter's concluding litany of intimate persons expands to include *all ages, all worlds, all mysteries,* its evocation of ever-widening communities of inclusion reveals Merton's enduring intuition that becoming a monk would never require breaking his inner ties with everyone and everything in his past. Becoming a monk would never mean he had to lose all things for God. As the writer paradoxically embraced the silence of a monk, Merton was discovering the best means for him, because it was a writer's precarious and thus high-tensioned means, to recover and keep all things for God.

Merton would write books, essays, poetry, letters, and journals all his monastic life as his monk's way of handing over to his most receptive readers, like his friend Bob Lax, the harvest of his inner experiences. Writing as a monk about his inner experiences became one of Merton's major spiritual exercises. Merton always discovered who he was becoming and might yet become by writing about everything that had propelled and was still driving him forward. Writing journals became Merton's way of living out more consciously the meaning of his life, step by significant step. Writing journals allowed him to savor and even taste again the complex flavors of everything he had always quickly gulped down of his life's rich juice.

He avowed that he wrote so that *life lived itself* through him (April 14, 1966). He wrote in his journals that writing was his means to *think and to live, even, to pray* (September 27, 1958). Particularly by writing journals, Merton incarnated and revealed the hidden, deeper patterns of his inner life. He documented in journals God's secret epiphanies to him between the lines of his everyday experiences.

Merton's journals collectively became his life's *book into which everything can go* (July 17, 1956). Writing journals was his way of gaining access to a center in himself, call it his soul, or call it what he called it, a *virgin point,* where he caught momentary glimpses of the widest dimensions of his deepest self in God. He wrote journals to stay awake and attentive to the life he was being given in all its particulars and to archive his conversations with every individual thing in his life that had spoken a *word* to him for his salvation.

The question of how Merton's journal writing has remained a powerful witness to the reality of others' inner experience is only partially answered by Merton's decision to allow his journal writing to be published. He needed to write journals as part of *a documentation demanded of [him] by the Holy Spirit* (October 22, 1952). Merton's writer's life, he eventually decided, would be the unique form by which his monk's life would become efficacious for others. He realized that the *words* he heard, in response to his mindfulness through an ordinary day, were *words* not only spoken to him for his own salvation but were also spoken through him for the salvation of others:

*In the last analysis what I am looking for in solitude is not happiness or fulfillment but salvation. Not "my own" salvation, but the salvation of everybody. . . . I am here for one thing: to be open, not to be "closed in" on any one choice to the exclusion of all others: to be open to God's will and freedom, to His love which comes to save me from all in myself that resists Him and says no to Him. This I must do not to justify myself, not to be right, not to be good, but because the whole world of lost people needs this opening by which salvation can get into [the world] through me. (June 24, 1966)*

Merton's extant journals from 1939 through 1968 have been published in seven volumes by Harper San Francisco. *The Intimate Merton: His Life from His Journals* culled entries from these seven volumes and presented chronologically in diary format his journals' major themes. By contrast, *A Year with Thomas Merton* features day-by-day reflections from his journals that range without chronological order through the twenty-nine years of extant journals. While they give the sense of reading a continuous day-by-day diary, the daily reflections in *A Year with Thomas Merton* are in fact separated by years, and yet they resonate with one another through themes of Merton's seeking God and listening for God's voice in solitude, of Merton's doing what monastic tradition calls "the work of the cell": learning to live with himself just as he was, through all his contradictory experiences, in the presence of a merciful and loving God.

Each journal entry in *A Year with Thomas Merton* unites with its companions by being a product of Merton's continually inclining his heart's ear, in obedience, to the speech a *day* made for his salvation. The first movement of his obedience was being present to a new day by waiting in silent receptivity until *day* spoke its "word" to him. His second move of obedience, *demanded of him by the Holy Spirit,* was to write down whatever of his dialogue with *day's* word for him that might prove meaningful for someone else.

This book's entry for December 31 is a beautifully adequate summary of what, after twenty-seven years of monastic life, Merton might have said of his life, conceived by him as a book into which everything was allowed to go. He writes that he knew he had experienced throughout his life the immense mercy of God. He knew himself atypical and unclassifiable as a monk and hermit: he had loved a wide variety of persons and things and had not forgone their physical company or their spiritual presence in his heart, mind, and writing. And even though mystically living out connections to all peoples, worlds, and times, Merton still considered his essential vocation to have been that of a solitary. He judged that all his speech and writing about God had been impertinent except for the writing in which he praised God out of his silences, for the writing in which he expressed his gratitude for the mysterious vocation of being both a Trappist monk and a writer, two seemingly opposed vocations that he had learned to hold together in a productive, creative tension. At the end of his day, Merton knew he would remain a gloriously and dramatically unsatisfied human being because he had learned the hard way that his very dissatisfaction with himself—always needing more of God's mercy, not less—was the secret fuel that had kept his life's affirming flame burning strong:

> *Lay in bed and realized what I was: I was happy. Said the strange word "happiness" and realized that it was there, not as an "it" or object. It simply was. And I was that. And this morning, coming down, seeing the multitude of stars above the bare branches of the wood, I was suddenly hit, as it were, with the*

*whole package of the meaning of everything: that the immense*
*mercy of God was upon me, that the Lord in infinite kindness*
*had looked down on me and given me this vocation out of love,*
*and that he had always intended this, and how foolish and triv-*
*ial had been all my fears and desperation. And no matter what*
*anyone else might do or say about it, however they might judge*
*or evaluate it, all is irrelevant in the reality of my vocation to*
*solitude, even though I am not a typical hermit. Quite the con-*
*trary, perhaps. It does not matter how I may or may not be classi-*
*fied. In the light of this simple fact of God's love and the form it*
*has taken in the mystery of my life, classifications are ludicrous,*
*and I have no further need to occupy my mind with them (if I*
*ever did)—at least in this connection.*

*The only response is to go out from yourself with all that*
*one is, which is nothing, and pour out that nothingness in grati-*
*tude that God is who He is. All speech is impertinent; it destroys*
*the simplicity of that nothing before God by making it seem as if*
*it had been "something." (December 9, 1964)*

It does remain, however, something of a mystery how a Trappist-
Cistercian monk, who lived out of his own specific moments in
history (1915–1968), by exposing his life's text can continue to be
a witness for readers so that they can make their own journeys
through their own uniquely experienced territories. Merton
wrote and prayed out of the unique roots of his own life, and yet
his artistic and spiritual legacy continues to communicate universal inner experiences that allow his readers, as they enter Merton's
inner life, to reenter the school of their own lives. There they can
rediscover and relearn for themselves the language Love speaks
when *the heavens are telling the glory of God; and the firmament pro-*
*claims his handiwork. Day to day pours forth speech, and night to night*

*declares knowledge. There is no speech, nor are there words; their voice is not heard; yet their voice goes out through all the earth and their words to the end of the world* (Psalm 19).

Navigating the text of his own life, Thomas Merton learned that Love is everybody's native language. Love's grammar binds us to everyone through all times and places. Love is the language of God's Book, into which everything God creates is always allowed to go. Love was the hidden ground of Merton's text, as Love is the hidden ground of ours, and Love's encoded message in Merton's and everyone's unique life paradoxically needs no translation. Test it for yourself in Merton's journal texts, bound together here within a fictive year. Place your heart's ear to this book's body and listen below its words for Love's ancient language, which you already know but will experience as ever new: the speech a *day* makes.

*Jonathan Montaldo*
*December 10, 2004*

# A Breath of Zen

Fidelity to grace in my life is fidelity to simplicity, rejecting ambition and analysis and elaborate thought, or even elaborate concern.

A breath of Zen blows all these cobwebs out the window.

It is certainly true that what is needed is to get back to the "original face" and drop off all the piled-up garments of thought that do not fit me and are not "mine"—but to take only what is nameless.

I have been absurdly burdened since the beginning of the year with the illusions of "great responsibility" and of a task to be done. Actually whatever work is to be done is God's work and not mine, and I will not help matters, only hinder them, by too much care.

Sunrise—an event that calls forth solemn music in the very depths of one's being, as if one's whole being had to attune itself to the cosmos and praise God for a new day, praise Him in the name of all the beings that ever were or ever will be—as though *now* upon me falls the responsibility of seeing what all my ancestors have seen, and acknowledging it, and praising God, so that, whether or not *they* praised God back then, themselves, they can do so *now* in me.

Sunrise demands this rightness, this order, this true disposition of one's whole being.

*January 20–21, 1963, IV. 291–92*

JANUARY 2

# The Silence in Yourself

Yesterday it looked like snow. Today there is deep snow, and the sun is out, and the cedars full of snow stand up against a bright blue sky and the white hills are in a sort of haze and the abbey buildings are golden. That is the way Gethsemani looks in winter and Frater Linus's box of Kodachromes is full of just such pictures.

Yesterday, when I was reading in the cemetery, I thought how the silence you find in yourself, when you enter in and rest in God, is always the same and always new, even though it is unchanging. For that silence is true life and, even though your body moves around (as mine did vigorously, being cold), your soul stays in the same place, resting in its life Who is God, now in winter just as it did before in summer, without any apparent difference, as if nothing had changed at all, and the passage of seasons had only been an illusion.

For the first time since the beginning of December, I went out to work to let some fresh air into my stuffy head and let a few phantasms fly away into the trees. We broke rock down on the road to the lower bottom, outside the enclosure, past the horse barn. How good it was to be out working with my brothers! And I felt this even about those who ordinarily rub me the wrong way! How good it is to have a rule in which simplicity and poverty and hardship play so large a part so that you can give yourself up to God by it!

*January 17 and 21, 1948, II.158–59*

# New Year's Darkness

The year struggles with its own blackness.

Dark, wet mush of snow under frozen rain for two days. Everything is curtained in purple greyness and ice. Fog gets in the throat. A desolation of wetness and waste, turning to mud.

Only New Year's Day was bright. Very cold. Everything hard and sparkling, trees heavy with snow. I went for a walk up the side of the Vineyard Knob, on the road to the fire tower, in secret hope of "raising the sparks" (as the Hassidim say), and they rose a little. It was quiet, but too bright, as if this celebration belonged not to the New Year or to any year.

More germane to this new year is darkness, wetness, ice and cold, the scent of illness.

But maybe that is good. Who can tell?

The morning was dark, with a harder bluer darkness than yesterday. The hills stood out stark and black, the pines were black over thin pale sheets of snow. A more interesting and tougher murkiness. Snowflakes began to blow when I went down to the monastery from the hermitage, but by 10:30 the sun was fairly out and it was rapidly getting colder.

Evening—new moon—snow hard crackling and squealing under my rubber boots. The dark pines over the hermitage. The graceful black fans and branches of the tall oaks between my field and the monastery. I said Compline and looked at the cold valley and tasted its peace. Who is entitled to such peace? I don't know. But I would be foolish to leave it for no reason.

*January 3 and 4, 1968, VII.32–33*

# The Speech of God Is Silence

For the first time in my life I am finding you, O Solitude. I can count on the fingers of one hand the few short moments of purity, of neutrality, in which I have found you. Now I know I am coming to the day in which I will be able to live without words, even outside my prayer. For I still need to go out into this no-man's-land of language, which does not quite join me to others and which throws a veil over my own solitude. I say "live without words." By *words* I mean the half-helpless and half-wise looks by which we seek one another's thoughts. But I do not abdicate all language, for there is the Word of God. This I proclaim and I live to proclaim it. I live to utter the Mass, the Canon, which implicitly contains all words, all revelation, and teaches everything. It is at the Canon and at the words of Consecration that all solitudes come into a single focus. There is the City of God gathered together in that one Word spoken in silence. The speech of God is silence. His Word is solitude. Him I will never deny, by His grace! Everything else is fiction, half-hiding the truth it tries to reveal. We are travelers from the half-world of language into solitude and infinity. We are strangers. Paper, I have not in you a lasting city. Yet, there is a return from solitude to make manifest His Name to them who have not known it. And then to re-enter solitude again and dwell in silence.

*January 11, 1950, II.158*

# Her Presence Demands My Love

A cold night. Woke up to find the night filled with the depth and silence of snow. Stayed up here in the hermitage for supper last night, but having cooked soup and cut up a pear and a banana for dessert, and made toast, finally came to the conclusion that it was all too elaborate. If there were no better reason for fasting, the mere fact of saving time would be a good enough reason. For the bowl and the saucepan have to be washed, and I have only a bucket of rainwater for washing, etc., etc. Taking only coffee for breakfast makes a lot of sense, because I can read quietly and sip my two mugs of coffee at leisure, and it really suffices for the morning.

There is a great need for discipline in meditation. Reading helps. The early morning hours are good, though in the morning meditation (one hour) I am easily distracted by the fire. An hour is not much, but I can be more meditative in the hour of reading that follows (and which goes much too fast). The presence of Our Lady is important to me. Elusive but I think a reality in this hermitage. Her influence is a demand of love, and no amount of talking will explain it. I need her and she is there. I should perhaps think of it explicitly more often.

In the afternoon, work takes up so much time, and there can be so much. Just keeping the place clean is already a big task. Then there is wood to be chopped, etc. The fire is voracious—but pleasant company.

*January 30, 1965, V.196–97*

# Winter Hermitage Under Black Pines

It is turning into the most brilliant of winters.

At 6:45—stepped out into the zero cold for a breath of air. Brilliance of Venus hanging as it were on one of the dim horns of Scorpio. Frozen snow. Deep wide blue-brown tracks of the tractor that came to get my gas tank the other day when everything was mucky. Bright hermitage settled quietly under black pines. I came in from saying the psalms of the Little Hours and the Rosary in the snow with my nose in pain and sinuses aching. Ears burn now in the silent sunlit room. Whisper of the gas fire. Blue shadows where feet have left frozen prints out there in the snow. I drank a glass of dry sherry and am warm! Lovely morning! How lovely life can be!

*January 5, 1968, VII. 33–34*

# The Sin of Wanting to Be Heard

The question of writing: definitely it has to be cut down, or changed.

Someone accused me of being a "high priest" of creativity. Or, at least, of allowing people to regard me as one. This is perhaps true.

The sin of *wanting to be a pontiff,* of wanting to be heard, of wanting converts, disciples. Being in a cloister, I thought I did not want this. Of course I did, and everyone knows it.

St. William, says the Breviary this night, when death approached, took off his pontifical vestments (what he was doing with them on in bed I can't imagine) and by his own efforts got to the floor and died.

So I am like him, in bed with a miter on. What am I going to do about it?

I have got to face the fact that there is in me a desire for survival as pontiff, prophet, and writer, and this has to be renounced before I can be myself at last.

*January 19, 1961, IV.87*

# Solitude and Gentleness

It is in deep solitude that I find the gentleness with which I can truly love my brothers. The more solitary I am, the more affection I have for them. It is pure affection, and filled with reverence for the solitude of others. Solitude and silence teach me to love my brothers for what they are, not for what they say. It is no longer a question of dishonoring them by accepting their fictions, believing in their image of themselves, which their weakness obliges them to compose, the wan work of communication. Yet there will, it is true, always remain a dialectic between the words of men and their being. This will tell something about them we would not have realized if the words had not been there.

Solitude is not merely a negative relationship. It is not merely the absence of people or of presence with people. True solitude is a participation in the solitariness of God—Who is in all things. Solitude is not a matter of being something *more* than other men, except by accident: for those who cannot be alone cannot find their true being and they are less than themselves. Solitude means withdrawal from an artificial and fictional level of being which men, divided by original sin, have fabricated in order to keep peace with concupiscence and death. But by that very fact the solitary finds himself on the level of a more perfect spiritual society—the city of those who have become real enough to confess and glorify God (that is, life) in the teeth of death. Solitude and society are formed and perfected in the Sacrifice of the Mass.

*January 12, 1950, II.398–99*

# Deepening the Present

I have entered the new and holy year with the feeling that I have somehow, secretly, been granted a new life and a new hope—or a return of the old life and hope I used to have.

The contemplative life becomes awfully thin and drab if you go for several days at a time without thinking explicitly of the Passion of Christ. I do not mean, necessarily, meditation, but at least attending with love and humility to Christ on the Cross. For His Cross is the source of all our life, and without it prayer dries up and everything goes dead.

A saint is not so much a man who realizes that he possesses virtues and sanctity as one who is overwhelmed by the sanctity of God. God is holiness. And therefore things are holy in proportion as they share Who He is. All creatures are holy in so far as they share in His being, but we are called to be holy in a far superior way—by somehow sharing His transcendence and rising above the level of everything that is not God.

Solitude is not found so much by looking outside the boundaries of your dwelling, as by staying within. Solitude is not something you must hope for in the future. Rather, it is a deepening of the present, and unless you look for solitude in the present, you will never find it.

*January 2–3, 1950, II.391–92*

# God Is the Room I Rest In

God's love takes care of everything I do. He guides me in all my work and in my reading, at least until I get greedy and start rushing from page to page. It is really illogical that I should get temptations to run off to another monastery and to another Order of monks. God has put me in a place where I can spend hour after hour, each day, in occupations that are always on the borderline of prayer. There is always a chance to step over the line and enter into simple and contemplative union with God. I get plenty of time alone before the Blessed Sacrament. I have gotten into the habit of walking up and down under the trees, or along the way of the cemetery, in the presence of God. And yet I am such a fool that I can consent to imagine that in some other situation I would quickly advance to a high degree of prayer. If I went anywhere else, I would almost certainly be much worse off than here. And, anyway, I did not come to Gethsemani for myself but for God. God is my order and my cell. He is my religious life and my rule. He has disposed everything in my life in order to draw me inward, where I can see Him and rest in Him. He has put me in this place because He wants me in this place, and if He ever wants to put me anywhere else, He will do so in a way that will leave no doubt as to who is doing it.

*January 14, 1947, II.36*

# With a Pure and Empty Heart

My great obligation is to obey God, and to seek His will carefully with a pure and empty heart. Not to try to impose my own order on my life but let God impose His. To serve His will and His order by realizing them in my own life. This means certainly a *deep consent* to all that is actually and manifestly His will for me.

After dinner—read the *Prometheus Bound* of Aeschylus. Shattered by it. I do not know when I have read anything so stupendous and so completely contemporary. I felt like throwing away everything and reading nothing but Aeschylus for six months. Like discovering a mountain full of diamond mines. It is like Zen—like Dostoevsky—like existentialism—like Francis—like the New Testament. It is inconceivably rich. I consider this a great grace. A great religious experience. Prometheus, archetypal representation of the suffering Christ. But we must go deep into this. Prometheus startles us by being more fully Christ than the Lord of our own clichés—I mean, he is free from all the falsifications and limitations of our hackneyed vision which has slowly emptied itself of reality.

*January 17 and 19, 1960, III.370*

# The Peace of Being Nothing Special

It seems to me that I have greater peace and am close to God when I am not "trying to be a contemplative," or trying to be anything special, but simply orienting my life fully and completely towards what seems to be required of a man like me at a time like this.

I am obscurely convinced that there is a need in the world for something I can provide and that there is a need for me to provide it. True, someone else can do it, God does not need me. But I feel He is asking me to provide it.

At the consecration of my Mass I suddenly thought of the words: "If you love me, feed my sheep!"

The wonder of being brought, by God, around a corner and to realize a new road is opening up, perhaps—which He alone knows. And that there is no way of traveling it but in Christ and with Him. This is joy and peace—whatever happens. The result does not matter. I have something to do for Him and, if I do that, everything else will follow. For the moment, it consists of prayer—thought—study, and above all care to form the South American postulants as He brings them to Gethsemani.

*January 23 and 24, 1958, III.159–60*

# Unlearning All Tension in Solitude

There is one thing I must do here at my woodshed hermitage, Saint Anne's (and may I one day live here and do it all day long), and that is to prepare for my death. But that means a preparation in *gentleness*. A gentleness, a silence, a humility that I have never had before—which seems impossible in the community, where even my compassion is tinged with force and strain.

But if I am called to solitude, it is, I think, to unlearn all tension, and get rid of the strain that has always falsified me in the presence of others and put harshness into the words of my mind. If I have needed solitude, it is because I have always so much needed the mercy of Christ and needed His humility and His charity. How can I give love unless I have much more than I have ever had?

Fine ideas in Max Picard's *World of Silence*. (A train whistle, like of the old time, sings in my present silence at St. Anne's, where the watch without a crystal ticks on the little desk.)

Foolish to expect a man "to develop all the possibilities that are within him." "The possibilities that are not fully realized nourish the substance of silence. Silence is strengthened by them and gives of this additional strength to the other potentialities that are fully realized."

"There is room for contradictions within the substance of silence. . . . A man who still has the substance of silence within him does not always need to be watching the movements of his inmost being."

*January 14 and 28, 1953, III.28–29*

# Thrown into Contradiction

God reveals Himself in the middle of conflict and contradiction—and we want to find Him outside all contradiction.

Importance of contradiction: the contradiction *essential* to my existence is the expression of the world's present: it is my contribution to the whole. My contradiction and my conflict are my part in the whole. They are my "place." It is in my insight and acceptance of contradiction that the world creates itself anew in and through my liberty—I permit God to act in and through me, making His world (in which all are judged and redeemed). I am thrown into contradiction: to realize it is mercy, to accept it is love, and to help others do the same is compassion. All this seems like nothing, but it is creation. The contradiction is precisely that we cannot "be creative" in some other way we would prefer (in which there is no contradiction).

*January 20, 1966, VI.354–55*

# One Dog's Good Afternoon

This afternoon—a quiet walk in the sun: again down by St. Bernard's pond. The Gannons' dog tagged along—the pretty collie bitch with a feathery tail—running busily into everything, immense interest in all kinds of smells, mysteries, secrets in the bushes and in the grass. She ran on the melting ice, rolled in the manure spread over the pasture (rolled twice!), came out of the brush with her tail full of dead leaves, and, in a final paroxysm of energy, chased a cat into the cow barn. A completely successful afternoon for *her* anyway!!

I had Martin Buber's *Ten Rungs* in my pocket and couldn't read a line of it, only looked at the sun, the dead grass, the green soft ice, the blue sky, and felt utterly blank. Will there never be any peace on earth in our lifetime? Will they never do anything but kill, and then kill some more? Apparently they are caught in that impasse: the system is completely violent and involved in violence, and there is no way out but violence, and that leads only to more violence. Really—what is ahead but the apocalypse?

*January 26, 1968, VII. 47*

# Content to Be Happy

You can make your life what you want. There are various ways of being happy. Why do we drive ourselves on with illusory demands? Happy only when we conform to something that is said to be a legitimate happiness? An approved happiness?

God gives us the freedom to create our own lives, according to His will, that is to say in the circumstances in which He has placed us. But we refuse to be content unless we realize in ourselves a "universal" standard, a happiness hypothetically prescribed and approved for all men of all time, and not just our own happiness. This, at least, is what I do. I am a happy person, and God has given me happiness, but I am guilty about it—as if being happy were not quite allowed, as if everybody didn't have it within reach somehow or other—and as if I had to justify God Himself by being zealous for something I do not and cannot have—because I am not happy in the same way as Pericles—or Khrushchev.

*January 21, 1961, IV.89*

# Weary of Words

Zero weather. Good work yesterday afternoon with the novices, cutting wood at the hermitage. Bright and cold. I went over to the Methodist Seminary at Asbury.

On the way over and back, stopped to take pictures at Shakertown. Marvelous, silent, vast spaces around the old buildings. Cold, pure light, and some grand trees. So cold my finger could no longer feel the shutter release. Some marvelous subjects. How the blank side of a frame house can be so completely beautiful I cannot imagine. A completely miraculous achievement of forms.

The moments of eloquent silent and emptiness in Shakertown stayed with me more than anything else—like a vision.

Tired of war, tired of letters, tired of books. Shaving today, saw new lines under the eyes, a new hollowness, a beginning of weariness. Well. So it is good.

What matters most is secret, not said. This begins to be the most real and the most certain dimension.

I had been secretly worried about my writing, especially on peace, getting condemned. Nothing to worry about. Whenever I am *really* wrong, it will be easy enough to change. But it is strange that such things should be regarded with suspicion. I know this is wrong. Weary of blindness, of this blindness that afflicts all men, but most of all of the blindness afflicting those who ought to see.

*January 12 and 19, 1962, IV.194–95*

# An Ecology of Silence

The new bells sound wonderful from the woods.

St. John's day—Frater Tarcisius and I walked all the way to Hanekamp's in the afternoon. Wonderful, quiet little valley! The silent house, the goats in the red sage grass, the dry creek, and Hanekamp's vineyard. The beautiful silence of the woods on every side! Frater Tarcisius looked about with such reverence that you would have thought he was seeing angels. Later we separated to pray apart in the thinned pine grove on the southeastern hillside. And I could see how simple it is to find God in solitude. There is no one else, nothing else. He is all there is to find there. Everything is in Him. And what could be more pleasing to Him than that we should leave all things and all company to be with Him and think only of Him and know Him alone, in order to give Him our love?

To be alone by being part of the universe—fitting in completely to an environment of woods and silence and peace. Everything you do becomes a unity and a prayer. Unity within and without. Unity with all living things—without effort or contention. My silence is part of the whole world's silence and builds the temple of God without the noise of hammers.

*December 29 and January 28, 1953, III.27, 29*

# Reality and the Ordinary

Still very cold and bright.

The best thing about the retreat has been working in the pig barn and then walking back alone, a mile and a half, through the snow.

I think I have come to see more clearly and more seriously the meaning, or lack of meaning, in my life. How much I am still the same self-willed and volatile person who made such a mess of Cambridge. That I have not changed yet, down in the depths, or, perhaps yes, I have changed radically somewhere, yet I have still kept some of the old, vain, inconstant, self-centered ways of looking at things. And that the situation I am in now has been given me to change me, if I will only surrender completely to reality as it is given me by God and no longer seek in any way to evade it, even by interior reservations.

Here at the hermitage, in deep snow, everything is ordinary and silent. Return to reality and to the ordinary, in silence. It is always there, if you know enough to return to it.

What is not ordinary—the tension of meeting people, discussion, ideas. This too is good and real, but illusion gets into it. The unimportant becomes important. Words and images become more important than life.

One travels all over vast areas, sitting still in a room, and one is soon tired of so much traveling.

I need very much this silence and this snow. Here alone can I find my way because here alone the way is right in front of my face and it is God's way for me—there really is no other.

*January 25 and 28, 1963, IV.293–95*

# Rediscovering Jesus

Today, in a moment of trial, I rediscovered Jesus, or perhaps discovered Him for the first time. But then, in a monastery you are always rediscovering Jesus for the first time.

His eyes, which are the eyes of Truth, are fixed upon my heart. Where His glance falls, there is peace: for the light of His Face, which is the Truth, produces truth wherever it shines. His eyes are always on us in choir and everywhere and in all times. No grace comes to us from heaven except He looks upon our hearts.

The grace of this gaze of Christ upon my heart transfigured this day like a miracle. It seems to me that I have discovered a freedom that I never knew before in my life and with this freedom a recollection that is no impediment to moderate action. I have felt that the Spirit of God was upon me, and after dinner, walking along the road beyond the orchard by myself under a cobalt blue sky (in which the moon was already visible), I thought that, if I only turned my head a little, I would see a tremendous host of angels in silver armor advancing behind me through the sky, coming at last to sweep the whole world clean. I did not have to mortify this fantasy as it did not arouse my emotions but carried me along on a vivid ocean of peace. And the whole world and the whole sky was filled with wonderful music, as it has often been for me in these days. But sitting alone in the attic of the garden house and looking at the stream shining in the bare willows and at the distant hills, I think I have never been so near to Adam's, my father's, Eden. Our Eden is the Heart of Christ.

*January 27 and 30, 1950, II. 403–4*

# My Deep Youthful Shyness

A bright, snowy afternoon, delicate blue clouds of snow blowing down off the frozen trees. Forcibly restrained myself from much work around the hermitage, made sure of my hour's meditation and will do more later. How badly I need it. I realize how great is the tempo and pressure of work I have been in down in the community—with many irons in the fire. True, I have in the community gained the knack of dropping everything and completely relaxing my attention and forgetting the work by going out and looking at the hills. Good that the novitiate work is not exceedingly absorbing. (Biggest trouble now is letter writing.)

Shall I look at the past as if it were something to analyze and think about? Rather, I thank God for the present, not for myself in the present, but for the present that is His and in Him. The past: I am inarticulate about it now. I remember irrelevant moments of embarrassment, and my joys are seen to have been largely meaningless. Yet, as I sit here in this wintry and lonely and quiet place, I suppose I am the same person as the eighteen-year-old riding back alone into Bournemouth on a bus out of the New Forest, where I had camped a couple of days and nights. I suppose I regret most my lack of love, my selfishness and glibness (covering a deep shyness and need of love) with girls who, after all, did love me, I think, for a time. My great fault was my inability really to believe it, and my efforts to get complete assurance and perfect fulfillment.

*January 30, 1965, V.197–98*

# Out to Sea Without Restraints

What more do I seek than this silence, this simplicity, this "living together with wisdom"? For me there is nothing else. Last night, before going to bed, realized momentarily what solitude really means: when the ropes are cast off and the skiff is no longer tied to land, but heads out to sea without ties, without restraints! Not the sea of passion, on the contrary, the sea of purity and love that is without care, that loves God alone immediately and directly in Himself as the All (and the seeming Nothing that is all). The unutterable confusion of those who think that God is a mental object and that to love "God alone" is to exclude all other objects to concentrate on this one! Fatal. Yet that is why so many misunderstand the meaning of contemplation and solitude, and condemn it. But I see too that I no longer have the slightest need to argue with them. I have nothing to justify and nothing to defend: I need only defend this vast simple emptiness from my own self, and the rest is clear. (Through the cold and darkness I hear the Angelus ringing at the monastery.) The beautiful jeweled shining of honey in the lamplight. Festival!

*January 31, 1965, V.200*

# Unveiling the Heart

Deep snow. A marvelous morning (early in the night hours) in which, among other things, I suddenly wrote a French poem.

Curious dimension of time: in four hours (besides writing this poem, getting breakfast and cleaning up) I reread a few pages of Burtt's book and perhaps twenty pages of Kitaro Nishida. That was all. But the time was most fruitful in depth and awareness, and I did not know what happened to all these hours.

Later I could see by the deer tracks that sometime in the dark before dawn a couple of deer had jumped the fence right out in the front of the hermitage—but I did not notice them. (Too dark, and with my desk light in front of me I do not see out when it is dark.)

As regards prayer—in the hermitage. To be snowed in is to be reminded that this is a place apart, from which praise goes up to God, and that my honor and responsibility are that praise. This is my joy, my only "importance." For it *is* important! To be chosen for this! And then the realization that the Spirit is given to me, the veil is removed from my heart, that I reflect "with open face" the glory of Christ (II Corinthians 3:12–18). It would be easy to remain with one's heart veiled, and it is not by any wisdom of my own, but by God's gift, that it *is* unveiled.

*January 23, 1966, VI. 10–11*

# Moments of Angelic Lucidity

I went down to the spring that feeds the stream running through Edelin's pasture. Wonderful clear water pouring strongly out of a cleft in the mossy rock. I drank from it in my cupped hands and suddenly realized it was years, perhaps twenty-five or thirty years, since I had tasted such water, no chemicals!! I looked up at the clear sky and the tops of the leafless trees shining in the sun: it was a moment of angelic lucidity. Said Tierce with great joy, overflowing joy, as if the land and woods and spring were all praising God through me. The sense of angelic transparency of everything, and of pure, simple, and total light. The word that comes closest to pointing to it is *simple.* It was all simple. But a simplicity to which one seems to aspire, only seldom to attain. A simplicity, that is, that has and says everything just because it is simple.

*January 6, 1965, V.187*

# I Begin to Awaken

There is an element of emptiness and anguish from the concentration of the annual retreat, but not much. Actually I feel more sure than I ever have in my life that I am obeying the Lord and am on the way He wills for me, though at the same time I am struck and appalled (more than ever!) by the shoddiness of my response. I am just beginning to awaken and to realize how much more awakening is to come. And how much is to be faced. How much I must admit and renounce ambition and agitated self-seeking in my work and contacts (I am so tied up in all this that I don't know where to start getting free!). But God will take care of me, for in my confusion and helplessness I nevertheless feel (believe in) His closeness and strength. I don't have to know and see how it will all come out.

My intention is, in fact, simply to "die" to the past somehow. To live more abandoned to God's will and less concerned with projects and initiatives. More detached from work and events, more solitary. To be one of those who entirely practices contemplation simply in order to follow Christ.

*January 25, 1965, V.195*

# Faithful to the Truth

In concluding this retreat:

1. There can be no doubt, no compromise, in my decision to be completely faithful to God's will and truth, and hence I must seek always and in everything to act for His will and in His truth, and thus to seek with His grace to be "a saint."

2. There must be no doubt, no compromise in my efforts to avoid falsifying this work of truth by considering too much what others approve of and regard as "holy." In a word, it may happen (or may not) that what God demands of me may make me look less perfect to others, and that it may rob me of their support, their affection, their respect. To become a saint therefore may mean the anguish of looking like, and in a real sense "being," a sinner, an outcast. It may mean apparent conflict with certain standards that may be wrongly understood by me or by others or by all of us.

3. The thing is to cling to God's will and truth in their purity and try to be sincere and to act in all things out of genuine love, in so far as I can.

*January 25, 1962, IV.198*

# The Necessity of Adoration

"Nothing is more necessary than to adore the living God," says the *Rule for Recluses.* It seems a platitude—really it is a deep, mysterious, unfathomable, living need—an imperative for one's whole life, a demand that is often forgotten and not met. I am in solitude precisely to confront *this* demand and others like it (in Zen terms, for example). I recognize I do not cope with the others really. Yet I must keep on with it, however much I fumble around. No one else can tell me what to do now: I have to try to find out for myself (of course people will come at the right time with the right word—books, too—but I have no one to *rely on.* This is my life and I don't pretend to understand it. Only, the mere playing of a role would be intolerable and mere living is also not enough, though at times it seems to resolve itself into that. There is living and then there is living.

*January 15, 1966, VI.7*

# Seeing the Center from Somewhere Else

The year of the dragon has so far distinguished itself by strong, lusty winds—great windstorm the other night, some trees blew down in the woods near the hermitage (one across the path going up). Pine cones and bits of branches all over the lawn.

The need for constant self-revision, growth, leaving behind, a renunciation of yesterday, yet in continuity with all yesterdays (to cling to the past is to lose one's identity with it, for this means clinging to what was not there). My ideas are always changing, always moving around one center, always seeing the center from somewhere else. I will always be accused of inconsistencies—and will no longer be there to hear the accusation.

"What makes us afraid is our great freedom in face of the emptiness that has still to be filled" (Karl Jaspers). And again these concluding words from the arresting little pamphlet on *The European Spirit:* "The philosophically serious European is faced today with the choice between opposed philosophical possibilities. Will he enter the limited field of fixed truth which in the end has only to be obeyed; or will he go into the limitless open truth? . . . Will he win this perilous independence in perilous openness, as in existential philosophy, the philosophy of communication in which the individual becomes himself on condition that others become themselves, in which there is no solitary peace but constant dissatisfaction and in which a man exposes his soul to suffering?"

*January 25 and 26, 1964, V.67–68*

# Going Nowhere, Having Nothing to Do

It is useless to simply substitute the "experience" of oneself as a hermit for the "experience" of oneself as active, as a "monk," as a "writer," etc. The same error is repeated in a new way. In reality the hermit life does imply a certain attrition of one's identity. In context a word that implies "loss of" identity. This must also be resisted: one does not live alone in order to become a vegetable. Yet the resistance does not take the form of asserting a social and evident identity of one who is going somewhere or doing something special. A curious kind of identity, then: "in God."

Merely living alone but continuing to engage in a lot of projects is not yet an authentic hermit life. The projects must go. Solitude demands an emptiness, an aimlessness, a going nowhere, a certain "having nothing to do," especially nothing that involves the growth and assertion of one's "image" and one's "career."

Distraction: the illusory expectation of some fulfillment, which in the end is only a human loneliness.

*Were you not forever distracted by expectation, as if everything were*
*announcing to you some (coming) beloved?*
*(Rainer Maria Rilke, lst* Duino Elegy*)*

*January 29, 1966, VI.356–57*

# On the Eve of a Birthday

Snow, silence, the talking fire, the watch on the table. Sorrow. I will get cleaned up (my hands are dirty). I will sing the psalms of my birthday.

No matter what mistakes and illusions have marked my life, most of it I think has been happiness and, as far as I can tell, truth. There were whole seasons of insincerity, largely when I was under twenty-one and followed friends that were not my own kind. But after my senior year at Columbia things got straight. I can remember many happy and illumined days and whole blocks of time. There were a few nightmare times in childhood. But at Saint Antonin, with Father, life was a revelation. Then again, at so many various times and places, in Sussex (at Rye and in the country), at Oakham, at Strasbourg, at Rome above all, in New York, especially upstate Olean and St. Bonaventure's. I remember one wonderful winter morning arriving at Olean to spend Christmas with Bob Lax. Arrivals and departures on the Erie were generally great. The cottage on the hill, too—then Cuba: wonderful days there. All this I have said before and the whole world knows it.

The profoundest and happiest times of my life have been in and around Gethsemani, and also some of the most terrible. Mostly the happy moments were in the woods and fields, alone, with the sky and the sun, and up here at the hermitage. And with the novices (afternoons at work).

*January 30, 1965, V.198–99*

# The Gift of My Life

*(Thomas Merton's birthday; born in 1915 in Prades, France)*

A lovely little icon arrived that Bob Rambusch got for us in Salonika, I believe. He had it cleaned in New York and here it is— not astonishingly beautiful but simple and holy and joyous. It radiates a kind of joy and strength that one would not look for or see, if one looked only superficially. I blessed this icon today (it had been sold and lost its consecration by the defiling touch of commerce) and I prayed aloud before it an Eastern prayer and hymn to the icon of Our Lady of Kazan. Her coming is a great grace—her presence a great comfort. I have placed the icon over the altar of Our Lady in the novitiate chapel.

Why was I always half-convinced I would die young? Perhaps a kind of superstition—the fear of admitting a hope of life which, if admitted, might have to be dashed. But now "I have lived" a fair span of life and, whether or not the fact be important, nothing can alter it. It is certain, infallible—even though that too is only a kind of dream. If I don't make it to sixty-five, it matters less. I can relax. But life is a gift I am glad of, and I do not curse the day when I was born. On the contrary, if I had never been born I would never have had friends to love and be loved by, never have made mistakes to learn from, never have seen new countries, and, as for what I may have suffered, it is inconsequential and indeed part of the great good which life has been and will, I hope, continue to be.

*January 31, 1960, III.372–73*

# The Climate of My Prayer

Our mentioning of the weather—our perfunctory observations on what kind of day it is—are perhaps not idle. Perhaps we have a deep and legitimate need to know in our entire being what the day is like, to *see* it and *feel* it, to know how the sky is grey, paler in the south, with patches of blue in the southwest, with snow on the ground, the thermometer at 18, and cold wind making your ears ache. I have a real need to know these things because I myself am part of the weather and part of the climate and part of the place, and a day in which I have not shared truly in all this is no day at all. It is certainly part of my life of prayer.

*February 27, 1963, IV.299–300*

# Bearing Witness to the Resurrection

A priest bears witness to the Resurrection by holding in his hands the Risen Christ—high over his head for all the people to see. And none of us see, except by faith. Faith itself is the light of the Resurrection, our sharing of the Resurrection. It is the effect of the Resurrection in our souls. By it we are buried and rise from the dead in Christ.

Gone are the days when "mysticism" was for me a matter of eager and speculative interest. Now, because it is my life, it is a torment to think about. Like being in the pangs of childbirth and reading an essay on mother love written by a spinster.

In choir I am happier than I have ever been there, extremely poor and helpless, often strained, hardly able to hold myself in place. "Expecting every moment to be my last." Sometimes it is a great relief to be distracted. There is a "presence" of God that is like an iron curtain between the mind and God.

But when I am at my toolshed hermitage, Saint Anne's, I am always happy and at peace no matter what happens. For here there is no need for anyone but God—no need of "mysticism."

A fly buzzes on the windowpane!

*February 24, 1953, III.35–36*

# The Fellowship of Stars and Crows

Bright morning—freezing, but less cold than before—and with a hint of the smell of spring-earth in the cold air. A beautiful sunrise, the woods all peaceful and silent, the dried old fruits on the yellow poplar shining like precious artifacts. I have a new level in my (elementary) star-consciousness. I can now tell where constellations may be in the daytime when they are invisible. Not many, of course! But for example: the sun is rising in Aquarius and so I know that in the blue sky overhead the beautiful swan, invisible, spreads its wide wings over me. A lovely thought, for some reason.

Since Hayden Carruth's reprimand I have had more esteem for the crows around here and I find, in fact, that we seem to get on much more peacefully. Two sat high in an oak beyond my gate as I walked on the brow of the hill at sunrise saying the Little Hours. They listened without protest to my singing of the antiphons. We are part of a ménage, a liturgy, a fellowship of sorts.

*February 13, 1968, VII.55–56*

# A Priest with the World as My Parish

Looking at the crucifix on the white wall of Saint Anne's—overwhelmed at the realization that I am a *priest,* that it has been given to me to know something of what the Cross means, that St. Anne's is a special part of my priestly vocation: the silence, the woods, the sunlight, the shadows, the picture of Jesus, Our Lady of Cobre, and the little angels in Fra Angelico's paradise. Here I am a priest with all the world as my parish. Or is it a temptation, the thought of this? Perhaps I do not need to remember the apostolic fruitfulness of this silence. I need only to be nothing and to wait for the revelation of Christ: to be at peace and poor and silent in the world where the mystery of iniquity is also at work and where there is also no other revelation. No, there is so much peace at St. Anne's that it is most certainly the heart of a great spiritual battle that is fought in silence. I who sit here and pray and think and live—I am nothing and do not need to know what is going on. I need only to hope in Christ and hear the big deep bell that now begins to ring and sends its holy sound to me through the little cedars.

This is the continuation of my Mass. This is still my Eucharist, my day-long thanksgiving, work, worship, my hoping for the perfect revelation of Christ.

*February 17, 1953, III.33*

# We Are Not Shadows of God

I cannot deny that it was a great joy to say the office in private, Lauds and Prime, especially with the sun coming up slowly and shining on the sunny pastures and on the pine woods of the dark knobs, which I see through the novitiate window. Lovely blue and mauve shadows on the snow, and the indescribably delicate color of the sunlit patches of snow. All the life of color is in the snow and the sky. The green of the pines is dull and brownish. The dead leaves, still clinging tenaciously to the white oaks, are also dull brown. The cold sky is very blue, and the air is dry and frozen so that, for the first time in years, I see and breathe the winters of New York and not the mild or ambivalent winters of Kentucky.

The strength of the cold, the austerity and power of the landscape, redeems the snow colors and delicate shadows from anything of pastel shading. I can think of no art that has rendered such things adequately—the nineteenth-century realists were so realistic as to be totally *unlike* what they painted. There is such a thing as *too close* a resemblance. In a way, nothing resembles reality less than the average photograph. Nothing resembles substance *less* than its shadow. To convey the meaning of something substantial, you have to use a sign, which is itself substantial and exists in its own right.

Man is the *image* of God and not the *shadow* of God.

*February 17, 1958, III.171*

# Every Next Instant Reveals God's Will

I can have one prayer—to belong to God, to be able to renounce the whole world and follow Him. I say that prayer now. When it pleases Him, He will show me what to do. When? Not next year, every next instant. If I love Him, I will hear.

*Anima mea in manibus meis semper:* "Constantly I take my life in my hands."

This is what I read in the Bible today:

Isaias 47:1 "Come down, sit in the dust, O virgin daughter of Babylon, sit on the ground: there is no throne for the daughter of the Chaldaeans, for thou shall not any more be called delicate and tender."

55:1 "All you that thirst, come to the waters; and you that have no money, make haste, buy, eat; come ye, buy wine and milk without money, and without any price."

58:10 "When thou shall pour out thy soul to the hungry and shall satisfy the afflicted soul, then shall thy light rise up in darkness, and thy darkness shall be as noonday."

*February 19, 1941, I.311*

# My Place in the Scheme of Things

Everything about this hermitage fills me with joy. There are lots of things that could have been far more perfect one way or the other—ascetically and "domestically." But it is the place God has given me after so much prayer and longing—but without my deserving it—and it is a delight. I can imagine no other joy on earth than to have a hermitage and to be at peace in it, to live in silence, to think and write, to listen to the wind and to all the voices of the wood, to live in the shadow of the big cedar cross, to prepare for my death and my exodus to the heavenly country, to love my brothers and all people, and to pray for the whole world and for peace and good sense among men. So it is "my place" in the scheme of things, and that is sufficient!

Reading some studies on St. Leonard of Port Maurice and his retirement house (*Ritiro*) and hermitage of the Incontro. How clearly Vatican II has brought into question all the attitudes that he and his companions took completely for granted: the dramatic bare-foot procession from Florence to the Incontro in the snow—the daily half-hour self-flagellation in common—etc. This used to be admired, if prudently avoided, by all in the Church. Depth psychology, etc., have made these things forever questionable—they belong to another age. And yet there has to be hardness and rigor in the solitary life. The hardness is there by itself. The cold, the solitude, the labor, the need for poverty to keep everything simple and manageable, the need for the discipline of long meditation in silence.

*February 24, 1965, V.209–10*

# Sealed Together in Christ

Can one say that by love the soul receives the very "form" of God? In St. Bernard of Clairvaux's language, this form, this divine likeness, is the identity we were made for. Thus we can say, *Caritas haec visio, haec similitudo est:* "Charity is this vision and this likeness." By love we are at once made like to God, and (in mystical love, pure love) we already "see" Him (darkly), that is, we have experience of Him as He is in Himself, and wisdom is the *medium quo cognoscitur:* "the medium by which He is known." The soul knows God in this effect, this love, in the same way (analogously) as it knows itself in the consciousness of its own existence and activity. I know God because I am aware of His life in me, and the Spirit bears witness to my conscience, crying out that God is my Father. Thus by loving we know God in God, and through God, for in love the Three Divine Persons are made known to us, sealing our souls, not with a static likeness, but with the impression of Their infinite Life. Our souls are sealed with fire. Our souls are sealed with Life. Our souls are sealed with the character of God as the air is full of sunshine. Glory to God in the highest, Who has sealed us with His holiness, sealed us all together, brothers and sisters in His Christ.

*February 12, 1950, II.409*

# Out of Touch and Left Behind

The "spiritual preoccupations" of this time—the post–Vatican II Conciliar years. (An imaginary era we have thought up for ourselves—*divertissement!*) I need perhaps to be *less* preoccupied with them, to show that one can be *free* of them, and go one's own way in peace. But there is inculcated in us such a *fear* of being out of everything, out of touch, left behind. This fear is a form of tyranny, a *law*—and one is faced with a choice between this law and true grace, hidden, paradoxical, but free.

An unformulated "preoccupation" of our time—the conviction that it is precisely in these (collective) *preoccupations* that the Holy Spirit is at work. To be "preoccupied with the current preoccupations" is then the best—if not the only—way to be open to the Spirit.

Hence one must know what everybody is saying, read what everybody is reading, keep up with everything or be left behind by the Holy Spirit. Is this a perversion of the idea of the Church—a distortion of perspective due to the Church's situation in the world of mass communications? I wonder if this anxiety to keep up is not in fact an obstacle to the Holy Spirit.

*February 24, 1966, VI.363*

# Blessings of Emptiness and Peace

I am glutted with books and a million trifles besides—articles on this and that. I balk at reading about Panama. I have had enough. (Yet I will read it because I am obliged in conscience to know at least vaguely what is happening.) Panama, Zanzibar, Cypress (Costas Papademas wrote from there, he flew back at Christmas), Kenya (Joy French wrote from there today—first time I have seen the new stamp of the independent nation), and then "the freeze" (on nuclear weapons) and various iniquities in Washington, and nonsense in Vietnam (new dictator), so on and so on. Does one have to read all this? Enough! Thank God tomorrow is Lent. I am glutted.

Today constant snow, ever so blinding, pale bright blue sky such as I have sometimes seen in England on rare days in East Anglia. All the trees heavy with snow and the hills hanging like white clouds in the sky. But much of the snow has melted off the trees and there is slight mist over the sunny valley. No jets, for a wonder! Only a train off towards Lebanon. Quiet afternoon! Peace! May this Lent be blessed with emptiness and peace and faith.

The woods echo with distant crows. A hen sings out happily at Andy Boone's, and snow falling from the trees makes the woods sound as though they were full of people walking through the bushes.

*February 11, 1964, V.75–76*

# Sunlight on a Vase of Carnations

Beauty of the sunlight falling on a tall vase of red and white carnations and green leaves on the altar in the novitiate chapel. The light and shade of the red, especially the darkness in the fresh crinkled flower and the light warm red around the darkness, the same color as blood but not "red as blood," utterly unlike blood. Red as a carnation. This flower, this light, this moment, this silence = *Dominus est,* eternity! Best because the flower is itself and the light is itself and the silence is itself and I am myself—all, perhaps, an illusion, but no matter, for illusion is nevertheless the shadow of reality and reality is the grace that underlies these lights, these colors, and this silence.

The "simplicity" that would have kept those flowers off the altar is, to my mind, less simple than the simplicity that enjoys them there, but does not need them to be there.

*February 4, 1958, III. 164–65*

# The Power of Jesus' Passion in Us

Ash Wednesday: the ashes themselves bring the mercy of the blessing of Christ, in sobriety and barefooted peace.

At St. Anne's the sun is as bright as the first day that it was created. The world is clean. There is sin in it, but Christ has overcome the world. Even on Ash Wednesday I begin to hear the silence of Easter.

Many birds, going north, were flying in the wind. They moved slowly against the blue sky and looked like a school of fish in clear West Indian waters. The sun shone through their wings and made them seem like red and orange fins.

I think of the unity of the Church in this her Lent (the lesson from the book of Joel brings this out: "Blow the trumpet and call the people together for the great fast!" Joel 1:14). The whole Church is called together and we realize that our Lent is united with the suffering of the martyrs and the fasts of the desert fathers and the good works and penances of all the saints. Whatever I can give to God and to other men is only the effect and manifestation in me of the power of the Passion of Jesus. I would reply to His action, and let Him show Himself in my life. This He will do in a way I have expected and not expected; planned and not planned; desired and not desired.

My decisions do not anticipate His coming: they manifest that He has come, if they be His decisions.

*February 18, 1953, III.34*

# Get Warm and Love God Any Way You Can

A great deal of wood I have for the fire is wet or not sufficiently seasoned to burn well—though finally this morning I got a pretty hot fire going with a big cedar log on top of it.

It is hard but good to live according to nature with a primitive technology of wood chopping and fires rather than according to the mature technology that has supplanted nature, creating its own weather, etc., etc. Yet there are advantages, too, in a warmed house and a self-stoking furnace. No need to pledge allegiance to either one. Get warm any way you can, and love God and pray.

I see more and more that now I must desire nothing else than to be "poured out as a libation," to give and surrender my being without concern. The cold woods make this more real. And the loneliness: coming up last night at the time of a very cold sunset, with two little birds still picking at crumbs I had thrown for them on the frozen porch. Everywhere else, snow. In the morning, coming down: all tracks covered by snow blown over the path by the wind, except tracks of the cat that hunts around the old sheep barn. Solitude = being aware that you are one man in this snow where there has been no one but one cat.

*February 2, 1965, V.201*

# An Untidy Holy Life

Today we commemorate Blessed Conrad—one of the Cistercian hermits.

I might as well say that in the novitiate I did not like the hermits of our Order. Their stories were inconclusive. They seemed to have died before finding out what they were supposed to achieve.

Now I know there is something important about the very incompleteness of Blessed Conrad: hermit in Palestine, by St. Bernard's permission. Starts home for Clairvaux when he hears St. Bernard is dying. Gets to Italy and hears St. Bernard is dead. Settles in a wayside chapel outside Bari and dies there. What an untidily unplanned life! No order, no sense, no system, no climax. Like a book without punctuation that suddenly ends in the middle of a sentence.

Yet I know that those are the books I really like!

Blessed Conrad cannot possibly be solidified or ossified in history. He can perhaps be caught and held in a picture, but he is like a photograph of a bird in flight—too accurate to look the way a flying bird seems to appear to us. We never saw the wings in that position. Such is the solitary vocation. For, of all men, the solitary knows least where he is going, and yet he is more sure, for there is one thing he cannot doubt: he travels where God is leading him. That is precisely why he doesn't know the way. And that too is why, to most other men, the way is something of a scandal.

*February 14, 1953, III.30–31*

# On Not Going Crazy for Christ

I have been reading about de Rancé, that old Trappist business of trying to starve and beat your way to sanctity and of assuming that your own efforts and energy are practically everything—beating your head against a brick wall at the end of a dead end in order to fulfill some particular negative ideal. Our Cistercian Fathers and St. Benedict knew better. So did the Little Flower. So did our Lord.

I don't know any universal solution to the problem of why monks go crazy, except yesterday it was such a beautiful day, and I walked under the trees and looked at the sunny hills, and listened to the quiet sunlight, and kicked the gravel with my feet and said, "What is there to go crazy about?" We have a wonderful vocation. Christ has brought us here to live: to live and breathe and be happy under His gaze, to play in His sight like children, while He takes care of us—to sing and fast and pray and (for me) to write books and to love all the time. It's not an effort; there is nothing to get excited about. Sure, I am distracted, I am vain, I am full of dumb books, and I get into interior arguments about the chant, so what? He knows I don't want to get into all that stuff, and He loves me.

I am happy that I can at least want to love God. Perhaps that is all I've got, but it is already all that is essential. And He will take care of the rest.

*February 22, 1948, II.172*

# Hidden Movements of Christ's Grace

I don't know what I have written that I could really call mine, or what I have prayed or done that was good that came from my own will. Whose prayer made me pray again to God to give me grace to pray? I could have fought for years by myself to reduce my life to some order (for that was what I was trying to do—even to ridiculous extremes and the most eccentric disciplines, keeping records of what I drank, trying to cut out smoking by reducing the number of cigarettes every day, noting down the numbers in a book . . . weighing myself every few days, etc.!), yet I would have slowly eaten myself out, I think. But someone must have mentioned me in some prayer; perhaps the soul of some person I hardly remember—perhaps some stranger in a subway, or some child—or maybe the fact that someone as good as Lilly Reilly happened to think I was a good guy served as a prayer—or the fact that Nanny might have said my name in her prayers moved the Lord God to send me a little grace to pray again or, first, to begin reading books that led me there again—and how much of it was brought on by the war? Or maybe Brahmachari in some word to the Lord in his strange language moved the Lord to help me pray again! These things are inscrutable and I begin to know them better when I can write them down. How many people have become Christians through the prayers of Jews and Hindus who themselves find Christianity terribly hard? We cannot know all the movements of Christ's grace.

*February 2, 1941, I.304–5*

# Absent from the Wedding Feast

Today was *the* prophetic day, the first of the real shining spring: not that there was not warm weather last week, not that there will not be cold weather again. But this was the day of the year when spring became truly *credible.*

The morning got more and more brilliant and I could feel the brilliancy of it getting into my own blood. Living so close to the cold, you feel the spring. And this is man's mission! The earth cannot *feel* all this. We must. But living away from the earth and the trees, we fail them. We are absent from the wedding feast.

There are moments of great loneliness and lostness in this solitude, but often then come other, deeper moments of hope and understanding, and I realize that these would *not be possible* in their purity, their simple, secret directions anywhere but in solitude. I hope to be worthy of them.

After dinner, when I came back to the hermitage, the whole hillside was so bright and new that I wanted to cry out, and I got tears in my eyes from it!

With the new comes also memory: as if that which was once so fresh in the past (days of discovery when I was nineteen or twenty) were very close again, and as if one were beginning to live again from the beginning. One must experience spring like that. A whole new chance! A complete renewal!

*February 17, 1966, VI.18–19*

# In the Darkness of My Empty Mind

The blue elm tree near at hand and the light blue hills in the distance: the red bare clay where I am supposed to plant some shade trees: these are before me as I sit in the sun for a free half hour between spiritual direction and work. Today, as I sit in the sun, big blue and purple fish swim past me in the darkness of my empty mind, this sea which opens within me as soon as I close my eyes. Delightful darkness, delightful sun, shining on a world which, for all I care, has already ended.

It does not occur to me to wonder whether we will ever transplant the young maples from the wood, yonder, to this bare leveled patch—the place where the old horse barn once stood. It does not occur to me to wonder how everything came to be transformed. I sit on a cedar log half chewed by some novice's blunt axe, and do not reflect on plans I have made for this place of prayer, because they do not matter. They will happen when they happen.

The hills are as pure as jade in the distance. God is in His transparent world, but He is too sacred to be mentioned, too holy to be observed. I sit in silence. The big deep fish are purple in my sea.

*February 26, 1952, II.467*

# Healing Our Flesh

Lent is a sunlit season.

*Carnivale*—farewell to the flesh. It is a poor joke to be merry about leaving the flesh, as if we were to return to it once again. What would be the good of Lent, if it were only temporary?

Jesus nevertheless died *in order to return* to His flesh; in order to raise His own body glorious from the dead, and in order to raise our bodies with Him. "Unless the grain of wheat, falling into the ground, dies, itself remains alone." So we cast off the flesh, not out of contempt, but in order to heal the flesh in the mercy of penance and restore it to the Spirit to which it belongs. And all creation waits in anguish for our victory and our bodies' glory.

God wills us to recover all the joys of His created world in the Spirit, by denying ourselves what is really no joy—what only ends in the flesh. "The flesh profits nothing."

*February 17, 1953, III.33*

# Solitude Is a Stern Mother

I see more and more that solitude is not something to play with. It is deadly serious. And much as I have wanted it, I have not been serious enough. It is not enough to "like solitude," or love it even. Even if you "like" it, it can wreck you, I believe, if you desire it only for your own sake. So I go forward (I don't believe I would go back. Even interiorly I have reached, at least relatively, a point of no return), but I go in fear and trembling, and often with a sense of lostness, and trying to be careful what I do because I am beginning to see that every false step is paid for dearly. Hence I fall back on prayer, or try to. Yet no matter, there is great beauty and peace in this life of silence and emptiness. But to fool around brings awful desolation. When one is trifling, even the beauty of the solitary life becomes implacable. Solitude is a stern mother who brooks no nonsense. The question arises: am I so full of nonsense that she will cast me out? I pray not, and think it is going to take much prayer.

*February 26, 1965, V.211*

# Where Your Treasure Is

Tremendous discovery. The *Brihad-Aranyaka Upanishad!*

*Kairos!* Everything for a long time has been slowly leading up to this, and with this reading a sudden convergence of roads, tendencies, lights, in unity!

A new door. (Looked at it without comprehension nine months ago.)

Yesterday's disgust with the trivial, shallow, contemporary stuff I am tempted to read! No time for that.

Scriptures. Greek patrology. Oriental thought. This is enough to fill every free corner of the day not given to prayer, meditation, duties.

This morning, the splendor of my Mass! Sun pouring in on the altar and in glory of reflected lights from the hammered silver chalice splashed all over the corporal and all around the Host. Deep quiet. The Gospel—"Do not fear, little flock." Where your treasure is, there your heart is also. May I learn the lessons of detachment, even from the little white house of St. Mary of Carmel. But no nonsense about not desiring solitude. On the contrary, to desire it in perfection and in truth. Interior and exterior.

*February 4 and 14, 1961, IV.92–93*

# The Wonder of God's Mercy

*(Merton becomes a novice at Gethsemani on February 22, 1942)*

Once again the 22nd—the day I received the habit of novice—comes around on the First Sunday of Lent. I received a Lenten book from the hands of my spiritual children, and in a short time I have become the spiritual father of many. Once again I am aware of the mystery of my vocation.

The greatest mystery is here at St. Anne's, my toolshed hermitage. Just as Baptism makes us potential martyrs, so also it makes us potential priests, potential monks, potential hermits.

I was clothed in this hermitage, when I received the habit of novice, without even knowing it. The black and white house indeed is a kind of religious habit—and a warm enough one when the stove is going.

All this is to say that this silence is Christ's love for me and bought by His death, and it purifies me in His sufferings and His Blood. I must receive it with compunction and love and reverence, lest His love be in vain.

When I am most quiet and most myself, God's grace is clear, and then I see nothing else under the sun. What else is there for us but to be tranquil and at peace in the all-enchanting wonder of God's mercy to us? It falls upon this paper more quietly than the morning sun, and then I know that all things, without His love, are useless, and in His love, having nothing, I can possess all things.

*February 22, 1953, III.34–35*

# Belonging Entirely to God

Certainly the solitary life makes sense only when it is centered on one thing: the perfect love of God. Without this, everything is triviality. Love of God in Himself, for Himself, sought only in His will, in total surrender. Anything but this, in solitude, is nausea and absurdity. But outside of solitude, one can be occupied in many things that seem to have and do have a meaning of their own. And their meaning can be and is accepted, at least provisionally, as something that must be reckoned with *until* such time as one can come to love God alone perfectly, etc. This is all right in a way, except that, while doing things theoretically "for the love of God," one falls in practice into complete forgetfulness and ignorance and torpor. This happens in solitude, too, of course, but in solitude, while distraction is evidently vain, forgetfulness brings nausea. But in society, forgetfulness brings comfort of a kind.

It is therefore a great thing to be completely vulnerable and to feel at once, with every weakening of faith, a total loss. Things that in community are legitimate concerns are seen in solitude to be also temptations, test, questionings: for instance, the skin trouble on my hands.

*February 27, 1965, V.211–12*

# He Made the Desert Holy

The song of my Beloved beside the stream. The birds descanting in their clerestories. His skies have sanctified my eyes, His woods are clearer than the King's palace. But the air and I will never tell our secret.

The first Sunday of Lent, as I now know, is a great feast. Christ has sanctified the desert, and in the desert I discovered it. The woods have all become young in the discipline of spring, but it is the discipline of expectancy only. Which one cuts more keenly? The February sunlight or the air? There are no buds. Buds are not guessed at or even thought of this early in Lent. But the wilderness shines with promise. The land is first in simplicity and strength. Everything foretells the coming of the holy spring. I had never before spoken freely or so intimately with woods, hills, buds, water, and sky. On this great day, however, they understood their position and they remained mute in the presence of the Beloved. Only His light was obvious and eloquent. My brother and sister, the light and the water. The stump and the stone. The tables of rock. The blue, naked sky. Tractor tracks, a little waterfall. And Mediterranean solitude. I thought of Italy after my Beloved had spoken and was gone.

*February 27, 1950, II.412*

# Christ Has Known Our Exile

At the end of the first Epistle of Saint Paul to the Corinthians: "I shall know even as I have been known."

It is in the passion of Christ that God has proved to us that He has "known" us. That He has recognized us in our misery. That He has found His lost image in our fallen state and reclaimed it for His own, cleansed in the charity of His Divine Son.

It is on the Cross that God has known us: that He has searched our souls with His compassion and experienced the full extent of capacity for wickedness: it is on the Cross that He has known our exile, and ended it, and brought us home to Him.

We have to return to Him though the same gate of charity by which He came to us. If we had to open the gate ourselves, we could never do it. He has done the work. It is for us to follow Him and enter in by all those things that go together to fulfill in us the law of charity, in which all virtues are complete.

*February 14, 1953, II. 31–32*

# Our Blindness

Although it is almost unbelievable to imagine this country being laid to waste, yet that is very probably what is going to happen.

Without serious reason, without people "wanting" it, and without them being able to prevent it, because of their incapacity to use the power they have acquired, they must be used by it.

Hence the absolute necessity of taking this fact soberly into account and living in the perspectives that it establishes—an almost impossible task.

1. *Preeminence of meditation* and prayer, of self-emptying, cleaning out, getting rid of the self that blocks the view of truth. The self that says it will be here and then that it will not be here.

2. *Preeminence of compassion* for every living thing, for life, for the defenseless and simple beings, for the human race in its blindness. For Christ, crucified in His image. Eucharistic sacrifice, without justification.

3. *Weariness of words,* except in friendship, and in the simplest and most direct kind of communication, by word of mouth or letter.

4. *Preeminence of the silent and inconclusive action*—if any presents itself. And meaningful suffering, accepted in complete silence, without justification.

*February 27, 1962, IV.205–6*

# Clinging to God

Yesterday in the morning, when I went out for a breath of air before my novice conference, I saw men working on the hillside beyond the sheep barn. At last the electric line is coming to my hermitage! All day they were working on the holes, digging and blasting the rock with small charges, young men in yellow helmets, good, eager, hardworking guys with machines. I was glad of them and of American technology, pitching in to bring me light, as they would for any farmer in the district. It was good to feel part of this, which is not to be despised, but is admirable. (Which does not mean that I hold any brief for the excess of useless developments in technology.)

Galley proofs of the little Gandhi book for New Directions came and I finished them in a couple of hours. A good letter from Morcelliana, and an architect in Madrid who will use two essays on art from *Disputed Questions,* etc., etc. Drawings from Lax. And a couple of the usual letters from crazy people. It is good to be part of that too! Vanity. But that is the thing about solitude. To *realize* how desperately we depend on the "existence" that recognition by others gives us, and how hopeless we are without it until God gives us feet to stand alone on. I have those feet sometimes, but once again, let me realize that there is no absolute "standing alone"—only awful poverty and insecurity and clinging to God in one's *need* of others, and greater appreciation of the smallest and most insignificant of communal verities.

*February 16, 1965, V.206–7*

# A Life of Clashes and Discoveries

I begin my jubilee year not exactly clear what I am doing, for everything is always beginning again. If everything in my life remains indefinite to some extent (though it is superficially definite), I accept this as a good thing. As a serious and perhaps troubling thing, always faced with possibilities, I must recognize that many of the "possibilities" are so illusory or so impossible as not to be worth considering. And at times I will not know which to consider, which not.

Coming to grips with my reality—(as if this were not going on all the time) coordinating, incorporating in a living regime all that I can reach to make relevant my presence here, on its way to ending. The religious depth of Ammonias, the perspicacity of Merleau-Ponty, even the tedious subtleties of Sartre, and always the Bible. Meetings of opposites, not carefully planned exclusions and mere inclusion of the familiar. A life of clashes and discoveries, not of repetitions: and yet also deep dread before God, and not trivial excitement.

*January 31 and February 2, 1964, V.68–69*

# A Bleak Extra Day

Bleak leap-year extra day. Black, with a few snowflakes, like yesterday when no snow stayed on the ground but there was sleet and the rain-buckets nearly filled. All the grass is white with, not snow, death.

A magazine in English—in Burma or somewhere (India?)—has an article by a Buddhist laywoman of her practice of meditation—emphasizing *mindfulness* of suffering in its existential reality, not escaping into ecstasy, etc. On one of the pages with this article, the following advertisement:

> If you use Balm
> Use only the *strongest* Balm
> de Songa's Dali Brand
> BURMA BALM (picture of jar—radiating light)
> So powerful yet only K1 a jar
> Relieves all pain—and quickly!
> From de Songa's of course.

Though it is still cold (with a bitterly biting wind) there were a few moments this afternoon when the coming of spring might almost be credible—perhaps because I so desire it after this cold winter. Out in St. Bernard's field, just as the clock was striking two, the sound of the bells came clear in a lull of the wind, and, with the wind down, the sun was suddenly warm. Fern-like walnut trees in the hollow stood as if ready for summer, and I looked at the distant valley and at the slight haze in the sky. Perhaps warm weather will once again be possible.

*February 24, 25, & 29, 1968, VII.57–58, 60*

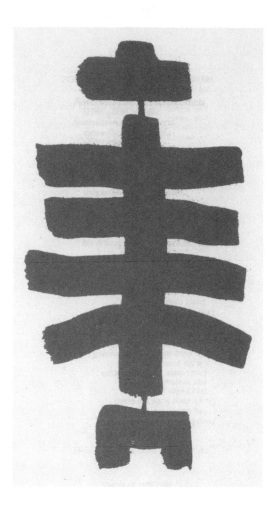

# In Me God Takes His Joy

Yesterday—more truly spring, and this is a spring dawn today, cold, but with birds singing. First time I have heard the whistling of the towhee this year. And the cardinals up in the woods to the west. The promise grows more and more definite. I look up at the morning star: in all this God takes His joy, and in me also, since I am His creation and His son, His redeemed, and member of His Christ. Sorrow at the fabulous confusion and violence of this world, which does not understand His love—yet I am called not to interpret or condemn this misunderstanding, only to return the love which is the final and ultimate truth of everything, and which seeks all men's awakening and response. Basically I need to grow in this faith and this realization, not only for myself but for all men.

To go out to walk slowly in this wood—this is a more important and significant means to understanding, at the moment, than a lot of analysis and a lot of reporting on the things "of the spirit."

*March 2, 1966, VI.23*

# The Comfort of Frogs

One thing the hermitage is making me see—that the universe is my home and I am nothing if not part of it. The destruction of the self that seems to stand outside the universe only as part of its fabric and dynamism. Can I find true being in God who has willed me to exist in the world? This I discover here in the hermitage, not mentally only but in depth. Especially, for example, in the ability to sleep. Frogs kept me awake at the monastery, not here—they are comfort, an extension of my own being—and now also the hum of the electric meter near my bed is nothing (although at the monastery it would have been intolerable). Acceptance of nature and even technology as my true habitat.

*March 2, 1965, V.212–13*

# With Contrite Hearts to God

Every day I mean to pray, especially in choir, for all the priests in the world who hear confessions and for all their penitents. I ask that everywhere this Sacrament may be administered and received in truth and justice and prudence and mercy and sorrow, and that priests and penitents may better know what they are doing and that they be filled with a great love and reverence for what they do. I ask that everywhere men may discover in themselves a great admiration for this Sacrament and may love it with their whole being, giving themselves entirely with contrite hearts to the mercy and truth of God, that His love may remake them in His own likeness—that is, that He may make them true.

Down there in the wooded hollow full of cedars I hear a great outcry of blue jays, and yonder is one of the snipes that are always flying and ducking around St. Joseph's hill. In all this I am reassured by the sweet, constant melody of my cardinals, who sing their less worldly tunes with no regard for any other sound on earth. And now the jays have stopped. Their tribulation rarely lasts very long.

Now I am under the sky. The birds are all silent except for some quiet bluebirds. But the frogs have begun singing their pleasure in all the waters and in the warm, green places where the sunshine is wonderful. Praise Christ, all you living creatures. For Him you and I were created. With every breath we love Him. My psalms fulfill your dim, unconscious song, O brothers in this wood.

*March 18 and 21, 1950, II.421–23*

# Looking in the Mirror of My Books

Yesterday *Seeds of Contemplation* arrived and it is very handsome. The best job of printing that has ever been done on any book by me. I can hardly keep my hands off it. Jay Laughlin says the burlap effect we have on the cover is really a material they are using now on the walls of nightclubs. Well, it is the Christian technique: sanctify the *saturnalia* and *lupercalia* with Christian liturgy: turn them into Christian feasts.

Every book that comes out under my name is a new problem. To begin with, every one brings with it an immense examination of conscience.

Every book I write is a mirror of my own character and conscience. I always open the final printed job with a faint hope of finding myself agreeable, and I never do.

The Passion and Precious Blood of Christ are too little in this new book—only hinted at here and there. Therefore the book is cold and cerebral. What is the good of trying to teach people to love God without preaching through Christ's wounds? The reason I do not do so is because I am still selfish. I find myself thinking about what we ought to get for dinner in Lent; about how to distribute signed complimentary copies of the *deluxe* edition of this book. I should never have gone into such a thing as a boxed special edition. I must be nuts.

*March 6, 1949, II.287*

# The Sparks of Truth

Fear of man and fear of God cannot coexist in one heart!

The wise follow the path of non-assertion and teach without words. —Lao Tzu

Beauty and *necessity* (for me) of the solitary life—apparent in the sparks of truth, small, recurring flashes of a reality that is *beyond doubt,* momentarily appearing, leading me further on my way. Things that need no explanation and perhaps have none, but which say: "Here! This way!" And with final authority.

It is for them that I will be held responsible. Nothing but immense gratitude! They cancel out all my mistakes, weaknesses, evasions, falsifications.

They lead further and further in that direction that has been shown me and to which I am called.

*March 2 and 6, 1966, VI.367*

# The Real in Front of My Nose

The solitary life reduces itself to a simple need—to make the choices that constantly imply preference for solitude fully understood (better: "properly" understood in relation to one's capacity at the moment). I find myself confronted with these choices repeatedly. They present themselves in their own way, and what they add up to these days is the question of emotional dependence on other people, simply, collectively—the community, friends, readers, other poets, etc. Over and over again I have to make small decisions here and there, in regard to one or other. Distractions and obsessions are resolved in this way. What the resolution amounts to, in the end: letting go of the imaginary and the absent and returning to the present, the real, what is in front of my nose. Each time I do this I am more present, more alone, more detached, more clear, better able to pray. Failure to do it means confusions, weakness, hesitation, fear—and all the way through to anguish and nightmares. It is not purely up to me to "succeed" each time. I cannot calculate the force of unidentified emotion that will well out of my unconscious. There are days of obscurity, frustrations, and crises when *nothing* is straight. However, I know my aim and I try at least to meditate.

So, when it comes to "preparing for death": in my case it means simply this reiterated decision for solitude as the reality called for me by God, as my penance and my cleansing, as my paying off debts, as my return to my right mind, and as my place of worship and prayer.

*March 8, 1966, VI.26*

# Love Makes Duty Beautiful

Yesterday, out in the beginning of a snowstorm, I dipped into the spiritual notes of Charles de Foucauld and was moved by their intensity. He speaks to God in a clear and vibrant voice, simple words, sentences of fire. This voice rings in the ear of your heart after you have put the book away and turned to other, less saintly voices, even though they may be religious voices, too. M. Lefèvre, who is teaching us chant, saw the book and told me how, some twenty-five years ago, it had made him weep and had driven him to the seminary. From which, he said, by the grace of God, he eventually emerged again into the world. I forget whether he has ten children or twelve.

God gives Himself to those who give themselves to Him. The way does not matter much, as long as it is the way He has chosen for us. I find that I can get just as close to God in studying the dry problems of moral theology as by reading the more burning pages of the mystics. For it is God's will that I, as a priest, should know my moral theology. Duty does not have to be dull. Love can make it beautiful and fill it with life. As long as we show lines of division between duty and pleasure in the world of the spirit, we will remain far from God and from His joy.

*March 9 and 10, 1950, II.417*

# My Unripeness in a Peace-Filled Luminosity

In a Zen koan someone said that an enlightened man is not one who seeks Buddha, or finds Buddha, but just an ordinary man who has *nothing left to do*. And yet mere stopping is not to arrive. To stop is to stay a million miles from it, and to do nothing is to miss it by the whole width of the universe. Yet how close it is, how simple it would be to have nothing more to do—if I had only done it. Meanwhile I am more content than I have ever been here with this unripeness, and thus I know that one day it will ripen, and one will see there had been nothing there at all, except an ordinary person with nothing to do in the first place.

The evening light. Purple coves and holes of shadow in the breasts of the hills and the white gable of Newton's house smiling so peacefully amid the trees in the middle of the valley. This is the peace and luminosity William Blake loved. Today after dinner a hawk, circling the novitiate and the church steeple, designed a free flight unutterably more pure than skating or music. How he flung himself down from on high and swooped up to touch lightly on the pinnacle of the steeple and sat there, then fell off to cut lovely curves all around the cedars, then off like an arrow to the south.

*March 10, 1963, IV.302*

# A Christian Remnant to Preach Peace

I am coming to see clearly the great importance of the concept of "realized eschatology"—the transformation of life and of human relations by Christ now (rather than an eschatology focused on future cosmic events—the Jewish poetic figures to emphasize the transcendence of the Son of God). "Realized eschatology" is the heart of genuine Christian humanism and hence its tremendous importance for the Christian peace effort, for example. The presence of the Holy Spirit, the call to repentance, the call to see Christ in man, the presence of the redeeming power of the Cross in the sacraments: these belong to the "last age," which we are in. But all these do not reveal their significance without a Christian mission of peace, the preaching of the Gospel of unity, peace, and mercy, the reconciliation of man with man, and so with God. This duty, however, does not mean that there will not at the same time be great cosmic upheavals. The preaching of peace by a remnant in an age of war and violence is one of the eschatological characteristics of the life of the Church. By this activity of the Church the work of God is mysteriously accomplished in the world.

*March 7, 1964, V.87*

# The Mud and Rain Are My Novice Masters

March is St. Benedict's month. Clearing thorn trees from the rocky shoulder over the middle bottom, where the new road is being made, I got to be good friends with his relic yesterday. How weary I am of being a writer. How necessary it is for monks to work in the fields, in the rain, in the sun, in the mud, in the clay, in the wind: these are our spiritual directors and our novice masters. They form our contemplation. They instill virtue in us. They make us stable as the land we live in. You do not get that out of a typewriter.

> For then are they truly monks: when they live by the
> labor of their hands, as our Fathers and the Apostles did.
> —*The Rule of St. Benedict* 48:8

*March 3, 1951, II.450*

# Seeding the Forest in Silence

The Communion antiphon sounded like bugles at the end of the Conventual Mass. This was because it is in the fifth tone and the fifth tone is full of melodies that echo in the new Jerusalem the silver trumpets that sounded in the temple of old. The sun is bright, and the spring is upon us, though the winds are cold. There are daffodils coming out by the door of the secular kitchen and in the beds outside this window. The Traxcavator roars merrily where they are trying to haul beams that weigh three tons up to the top floor of the new brothers' novitiate. And for my own part, I came out of Mass thinking about the trench where Frater John of God and I made haste to heel six thousand seedlings for the forest on Saturday afternoon. Today I hope to take about twenty novices out to the section of woods behind Donahue's and start planting these seedlings in the places we logged most heavily last winter.

When your tongue is silent, you can rest in the silence of the forest. When your imagination is silent, the forest speaks to you. It tells you of its unreality and of the Reality of God. But when your mind is silent, then the forest suddenly becomes magnificently real and blazes transparently with the Reality of God. For now I know that the Creation, which at first seems to reveal Him in concepts, then seems to hide Him by the same concepts, finally *is revealed in Him,* by the Holy Spirit. And we who are in God find ourselves united in Him with all that springs from Him. This is prayer, and this is glory!

*March 17, 1952, II.470–71*

# To Love and Serve Society

Came up to the hermitage at 4 a.m. The moon poured down silence over the woods, and the frosty grass sparkled faintly. More than two hours of prayer in firelight. The sun appeared and rose at 6:45. Sweet pungent smell of hickory smoke, and silence, silence. But birds again—presence, awareness. Our sorry idiot life, our idiot existence, idiot not because it has to be but because it is not what it could be with a little more courage and care. In the end it all comes down to renunciation, the "infinite bonding" without which one cannot begin to talk of freedom—but it must be renunciation, not mere resignation, abdication, "giving up." There is no simple answer, least of all in the community. The ordinary answers tend to be confusing and to hide the truth, for which one must struggle in loneliness—but *why in desperation?* This is not necessary.

"All the moral wretchedness as we see it about us is *our* wretchedness and *our* weakness," says Hromadka, in a powerful article about the Christian's concern for the (godless) man of today. From such a one I am willing to learn. He says the obligation of the Christian in socialist society is first to understand that society, to love it and serve its spiritual needs, and to bring up children in truthfulness for the sake of helping in the task of building a new world. "Not with groaning but with joyful love for the man of this modern world of ours we want to bring a service which no one can bring in our stead."

*March 26 and 27, 1964, V. 92–93*

# All Day the Frogs Sing

As soon as I get into a cell by myself I am a different person! Prayer becomes what it ought to be. Everything is very quiet. The door is closed but I have the window open. It is warm—grey clouds fly all night—and all day the frogs sing.

Now it is evening. The frogs still sing. After the showers of rain around dinnertime, the sky cleared. All afternoon I sat on the bed rediscovering God, rediscovering myself, and the office and Scripture and everything.

It has been one of the most wonderful days I have ever known in my life, and yet I am not attached to that part of it either. My pleasure or the contentment that I may have experienced out of silence and solitude and freedom from all care does not matter. But I know that is the way I ought to be *living:* with my mind and senses silent, contacts with the world of business and war and community troubles severed—not solicitous for anything high or low or far or near—not pushing myself around with my own fancies or desires or projects—and not letting myself get hurried off my feet by the excessive current of activity that flows through Gethsemani with full force.

*March 19, 1948, II.185*

# Love That Forgets It Was Born in Sorrow

My soul is trying to awaken and discover again the beauty of penance. I am ashamed of having made so many confessions of my faults in the monastery with so little sorrow and so feeble a hope of doing better. I want to say, over and over again, that I am sorry. I do not know how I can go on living unless I convince you, Jesus, that I am really sorry. The psalms say this better than I ever could. I am sorry that it has taken me so long to begin to discover the psalms. I am sorry that I have not lived them.

I am sorry for having let myself become so stupid and so torpid, thinking more of myself than of what I owe to your Love—and I owe You everything. Forgive me for paying so little attention. Without compunction and deep sorrow, contemplation is likely to be nothing more than a kind of idolatry. How can I love You if I do not know who I am and who You are? And how can I know this without sorrow? Jesus, I no longer want to have anything to do with love that forgets that it was born in sorrow, and therefore forgets to be grateful. Otherwise I will only go on lying to You, and I want to be done with insincerity forever and forever.

*March 18, 1950, II.420*

# God Is All in Christ

Went out to work clearing brush near the lake by the Bardstown Road yesterday and got my eyes infected. Conjunctivitis, they say. During the night office and especially during my Mass it was extremely painful today. Now I know what Gerard Manley Hopkins was talking about when, after correcting hundreds of exam papers, he said he felt as if his eyes were full of lemon juice. Got the thing fixed up with ointment and even bandaged, and it was better. Practically no reading all day—spent a lot of time "empty" and it was a happy, salutary day—a gift from God!

One thing Christ has said: "He who sees me sees the Father also."

In emptying Himself to come into the world, God has not simply kept His reality in reserve, in a safe place, and manifested a kind of shadow or symbol of Himself. He has emptied Himself and is *all* in Christ. Christ is not simply the tip of the little finger of the Godhead, moving in the world, easily withdrawn, never threatened, never really risking anything. God has acted and given Himself totally. He has become not only one of us but even our very selves.

*March 24 and 25, 1960, III.380–81*

# My Ruin Is My Fortune

In the Penitential Psalms, Christ recognizes my poverty in His poverty. Merely to see myself in the psalm is a beginning of being healed. For I see myself through His grace. His grace is working; therefore I am on my way to being healed. O the need of that healing! I walk from region to region of my soul and I discover that I am a bombed city.

When I meditated on Psalm 6—"Lord, not in thy fury"—I caught sight of an unexpected patch of green meadow along the creek on our neighbor's land. The green grass under the leafless trees and the pools of water after the storm lifted my heart to God. He is so easy to come to when even grass and water bear witness to His mercy. "I will water my couch with tears."

I have written about the frogs singing. Now they sing again. It is another spring. Although I am ruined, I am far better off than I have ever been in my life. My ruin is my fortune.

*March 3, 1953, III.39*

# Freedom Within Boundaries

Cold day with sun. The snow melts slowly.

A jet plane swooped low over the monastery with an interesting roar and then started climbing beautifully into the north, at great speed, with a flight I could not help but love and admire. In a few seconds it was high enough for the exhaust to come out white in a long trail.

Perhaps I have been struggling with an illusory idea of freedom, as if I were not, to a great extent, bound by my own history, the history of Gethsemani, of the country where I have become a citizen, etc. There are only certain very limited and special avenues of freedom open to me now, and it is useless to fight my way along where no issue is possible. This is true not only exteriorly but even interiorly and spiritually. To say that God can open up new ways is perhaps, among other things, to admit only that He has provided ways for me of which I cannot yet be aware, since I am too intent upon imaginary and experimental ones.

*March 18, 1960, III.379–80*

# The World Is Our Mother

I have come to the monastery to find my place in the world, and if I fail to find this place, I will be wasting my time in the monastery.

It would be a grave sin for me to be on my knees in this monastery, flagellated, penanced, though not now as thin as I ought to be, and spend my time cursing the world without distinguishing what is good in it from what is bad.

Wars are evil, but the people involved in them are good, and I can do nothing whatever for my own salvation or for the glory of God if I merely withdraw from the mess people are in and make an exhibition of myself and write a big book saying, "Look! I'm different!" To do this is to die. Because any man who pretends to be either an angel or a statue must die the death.

Coming to the monastery has been, for me, exactly the right kind of withdrawal. It has given me perspective. It has taught me how to live. And now I owe everyone else in the world a share in that life. My first duty is to start, for the first time, to live as a member of the human race, which is no more (and no less) ridiculous than I am myself. And my first human act is the recognition of how much I owe everybody else. There *is* a world which Christ would not pray for. But the world was also made by God and is good, and unless that world is our mother, we cannot be saints, because we cannot be saints unless we are first of all human.

*March 3, 1951, II.451*

# Shining Like the Sun

*(Feast of St. Joseph; Merton makes Solemn Vows at*
*Gethsemani on March 19, 1947)*

Yesterday, in Louisville, at the corner of Fourth and Walnut, suddenly realized that I loved all the people and that none of them were or could be totally alien to me. As if waking from a dream—a dream of my separateness, of the "special" vocation to be different. My vocation does not really make me different from the rest of men or put me in a special category except artificially, juridically. I am still a member of the human race, and what more glorious destiny is there for man, since the Word was made flesh and became, too, a member of the Human Race!

Thank God! Thank God! I am only another member of the human race, like all the rest of them. I have the immense joy of being man, a member of a race in which God Himself became incarnate. As if the sorrows and stupidities of the human condition could overwhelm me, now that I realize what we all are. And if only everybody could realize this! But it cannot be explained. There is no way of telling people that they are all walking around shining like the sun.

*March 19, 1958, III. 181–83*

# My Divinely Appointed Place

God has brought me to Kentucky, where the people are, for the most part, singularly without inhibitions. This is the precise place He has chosen for my sanctification. Here I must revise all my own absurd plans, and take myself as I am, Gethsemani as it is, and America as it is—atomic bomb and all. It is utterly peculiar, but nonetheless true, that, after all, one's nationality should come to have a meaning in the light of eternity. I have lived for thirty-six years without one. Nine years ago I was proud of the fact. I thought that, to be a citizen of heaven, all you had to do was throw away your earthly passport. But now I have discovered a mystery: that the ladies in the Office of the Deputy Clerk of the Louisville District are perhaps in some accidental way empowered to see that I am definitely admitted to the Kingdom of Heaven forever.

For now I am beginning to believe that perhaps the only, or at least the quickest, way that I shall become a saint is by virtue of the desires of many good people in America that I should become one. Last night I dreamt I was telling several other monks, "I shall be a saint," and they did not seem to question me. Furthermore, I believed it myself. If I do—(I shall)—it will be because of the prayers of other people who, though they are better than I am, still want me to pray for them.

*March 3, 1951, II.452*

# Christ Is My Own Kind

In Louisville I bought marvelous books for a few pennies—
including *The Family of Man* for fifty cents. All those fabulous pictures. And again, no refinements and no explanations are
necessary! How scandalized some would be if I said that this
whole book is to me a picture of Christ, and yet that is the Truth.
There, there is Christ in my own Kind, my own Kind—*Kind,*
which means "likeness" and which means "love" and which means
"child." Mankind. Like one another, the dear "Kind" of sinners
united and embraced in only one heart, in only one Kindness,
which is the Heart and Kindness of Christ. I do not look for sin in
you, Mankind. I do not see sin in you anymore today (though we
are all sinners). There is something too real to allow sin any longer
to seem important, to seem to exist, for it has been swallowed up,
it has been destroyed, it is gone, and there is only the great secret
between us that we are all one Kind, and what matters is not what
this or that one has committed in his heart, separate from the others, but the love that brings him back to all the others in the one
Christ, and this love is not our love but the Divine Bridegroom's.
It is the Divine Power and the Divine Joy—and God is seen and
reveals Himself as man, that is, in us, and there is no other hope of
finding wisdom than in God-manhood: our own manhood transformed in God!

*March 19, 1958, III.182–83*

# The New Man

The old and the new.

For the "old man," everything is old: he has seen everything or thinks he has. He has lost hope in anything new. What pleases him is the "old" he clings to, fearing to lose it, but he is certainly not happy with it. And so he keeps himself "old" and cannot change: he is not open to any newness. His life is stagnant and futile. And yet there may be much movement—but change that leads to no change. *Plus ça change, plus c'est la même chose.*

For the "new man" everything is new. Even the old is transfigured in the Holy Spirit and is always new. There is nothing to cling to, there is nothing to be hoped for in what is already past— it is nothing. The new man is he who can find reality where it cannot be seen by the eyes of the flesh—where it is not yet— where it comes into being the moment he sees it. And would not be (at least for him) if he did not see it. The new man lives in a world that is always being created, and renewed. He lives in this realm of renewal and creation. He lives in life.

The old man lives without life. He lives in death, and clings to what has died precisely because he clings to it. And yet he is crazy for change, as if struggling with the bonds of death. His struggle is miserable, and cannot be a substitute for life.

Thought of these things after Communion today, when I suddenly realized that I had, and for how long, deeply lost hope of "anything new." How foolish, when in fact the newness is there all the time.

*March 18, 1959, III.269*

# Prodigals Going Home

Yesterday afternoon, when Fr. Amadeus was preaching to us about the Holy Ghost in the infirmary chapel, Fr. George came bursting in, made the sign of "Thank you" three or four times, and departed. Last night he came down and wandered around the monastery.

Reverend Father, who used to be the infirmarian, says that sometimes, when they are near death, they get this urge to travel.

There was a Brother Mary up there who used to be the gate-keeper. He was dying. He had a wooden leg and a cane. He used to take his cane and go clumping around instead of staying in bed. They hid his wooden leg. He found it behind the door, and put it on and got going. They hid it again, in a closet where he couldn't find it. He lay in bed waving his hand and making signs, "The cane! The cane!"

There was another Brother who was dying. It was summer, very hot. He was in bed with very few clothes on. They found him walking out of the infirmary with nothing on him but a shirt. "Where are you going?" they asked him. "Nebraska!" he said. Nebraska is where he used to live.

I think I am beginning to understand something about the fifteenth chapter of St. Luke's Gospel—the lost sheep, the lost drachma, the Prodigal Son. Our dearest Lord is showing that He means everything about the fatted calf and the rejoicing to be taken literally, and that He means to pour out every kind of happiness in rivers upon those who ran away from His mercy but could not escape it.

*March 15 and 21, 1949, II.292, 295*

85

# A Moment of Clarity

A flash of sanity: the momentary realization that there is *no need* to come to certain conclusions about persons, events, conflicts, trends, even trends toward evil and disaster, as if from day to day, and even from moment to moment, I had to know and *declare* (at least to myself) that this is so and so, this is good, this is bad. We are heading for a "new era" or we are heading for destruction. What do such judgments mean? Little or nothing. Things are as they are in an immense whole of which I am a part and which I cannot pretend to grasp. To say I grasp it is immediately to put myself in a false position, as if I were "outside" it. Whereas to be "in" it is to seek truth in my own life and action, moving where movement is possible and keeping still when movement is unnecessary, realizing that things will continue to define themselves and that the judgments and mercies of God will clarify themselves and will be more clear to me if I am silent and attentive, obedient to His will, rather than constantly formulating statements in this age which is smothered in language, in meaningless and inconclusive debate in which, in the last analysis, nobody listens to anything except what agrees with his own prejudices.

*March 2, 1966, VI.366*

# Only One Is Your Teacher

The feast of Saint Thomas Aquinas, the Angelic Doctor, falls this year on the Tuesday of the Second Week in Lent. So there is a very striking coincidence in the liturgy: the Gospel of the feast speaks of the true Teachers, the salt of the earth, who "do and teach" and whose *works* shine before men. The Gospel for Tuesday in the Second Week of Lent speaks of the false teachers who have sat in the chair of Moses and have not done the works of Moses, that is, they have not kept the laws they talked about. Yet they have done works that have been dazzling in the eyes of men and have done them in order to shine before men, to have the first places in the synagogues and to be called Rabbi. The theme of both the feast and the ferial day is summed up in the line *Unus est Magister vester, Christus:* "Only one is your Teacher, Christ." It is Jesus Who teaches us in and through St. Thomas Aquinas and in St. Bonaventure and St. Augustine and in all the other doctors of the Church. We have no other Father and no other Doctor than Christ. It is Jesus Whose works shine in the lives of the saints. It is Jesus Who manifests Himself to us through the words of the Fathers and the theologians. The false doctors preach their own sanctity and Christ is not seen or heard in them. But the true teachers preach the sanctity of Christ, and He shines through them. He it is Whose Truth has made them holy.

*March 7, 1950, II.416*

# One Spirit Praying in All

Contemplative prayer is the recognition that we are the Sons of God, an experience of Who God is, and of His love for us, flowing from the operation of that love in us. Contemplative prayer is the voice of the Spirit crying out in us, "Abba, *Pater.*" In all prayer it is the Holy Spirit who prays in us, but in the graces of contemplation He makes us *realize,* at least obscurely, that it is He who is praying in us with a love too deep and too secret for us to comprehend. We exult in the union of our voice with His voice, and our soul springs up to the Father, through the Son, having become one flame with the Flame of their Spirit. The Holy Spirit is the soul of the Church, and it is to His presence in us that is attributed the sanctity of each one of the elect. He prays in us now as the Soul of the Church and now as the life of our own soul—but the distinction is real only in the external order of things. Interiorly, whether our prayer is private or public, it is the same Spirit praying in us: He is really touching different strings of the same instrument.

*March 21, 1950, II.422*

# A Preference for the Chant of Frogs

Warmer. Rain in the night. Frogs again. At first the waterhole (four feet long at most) had one frog or two. Now they are a small nation, loud in the night. The innocent nation, chanting blissfully in praise of the spring rain. Last evening I pruned a few little trees—including the beeches I had planted.

Today I have to go down to see Fr. Vernon Robertson, who evidently wants me to get involved in something—and I will try not to. He has been pestering me to come to Louisville to give a talk at Bellarmine College. And this is confirming me in my resolution to keep *out* of all that.

Almost every day I have to write a letter to someone refusing an invitation to attend a conference, or a workshop, or to give talks on the contemplative life, or poetry, etc. I can see more and more clearly how for me this would be a sheer waste, a Pascalian diversion, participation in a common delusion. (For others, no: they have the grace and mission to go around talking.) For me what matters is silence, meditation—and writing: but writing is secondary. To willingly and deliberately abandon this to go out and talk would be stupidity—for me. And for others, retirement into my kind of solitude would be equally stupid. They could not do it—and I could not do what they do.

*March 16, 1968, VII. 68*

# Offering Christ Our Sorry World

The center of all spiritual life is Christ in His Mass, Christ our Pasch who is slain and "dies now no more" but "draws all things to Himself," that we who are baptized in His death, crucifying our flesh and its desires, may live His life with a life hidden in Christ in God. And the heart of all life is not merely the static presence of the Blessed Sacrament, although Christ is truly living in our tabernacles, but above all in the *action* of the Mass, which is the center of all contemplation, an action in which the Christian family is gathered around Christ and in which Christ in His Body glorifies His Father. A sacrament of living unity in which the Love Who is God unites men to God and men to one another in Christ. When the Mass recovers its meaning, then devotion to the Blessed Sacrament reserved in the Tabernacle acquires its own true meaning and begins to live. Then the whole interior life is unified and vitalized and every department of it flows with life. In fact, "departments" and "sections" of one's life cease to exist in isolation and everything functions together.

I go to the altar offering Christ a sorry world to give to His Father in Thanksgiving, a world transformed into His own human life by our union with Him and His union with us in His Sacrifice and our Sacrifice which is His Pasch.

O God, give peace to your world. Give strength to the hearts of men. Raise us up from death in Christ. Give us to eat of His immortality and His glory. Give us to drink of the wine of His Kingdom.

*March 25, 1948, II.191–92*

# Grateful for Another Miracle

Shall I reread the bits in St. John of the Cross's *The Ascent of Mount Carmel* about the memory? They seem to do me so much good—always. Year after year, returning to them. In what sense do they make a difference in my life?

This *Journal*—the one I am writing right now. Apparently I have not yet written enough of it to become completely solitary and to be able to do without it. It is useless to drop the thing and say I am solitary just because I am not writing a *Journal,* when, in fact, the writing could help me find my way to where I am supposed to be traveling.

So I read about "forgetting" and write down all I remember. And somehow there is no contradiction here. It is simply a somewhat peculiar way of becoming a saint. I by no means insist that it is sanctity. All I say is that I must do what the situation seems to demand, and sanctity will appear when out of all this Christ, in His own good time, appears and manifests His own glory.

Tenderness of the Epistle, austerity of the Gospel in this morning's Mass, the Vigil of Passion Sunday. Last night, before Compline, out by the horse barn, looking at the orchard and thinking about what St. John of the Cross said about having in your heart the image of Christ crucified.

Confusion and fog pile up in your life, and then, by the power of the Cross, things once again are clear, and you know more about your wretchedness and you are grateful for another miracle.

*March 4 and 10, 1951, II.452–53*

# Setting My House in Order

Cold again. I took a good walk in the woods, watching the patterns of water in my quiet favorite creek. Then walked up and down in the sheltered place where we used to go for Christmas trees, thinking about life and death—and how impossible it is to grasp the idea that one must die. And what to do to get ready for it! When it comes to setting my house in order, I seem to have no ideas at all.

In the evening, stood for about fifteen minutes on the porch watching deer, etc., through the field glasses. The deer, five of them, were out by the brush piles beyond my fence, barely a hundred yards—less perhaps—from the hermitage. Hence I could see them very clearly and watch all their beautiful movements—from time to time they tried to figure me out, and would spread out their ears at me, and stand still, looking, and there I would be gazing right back into those big brown eyes and those black noses. And one, the most suspicious, would lift a foot and set it down again quietly, as if to stomp—but in doubt about whether there was a good reason. This one also had a stylish, high-stepping trot routine which the others did not seem to have. But what form! I was entranced by their perfection!

*March 6, 1966, VI.25*

# The Return to the Father

One thing very clear after Mass: the "return to the Father." The nonentity and insufficiency of all other concerns. A going clear out of the midst of all that is transitory and inconclusive. The return to the Immense, the Primordial, the Unknown, to Him Who Loves, to the Silent, to the Holy, to the Merciful, to Him Who is All.

The misdirectedness, the folly, the inanity of all that seeks anything but this great return, the whole meaning and heart of all existence. The absurdity of movements, of the goals that are not ultimate, the purposes that are "ends of the line" and, therefore, do not even begin.

To return is not to "go back" in time, but a going forward, a going beyond. To retrace one's steps is nothing on top of nothing, vanity of vanities, a renewal of the same absurdity twice over, in reverse.

To go beyond everything, to leave everything and press forward to the End and to the Beginning, to the ever new Beginning that is without End. To obey Him on the way in order to reach Him in Whom I have begun, Who is the Way and the End—(the Beginning).

*March 22, 1961, IV.101*

# Love Flowers When It Is Obedient

Dawn is beginning (5:30) on a mild spring morning. Holy Week is about to begin and I was never more conscious of its solemnity and its importance. I am a Christian, and a member of a Christian community. I and my brothers are to put aside everything else and recognize that we belong not to ourselves but to God in Christ. That we have vowed obedience, which is intended to unite us to Christ "obedient unto death—even the death of the Cross." That without our listening and attention and submission, in total self-renunciation and love for the Father's will, in union with Christ, our life is false and without meaning. But in so far as we desire, with Christ, that the Father's will may be done in us, as it is in heaven and in Christ, then even the smallest and most ordinary things are made holy and great. And then in all things the love of God opens and flowers, and our lives are transformed. This transformation is a manifestation and advent of God in the world.

One of the fruits of a solitary life is a sense of the absolute importance of *obeying God*—a sense of the need to obey and to seek His will, to choose freely to see and accept what comes from Him, not as a last resort, but as one's "daily super-substantial bread." Liberation from automatic obedience into the seriousness and gravity of a free choice to submit. But it is not easy to see always where and how!

*April 9, 1965, V.226–27*

# Our Responsibility Toward Creation

"Obedient unto death. . . ." Perhaps the most crucial aspect of Christian obedience to God today concerns the responsibility of the Christian in a technological society toward God's creation and God's will for His creation. Obedience to God's will for nature and for man—respect for nature and for man—in the awareness of our power to frustrate God's designs for nature and for man—to radically corrupt and destroy natural goods by misuse and blind exploitation, especially by criminal waste. The problem of nuclear war is only one facet of an immense, complex and unified problem.

There are very grave problems in the implications of certain kinds of Christian outlooks on "the world." The crux of the matter seems to be to what extent a Christian thinker can preserve his independence from obsessive modes of thought about secular progress. (Behind which is always the anxiety for us and for the Church to be "acceptable" in a society that is leaving us behind in a cloud of dust.) In other words, where is our hope? If in fact our hope is in a temporal and secular humanism of technological and political progress, we will find ourselves, in the name of Christ, joining in the stupidity and barbarism of those who are despoiling His creation in order to make money or get power for themselves. But our hope must be in God. And he who hopes in God will find himself sooner or later making apparently hopeless and useless protests against the barbarism of power.

*April 15, 1965, V.227–28*

# A Time of Wordless Deepening

Yesterday, on orders from Brother Clement and Reverend Father, I marked the trees Andy Boone is to cut, down in the hollow behind the hermitage, where the spring is. What a tangle of brush, saplings, vines, fallen trees, honeysuckle, etc.! Marks of deer everywhere. A fire in there would be awful. I hope we can get a space of an acre or so good and clear between here and the spring, and keep it clear. And I can use the spring, for I need it. All this is the geographical unconscious of my hermitage. Out in front, the "conscious mind," the ordered fields, the wide valley, tame woods. Behind, the "unconscious"—this lush tangle of life and death, full of danger, yet where beautiful things move, the deer, and where there is a spring of sweet, pure water—buried!

Light rain all night. The need to keep working at meditation—going to the root. Mere passivity won't do at this point. But activism won't do either. A time of wordless deepening, to grasp the inner reality of my nothingness in Him Who Is. Talking about it in these terms seems absurd. Seems to have nothing to do with the concrete reality that is to be grasped. My prayer is peace and struggle in silence, to be aware and true, beyond myself, and to go outside the door of myself, not because I will it, but because I am called and must respond.

*April 3 and 4, 1965, V.224*

# An Ever-Ancient New Creation

The power of the Easter Vigil liturgy in part stems from the fact that so many vestiges of primitive nature rites are included and sanctified in it. Mystery of fire and mystery of water. Mystery of spring: *Ver sacrum*. Fire, water and spring made sacred and meaningful theologically by the Resurrection of Christ, the new creation. Instead of stamping down the force of new life in us (and turning it into a dragon), let it be sweetened, sanctified and exalted, a figure of the life of the Spirit which is made present in our heart's love by the Resurrection.

One unquestionable improvement in the liturgy of Holy Week is the recovery of the more ancient tone for the singing of the Passion. It is splendidly austere and noble. Tremendously moving, like great tolling Flemish bells stirring whole populations in medieval cities, or like the stone sides of the Cistercian churches of the twelfth century which echoed to those tones. The chant was a mighty and living presence, binding us together in mystery. A great eloquence and sobriety that has almost been lost from the world but has been recovered. This eloquence, though, is stubborn, it is in man, it will not go. Christ preserves it, as He preserves us, from our own vulgarity.

*April 1, 1961, IV.104–5*

# Baptized by Darkness

The darkness is thinning and expects the sun. Birds begin to sing. No Mass. Everything is waiting for the Resurrection.

At the end of the night office, when the whole choir sank into the darkness of death and chanted without the faintest light, I thought of the darkness as a luxury, simplifying and unifying everything, hiding all the accidents that make one monk different from another monk, and submerging all distinctions in plain obscurity. Thus we are all one in the death of Christ. The darkness that descends upon us at the end of Lauds hears us sing the *Benedictus,* the canticle of thanksgiving for the Light who is to be sent. Now He is sent. He has come. He has descended into the far end of night, gathered our Fathers, the Patriarchs and Prophets, to Himself in Limbo. Now we will all be manifest. We will see one another with white garments, with palm branches in our hands. The darkness is like a font from which we shall ascend washed and illumined, to see one another, no longer separate, but one in the Risen Christ.

*April 8, 1950, II.428*

# Easter's Clean Taste

The grace of Easter is a great silence, an immense tranquility and a clean taste in your soul. It is the taste of heaven, but not the heaven of some wild exaltation. The Easter vision is not riot and drunkenness of spirit, but a discovery of order above all order—a discovery of God and of all things in Him. This is a wine without intoxication, a joy that has no poison in it. It is life without death. Tasting it for a moment, we are briefly able to see and love all things according to their truth, to possess them in their substance hidden in God, beyond all sense. For desire clings to the vesture and accident of things, but charity possesses them in the simple depths of God.

If Mass could only be, every morning, what it is on Easter morning! If the prayers could always be so clear, if the Risen Christ would always shine in my heart and all around me and before me in His Easter simplicity! For His simplicity is our feast. This is the unleavened bread which is manna and the bread of heaven, this Easter cleanness, this freedom, this sincerity. Give us always this bread of heaven. Slake us always with this water that we might not thirst forever!

This is the life that pours down into us from the Risen Christ, this is the breath of his Spirit, and this is the love that quickens His Mystical Body.

*April 9, 1950, II.429–30*

APRIL 7

# A Speech Formed in Silence

The mystery of speech and silence is resolved in the Acts of the Apostles. Pentecost is the solution. The problem of language is the problem of sin. The problem of silence is also a problem of love. How can a man really know whether to write or not, whether to speak or not, whether his words and his silence are for good or for evil, for life or for death, unless he understands the two divisions of tongues—the division of Babel, when men were scattered in their speech because of pride, and the division of Pentecost, when the Holy Ghost sent out men of one dialect to speak all the languages of the earth and bring all men to unity: that they may be one, Father, Thou in Me and I in them, that they may be one in Us.

The Acts of the Apostles is a book full of speech. It begins with tongues of fire. The Apostles and disciples come downstairs and out into the street like an avalanche, talking in every language. And the world thought they were drunk. But before the sun had set, they had baptized three thousand souls out of Babel into the One Body of Christ. At Pentecost we sing of Whom they spoke. The false Jerusalem, the old one that was a figure and had died, could not prohibit them from speaking (Acts 4). But the more they loved one another and loved God, the more they declared His word. And He manifested Himself through them. That is the only possible reason for speaking—it justified speaking without end, as long as the speech formed is from silence and brings your soul again to silence.

*April 14, 1950, II.430–31*

# A Task to Spiritualize the World

The task of a priest is to spiritualize the world. He raises his consecrated hands, and the grace of Christ's resurrection goes out from him to enlighten the souls of the elect and of them that sit in darkness and the shadow of death. Through his blessing material creation is raised up and sanctified and dedicated to the glory of God. The priest prepares the coming of Christ by shedding upon the whole world the invisible light that enlightens every man that comes into the world. Through the priest the glory of Christ seeps out into creation until all things are saturated in prayer.

All week I have been thinking of the inestimable greatness and dignity of faith. Faith is higher and more perfect than all knowledge that is accessible to us on earth. The only really valuable experience is a deepening and intensification of faith by love and the gifts of the Holy Ghost—an intensification that only simplifies our faith and makes it more clear by purifying it of every created image and species. So that the purest experience of all begins with the realization of how far faith transcends experience. Our only true greatness is in the humility of living faith. The simpler and purer our faith is, the closer it brings us to God, Who is infinitely great. That is why everyone who humbles himself shall be exalted, and everyone who exalts himself, in the appetite for great lights and extraordinary experiences and feelings and mystical consolations, shall be humbled. Because the richer he desires to be in these things, the poorer he will be in the sight of God, in Whose eyes greatness is nothing.

*April 16 and 18, 1950, II.431–32*

# The Peace of Submerged Dragons

A gay, bright, glorious day and a very fine Easter such as I do not remember for a long time. The Vigil was tremendous for me and the glory of Christ was in it. There has been splendor in everything (including the emptiness of Good Friday morning, when rain came down in torrents and I stayed in the hermitage).

Yesterday—reading bits of Dame Julian of Norwich and today I began Gregory of Nyssa's homilies on the Canticle.

"There is not a more dangerous tendency in history than that of representing the past as if it were a rational whole and dictated by clearly defined interest," says Huizinga. What about the present? An even greater error.

Fr. Sylvanus was in town to go to the doctor and brought back a newspaper story about a man in the Kentucky mountains, a former coal miner, who for thirteen years has been living as a hermit, with a dog, in a pitiful little shack without even a chimney and with an old car seat for a bed. "Because of all these wars." A real desert father, and probably not too sure why.

The hills are suddenly dark blue. Very green alfalfa in the bottoms. Yellow or mustard or sienna sage grass in my own field. Here there is no impatience. I am a submerged dragon. The peace of the Easter Alleluias.

*April 2 and 7, 1961, IV.105–6*

# Relax and Live

Quiet, grey afternoon. It is warmer. Birds sing. There will be more rain. Cocks crowing in the afternoon silence, very distant.

A thunderstorm. The first I have sat through in the hermitage. Here you really can *watch* a storm. White snakes of lightning suddenly stand out in the sky and vanish.

The valley is clouded with rain as white as milk. All the hills vanish.

The thunder cracks and beats. Rain comes flooding down from the roof eaves, and grass looks twice as green as before.

Not to be known, not to be seen.

Father Gabriel Sweeney, the little white-haired Passionist who is in the novitiate, who asked to leave before Easter, and was dissuaded by Reverend Father, stands with a piteous expression in the novitiate library reading *Relax and Live*. Sooner or later they come to that.

The evening sky over the valley. Long lines of clouds traveling in strong cold wind toward the east.

*Janua Coeli:* the Gate of Heaven. How different prayer is here at the hermitage. Clarity—direction—to Christ the Lord for the great gift—the passage out of this world to the Father, entry into the kingdom. I know what I am here for. May I be faithful to this awareness.

*April 15 and 16, 1961, IV.107–8*

# My Art of Confession and Witness

The work of writing can be for me, or very close to, the simple job of *being:* by creative reflection and awareness to help life itself live in me, to give its *esse* an existent, or to find a place, rather, in *esse* by action, intelligence, and love. For to write is to love: it is to inquire and to praise, to confess and to appeal. This testimony of love remains necessary. Not to reassure myself that I am ("I write, therefore I am"), but simply to pay my debt to life, to the world, to other men. To speak out with an open heart and say what seems to me to have meaning. The bad writing I have done has all been authoritarian, the declaration of musts, and the announcement of punishments. Bad because it implies a lack of love, good insofar as there may yet have been some love in it. The best stuff has been more straight confession and witness.

*April 14, 1966, VI. 371*

# Staying Found

Good Shepherd Sunday. Jesus, the "Shepherd and Bishop" of our souls, gave me many graces appropriate to this day. "I know mine and mine know me" (John 10:14). "My sheep hear my voice." I read over St. John of the Cross's *Cautions,* which were the things I had in mind to keep when I made my solemn profession, and I see to my dismay how much I had forgotten them.

I went to Fr. Placid in the confessional and he told me I was too restless and that what I was looking for (union with God) was right in front of my nose and I couldn't see it. Also, there was no earthly reason why any amount of work should prevent my union with God, provided it is His will.

And all that is true. My mind is scattered among things, not because of my work, but became I am not detached, and I do not attend first of all to God. On the other hand, I do not attend to Him because I am so absorbed in all these objects and events. I have to wait on His grace. But how stubborn and slow my nature is. And how I keep confusing myself and complicating things for myself by useless twisting and turning.

What I need most of all is the grace to really accept God as He gives Himself to me in every situation. "He came unto His own and His own received Him not."

Good Shepherd, You have a wild and crazy sheep in love with thorns and brambles. But please don't get tired of looking for me! I know You won't. For You have found me. All I have to do is stay found.

*April 11, 1948, II.198–99*

# Nothing Counts Except Love

One thing has suddenly hit me—that nothing counts except love; that a solitude that is not simply the wide-openness of love and freedom is nothing. Love and solitude are the one ground of true maturity and freedom. Solitude that is just solitude and nothing else (i.e., *excludes* everything else but solitude) is worthless. True solitude embraces everything, for it is the fullness of love that rejects nothing and no one, and is open to All in All.

After several days of rain the sky is clearing. Afternoons at the hermitage become once again possible. I walked a bit in the woods, under the pines, and again plan work, study, ideas, not to affirm myself but to give to others. Anything I have that is good is worth sharing. What is not worth sharing is not worth bothering about. What is "mine" is tolerated only insofar as I am willing to share it with everybody.

I see this as ambiguous though. It needs qualification.

I have got to be faithful, detached, obedient, concerned not only for my own life as I want to live it, but for God's will, which remains to be realized in and through me. That is all.

*April 14, 1966, VI.40*

# Bearing Witness to What Is Simple

Is there not a false eschatology of the "new heaven and new earth" which places its hope in the power of science to transform earth and heaven into places of happiness and bliss? (With God or without Him for that matter.) Is the true prospect rather that the stupidity and pride of man will ruin the earth, and that God will restore it through charity and the tears of the poor, the "remnant" and the saints? I am not saying this false eschatology is in that article of K. V. Truhlar's, which has excellent things in it—but theologians occupied with the Christian and the world are not sufficiently aware of what technology is doing to the world and, in failing to make distinctions, they tend to embrace all manifestations of progress without question in "turning to the world" and in "Christian temporal action." Hence inevitably we get Christians in the U.S. supporting a criminally stupid military adventure in Vietnam.

There is no question for me that my one job as monk is to live the hermit life in simple, direct contact with nature, primitively, quietly, doing some writing, maintaining such contacts as are willed by God, and bearing witness to the value and goodness of simple things and ways, and loving God in it all. I am more convinced of this than of anything contingent upon my life, and I am sure it is what He asks of me. Yet I do not always respond with simplicity.

*April 15, 1965, V.228–29*

# A Nation of Fetishes

The great sin, the source of all other sins, is idolatry. And never has it been greater, more prevalent, than now. It is almost completely unrecognized—precisely because it is so overwhelming, total. It takes in everything. There is nothing else left. Fetishism of power, machines, possessions, medicine, sports, clothes, etc., all kept going by greed for money and power. The Bomb is only one accidental aspect of the cult. Indeed, the Bomb is not the worst. We should be thankful for it as a sign, a revelation of what all the rest of our civilization points to: the self-immolation of man to his own greed and his own despair. And behind it all are the principalities and powers whom man serves in his idolatry. Christians are as deeply involved in this as everyone else.

This is clearly one of the most important and inescapable messages of the Bible: that unless man turns from his idols to God, he will destroy himself, or rather this idolatry will prove itself to be his destruction. (The idolater is already self-destroyed.) The other thing: man as a whole will not change. He will destroy himself. The Bible sees no other end to the story. But Christ has come to save from this destruction all who seek to be saved. In and through them He will recreate the world. By no means are we to interpret this to mean that enlightened ethics and polite good intentions are going to make technological society safe for man, and that the new creation will be in fact the technological paradise (plus a renewed liturgy!).

*April 17, 1965, V.230–31*

# Death in the Newspapers

There is so much death in the newspapers that no one dies in them anymore and no one lives in them. There are neither lives nor deaths in our press, only a stream of words passing over the living and the dead without ever touching them.

In the monastery, or at any rate in choir, I have been forgetting how to think—and only in the past few days have I woken up to the fact that this is very dangerous! I mean the constant, habitual passivity we get into. No matter how honest the surroundings and how clean the doctrine believed in them, no man can afford to be passive and to restrict his thinking to a new rehearsal, in his own mind, of what is being repeated all around him.

But we are not as honest as we think, and our doctrine is not as pure as we hope it is. I least of all can afford to be passive in this place.

One must constantly be asking himself—"What do I mean by this? Am I saying what I mean? Have I understood what this implies? Have I some notion of the *consequences* of what I am saying?" I am particularly bad on the last question because usually I think on paper, that is, I often do not really know what I think until it is set out before me in black and white: then I can agree or disagree.

*April 30 and May 2, 1958, III. 198–99*

# We Are All Afflicted with Illusion

My present view—provisionally:

*a.* "The world," in the sense of collective myths and aspirations of contemporary society, is not to be unconditionally accepted or rejected, because whether we like it or not, we are all part of it and there is a sense in which it has to be accepted.

*b.* But I refuse an optimism that blesses *all* these myths and aspirations as "temporal values" and accepts *all* projects of man's society as good, progressive, and laudable efforts in which all are to cooperate. Here one certainly has to distinguish. War in Vietnam—no; civil rights—yes; and a huge area of uncertainties, official projects dressed up in approved inanities.

*c.* I am convinced of the sickness of American affluent society. To bless that sickness as a "temporal value" is something I absolutely refuse. Love of "the world" in this case means understanding and love of the millions of people *afflicted by* the sickness and suffering from it in various ways: compassion for them, desire to liberate them from their obsessions (how can anyone do it? We are all afflicted), to give them some measure of sanity and authenticity.

*d.* The error is in rejecting the sick and condemning them along with the sickness.

*e.* The only right way: to love and serve the man of the modern world, but not simply to succumb, with him, to all his illusions about the world.

*April 30, 1958, III.198*

# Taking Political Action

Bright noon sun and warmth. I left the refectory early and, as I was hurrying across the Night Pasture, I could hear the echo of Fr. Raymond's urgent shouts (he is reader in the refectory) relayed over a loudspeaker in the empty barns and in the farm building. It is characteristic of us that all our noise has to be heard *everywhere*.

To what extent is it simply a temptation for me to want to take some political position, as distinct from an ethical one? Are the two separable, for instance, where war is concerned? One thing is sure—it is beginning to be clear that opposition to nuclear war is something else than being simply a "pacifist." Also, opposition on the moral level demands some kind of open expression of one's position.

The question is—how to clearly, definitely and openly make such a stand without lending oneself to exploitation by one or another of the big power groups?

Reading Chuang Tzu. I wonder seriously if the answer, the only possible answer, does not lie hid far below the political and ethical levels. Ethics, and politics, certainly, but only in passing, only as a "night's lodging"? When all action has somehow become absurd, shall one act merely because at some other times action was once expected and significant? Like setting the dinner table in a time of starvation when you have no food, but setting it out anyway, out of habit?

*April 8, 1961, IV.106–7*

# The Irrelevant Middle Ages?

I wonder if I have not said ill-considered things about Christian traditions—things that will only add to the present confusion, motivated by some obscure desire to protect my own heart against wounds by inflicting them myself (i.e., the wounds of loss and separation: as if I were saying, since the Middle Ages are no longer relevant to us, I might as well be the first to admit it and get it over with. But *are* the Middle Ages irrelevant? Of course not, and I have not begun to believe it! And it is part of my vocation to make observations that preserve a living continuity with the past, and with what is good in the past!).

The study of medieval exegesis is a way of entering into the Christian experience of that age, an experience most relevant to us, for if we neglect it, we neglect part of our own totality in Henri de Lubac, Hans Urs von Balthasar, etc. But it must not be studied from the outside. Same idea in Kitaro Nishida on Japanese culture and the Japanese view of life. I have a real sense this Easter that my own vocation demands a deepened and experiential study, *from within* (by connaturality), of the medieval tradition as well as of, to some extent, Asian tradition and experiences, particularly Japanese, particularly Zen: i.e., in an awareness of a common need and aspiration with these past generations.

*April 18 and 19, 1965, V.231–32*

# God's Vestige in His Creatures

Yesterday I was sitting in the woodshed reading and a little Carolina wren suddenly hopped onto my shoulder and then onto the corner of the book I was reading and paused a second to take a look at me before flying away.

There is something you cannot know about a wren by cutting it up in a laboratory and that you can know only if it remains fully and completely a wren, itself, and hops on your shoulder if it feels like it.

A tame animal is already invested with a certain falsity by its tameness. By becoming what we want it to be, it takes a disguise that we have decided to impose upon it.

Even a wild animal merely "observed" is not seen as it really is, but rather in the light of our investigation (color changed by fluorescent lighting). But people who watch birds and animals are already wise in their way.

I want not only to observe but to *know* living things, and this implies a dimension of primordial familiarity that is simple and primitive and religious and poor. This is the reality I need, the vestige of God in His creatures.

*April 5, 1958, III.189–90*

APRIL 21

# The Paradise Season

It is already hot as summer. Everything is breaking into leaf, and the pine saw fly worms are all over the young pines.

This morning I sat in the monastery dentist's chair having my teeth cleaned and X-rayed, while the students banged and walloped next door demolishing the old library.

Early mornings are now completely beautiful—with the Easter moon in its last quarter high in the blue sky, and the light of dawn spreading triumphantly over the wide, cool green valley. It is the paradise season!

Then yesterday Flannery O'Connor's new book, *Everything That Rises Must Converge,* arrived, and I am already well into it, grueling and powerful! A relentlessly perfect writer, full of tragedy and irony. But what a writer! And she knows every aspect of the American meanness, and violence, and frustration. And the Southern struggle of will against inertia.

A pine warbler was caught in the novitiate scriptorium, beating against the window, and I got a good look at him letting him out. A couple of towhees are all around the hermitage.

*April 23, 1965, V.232–33*

# My Old Freedom in the Silence
# of "What Is"

Once again the old freedom, the peace of being without care, of not being at odds with the real sense of my own existence and with God's grace to me. Far better and deeper than any consolation of eros. A sense of stability and substantiality—of *not* being deceived. Though I know there was much good in our love—M.'s and mine—I also see clearly how deceptive it was and how it made me continually lie to myself. How we both loved each other and lied to each other at the same time. How difficult it must be to keep going *in truth* in a marriage. Heroic! For me the other truth is better: the truth of simply getting along without eros and resting in the silence of "what is." The deep inner sustaining power of silence. When I taste this again, so surely, after so long, I know what it means to repent of my infidelity and foolishness; yet at the same time I do not try to build up again anything that was properly torn down. It was good that I (we) went through the storm: it was the only way to learn a truth that was otherwise inaccessible.

All the old desires, the deep ones, the ones that are truly mine, come back now. Desire of silence, peace, depth, light. I see I have been foolish to let myself be so influenced by the current trends, though they perhaps have their point. On the other hand, I know where my roots really are—in the mystical tradition, not in the active and anxious secular city business. Not that I don't have an obligation to society. This evening on the porch I sang the Alleluias and the Introit of tomorrow's Mass.

*April 10 and 15, 1967, VI.217–18*

# The Crooked Tree

As long as I do not pretend I suffer, as long as I do not trade in false coin nor camp too much upon flowers, nor claim that I have disappeared, my brothers' prayers can always mend me. The windows are open. Let the psalms fly in. Prime each morning makes me safe and free. The Day Hours sustain me with their economy. By night I am buried in Christ. At 3 a.m. I wear the old white vestments and say the Mass of the Blessed Virgin. Through the gaps in my own prayer come the psalms of the night office that I discovered again in the woods yesterday afternoon.

There, there is the crooked tree, the moss with my secrets, those pines upon that cliff of shake, the valley living with the tunes of diesel trains. Nobody knows the exact place I speak of, and why should I tell them? For every man is his own Jacob. He wakes up at the foot of his own ladder and sees the angels going up and down, with God at the top of the ladder. And thus he wakes up in his own unrecognizable house, his gate of heaven.

*April 22, 1951, II. 456–57*

# Liberation Day

Evening. A full moon rising over the sharply outlined valley. Everything cool, green and very clear. I should have gone out for a long walk this afternoon but I had to write letters and then I have acquired a tape recorder and had to fool with it a little to make sure I know how to work it. It is a very fine machine and I am abashed by it. I take back some of the things I have said about technology.

I have made this day a sort of perplexed celebration—said Mass for M. and her fiancé and honestly hope they will get back in love again; in fact, by now, they probably are. And that they will be happy in marriage someday soon . . . and so on. I am sure there is no real problem. At least, I tell myself so. M. may want to hold on to me sentimentally in some way, but I am convinced that the real love is more or less over between us, though we shall always be fond of each other I am sure.

So in a way it is a liberation day—and I have made up my mind to be what I am supposed to be. (Finally!)

Actually it is a most happy evening—could not be more perfect. I have some bourbon (Tommie O'Callaghan brought some) and am playing an ancient Django Reinhardt record that brings back the thirties. (Regression?) Perhaps in a little while I shall go out and stroll around under the trees. And try to tell myself that I am not really sad at all.

*April 22, 1967, VI.22–33*

# Loyal to the Truth

The Truth is a Way and a Person—and a Way and a Person have to be found and followed. Truth is to be lived. There are, in fact, no simple formulas that will suffice once for all. True, there are principles. But a principle is worthless if it is usually known and not applied. And if we apply it, we have to have regard for circumstances that make the principle true in a unique way in this unique case—or that perhaps calls into action some entirely different principle that gives the lie to the first.

How hard it is to be loyal to the Truth when most of the time you do not see any of it! Thus loyalty demands constant criticism, constant rejection of empty formulas, of words used to evade the struggle and to allay anguish, rather than to find Truth or express it. And can we use words simply to *find* Truth? Is this not an illusion?

There grows in me an immense dissatisfaction with all that is merely passively accepted as truth, without struggle and without examination. Faith, surely, is not passive, and not an evasion. And today, more than ever, the things we believe, I mean especially the things we accept on *human faith*—reported matters of "fact," questions of history, of policy, of interpretation, of wants—they should be *very few*. In great spheres we should believe little or nothing, except what is obviously and incontrovertibly true—that the atomic bomb was dropped on Nagasaki, for instance.

*April 20, 1958, III.192*

# Heavenliness in the Nature of Things

Real spring weather—these are the precise days when everything changes. All the trees are fast beginning to be in leaf, and the first green freshness of a new summer is all over the hills. Irreplaceable purity of these days chosen by God as His sign!

Mixture of heavenliness and anguish. Seeing "heavenliness" suddenly, for instance, in the pure white of mature dogwood blossoms against the dark evergreens in the cloudy garden. "Heavenliness" too of the song of the unknown bird that is perhaps here only for these days, passing through, a lovely, deep, simple song. Seized by this "heavenliness" as if I were a child—a child's mind I have never done anything to deserve to have and which is my own part in the heavenly spring. Not of this world, or of my making. Born partly of physical anguish (which is really not there, though. It goes quickly). Sense that the "heavenliness" is the real nature of things, *not* their nature, but the fact they are a gift of love and of freedom.

*April 23, 1964, V.99*

# Everything Transfigured

*(Merton celebrates his first Mass in his hermitage's new Chapel on April 27, 1968)*

The icon of St. Elias, which Jack Ford brought me from St. Meinrad's, and which yesterday I put up on the east wall of my hermitage. Fabulously beautiful and delicate and strong. A great red transparent globe of light, with angelic horses rearing in unison, and angels lifting it all up to the blackness of the divine mystery—from, below, the dark curve and shelves of the mountain from which Eliseus reaches into the globe to touch the mantle of the prophet, who stands in a little, finely drawn, very simple Russian peasant's cart (in the globe of fire!).

Below, Elias sleeps: that was before, when he had sorrow. The angel leans over him and mentions the hearth-cake to the sleeping prophet.

What a thing to have by you! It changes everything! Transfiguring everything!

Outside the door, a double bloom on one large violet iris, standing out of the green spears of the daylilies. And on the tongue of one bloom walks a great black-gold bee, the largest honeybee I ever saw. To be part of all this is to be infinitely rich.

*April 24, 1963, IV.315–16*

# Walking Heaven's Ground

Heavenliness—again. For instance, walking up into the woods yesterday afternoon—as if my feet acquired a heavenly lightness from contact with the earth of the path. As though the earth itself were filled with an indescribable spirituality and lightness, as if the true nature of the earth were to be heavenly, or rather as if all things, in truth, had a heavenly existence. As if existence itself was heavenliness. The same—at Mass, obviously. But with a new earthy and yet pure heavenliness of bread. The ikons, particularly of St. Elias and his great red globe of light, and the desert gold, the bird red on the mountain: all transformed!

*April 24, 1964, V.99*

# Only One Unhappiness

Day of Recollection. If I were to make any resolutions, it would be the same old ones—no need to make them—they have been made. No need to reflect on them—it doesn't take much concentration to see how I keep them. I struggle along. It is useless to break your head over the same old details week after week and year after year, pruning the same ten twigs off the top of the tree. Get at the *root:* union with God. On these days of recollection drop everything and hide in yourself to find Him in the silence where He is hidden within you, and listen to what He has to say.

There is only one thing to live for: love. There is only one unhappiness: not to love God. That is what pains me on these days of recollection, to see my own soul so full of movement and shadows and vanities, cross-currents of dry wind stirring up the dust and rubbish of desire. I don't expect to avoid this humiliation in my life, but when will I become cleaner, more simple, more loving? "Have mercy on me, O God. My sin is always before me."

*April 20, 1947, II.64–65*

# We Have Work to Accomplish

Most important of all—Man's creative vocation to prepare, consciously, the ultimate triumph of Divine Wisdom. Man, the microcosm, the heart of the universe, is the one who is called to bring about the fusion of cosmic and historic processes in the final invocation of God's wisdom and love. In the name of Christ and by his power, Man has a work to accomplish—to offer the cosmos to the Father, by the power of the Spirit, in the Glory of the Word. Our life is a powerful Pentecost in which the Holy Spirit, ever active in us, seeks to reach through our inspired hands and tongues into the very heart of the material world created to be spiritualized through the work of the Church, the Mystical Body of the Incarnate Word of God.

If I can unite in *myself,* in my own spiritual life, the thought of the East and the West, of the Greek and Latin Fathers, I will create in myself a reunion of the divided Church, and from that unity in myself can come the exterior and visible unity of the Church. For if we want to bring together East and West, we cannot do it by imposing one upon the other. We must contain both in ourselves and transcend both in Christ.

*April 25 and 28, 1957, III.85–87*

# Learning Love's Language

I live in the woods out of necessity. I get out of bed in the middle of the night because it is imperative that I hear the silence of the night, alone, and, with my face on the floor, say psalms, alone, in the silence of the night.

It is necessary for me to live here alone without a woman, for the silence of the forest is my bride and the sweet dark warmth of the whole world is my love, and out of the heart of that dark warmth comes that secret which is only heard in silence, but it is the root of all the secrets that are whispered by all the lovers in their beds all over the world. I have an obligation to preserve the stillness, the silence, the poverty, the virginal point of pure nothingness which is at the center of all other loves. I cultivate this plant silently in the middle of the night and water it with psalms and prophecies in silence. It becomes the most beautiful of all the trees in the garden, at once the primordial paradise tree, the *axis mundi,* the cosmic axle, and the Cross.

It is necessary for me to see the first point of light that begins to be dawn. It is necessary to be present alone at the resurrection of Day in solemn silence at which the sun appears, for at this moment all the affairs of cities, of governments, of war departments, are seen to be the bickering of mice. I receive from the eastern woods, the tall oaks, the one word DAY. It is never the same. It is always in a totally new language.

*May 1965, V.240–41*

# Being in One Place

A cool and lovely morning, clear sky, ever-changing freshness of woods and valley! One has to be in the same place every day, watch the dawn from the same house, hear the same birds wake each morning to realize how inexhaustibly rich and different is "sameness." This is the blessing of stability, and I think it is not evident until you enjoy it alone in a hermitage. The common life distracts you from life in its fullness. But one must be able to share this fullness, and I am not for a complete and absolute solitude without communication (except temporarily).

Yesterday was St. Bede's day (he died on Ascension Day, 735). He is one of the saints I most love, and the simple story of his life and death fill me with love and joy. The afternoon was peaceful and marvelous—a nice walk and meditation at St. Malachy's field, then came back and gave a conference on Philoxenus. The simplicity and innocence of the monks is a real joy, a shining joy, so evident one does not notice it. Yet I must say that concelebration in the morning did nothing to express the reality of love and oneness in Christ that is actually here. The singing was timid and depressing, and I must say that we are not anywhere near properly realizing and manifesting what it is all about.

The flycatchers, tamer and tamer, play about on the chairs and baskets on my porch, right in front of this window, and they are enthralling. Wrens come too, less frequently.

*May 28 and 30, 1965, V.251–52*

# Day of a Stranger

The hills are blue and hot. There is a brown, dusty field in the bottom of the valley. I hear a machine, a bird, a clock. The clouds are high and enormous. In them, the inevitable jet plane passes: this time probably full of fat passengers from Miami to Chicago, but presently it will be a plane with a bomb in it. I have seen the plane with the bomb in it fly low over me, and I have looked up out of the woods directly at the closed bay. Like everyone else, I live under the bomb. But, unlike most people, I live in the woods. Do not ask me to explain this. I am embarrassed to describe it. I live in the woods out of necessity. I am both a prisoner and an escaped prisoner. I cannot tell you why, born in France, my journey ended here. I have tried to go further but I cannot. It makes no difference. When you are beginning to be old, and I am beginning to be old, for I am fifty, both times and places no longer take on the same meaning. Do I have a "day"? Do I spend my "day" in a "place"? I know there are trees here. I know there are birds here. I know the birds in fact very well, for there are exactly fifteen pairs of birds living in the immediate area of my cabin and I share this particular place with them: we form an ecological balance. This harmony gives "place" a different configuration.

*May 1965, V.239*

# History and the Passion of Christ

The bombing goes on in Vietnam. The whole thinking of this country is awry on war: basic conviction that force is the only thing that is effective. That doubtless it is in many ways not "nice" but one must be realistic and use it, with moral justification so as not to be just gangsters as "they" are (the enemy). Thus there is determination to settle everything by force and to make sure one's force is verbally justified.

It is not altogether easy to make an act of faith that all of history is in God's hands. But history *is* in the hands of God, and the decisions of men lead infallibly to the full expression of what is really hidden in them and in their society. The actions of the U.S. in Asia are God's judgment on the U.S. We have decided that we will police the world—by the same tactics used by the police in Alabama: beating "colored people" over the head because we believe they are "inferior." In the end, an accounting will be demanded.

We have to see history as a book that is sealed and opened by the Passion of Christ. But we still read it from the viewpoint of the Beast. Passion of Christ = the passion of the poor, the underprivileged, etc. Viewpoint of the Beast: self-righteousness and cruelty of power. Hubris of human might and technological efficiency. But the same cruelty is bred by this hubris in the weak, who grow strong by resisting it and overcoming it—to be proud in their turn. Christ remains in agony until the end of time, and in His agony Christ triumphs over all power.

*May 22, 1965, V.249–50*

# The Return to Unity

Lightning, thunder and rain on and off all night. The lovely grey-green valley, misty clouds sweeping low over the hills and forest out there in the South, iron dark clouds heavy above them.

As I have been asked to write a piece on Paul the Hermit (died ca. 340), I reread his *Vita* by St. Jerome. A work of art, really, with plenty of monastic theology in its symbolism. A beautiful piece of writing, with deep mystical and psychological implications—so that whether or not it is "historical" is irrelevant. It awakens a kind of inner awareness of psychic possibilities which one so easily forgets and neglects. The return to unity, to the ground, the paradisial inner sacred space where the archetypal man dwells in peace and in God. The journey to that space, through a realm of aridity, dualism, dryness, death. The need of courage and of desire. Above all faith, praise, obedience to the inner voice of the Spirit, refusal to give up or to compromise.

What is "wrong" in my life is not so much a matter of "sin" (though it is sin, too), but a matter of *unawareness*, lostness, slackness, relaxation, dissipation of desire, lack of courage and decision, so that I let myself be carried along and dictated by an alien movement. The current of "the world," which I know is not mine. I am always being diverted into a way that is not my way and is not going where I am called to go. And only if I go where I must go can I be of any use to "the world." I can serve the world best by keeping my distance and my freedom.

*May 14, 1967, VI.234–35*

# Every Day I Kill Isaac

Every day I get some idea of what is in myself, when I have to swallow my own ideas about chant, the interior life, solitude, the Cistercian vocation, etc., etc. Every day I kill Isaac—my beautiful dream about a silent, solitary, well-ordered life of perfect contemplation and perfect monastic observance, with no intrusion from the world, no publicity, no best-selling books, just God and that nice, archaic little Carthusian cell!! I have to make that blind act of faith that God and our Lady are drawing me—*per crucem*—through the Cross—to something better, which I will probably never see this side of heaven.

At the beginning of May, I think: our Lady is coming gradually to be the *whole* of my interior life. The more I leave everything to her, the simpler everything becomes, and the easier I travel. And this morning I was reading marvelous things in Adam of Perseigne about Mary being "the way." She is that. Through her we come quickly to—everything.

At Mass I have hardly been able to think of anything but our Lady. Either that, or else I sink down into the depths where God is found alone. But to do that is to be occupied implicitly with her, for she is the way there. Yet I do not say I do all this easily—I am surrounded by distractions and yet drawn into this love of her in spite of them.

More and more I abandon anything of my own that might seem to be a "technique" of prayer and throw myself upon her mercy, leaving myself to be moved and guided by her, certain that she alone, by God's dispensation and decree, can help my helplessness.

*May 1 and 5, 1949, II.307–8*

# Loving the Place and the Brothers

God brought me here, and I simply cannot be thinking of going anywhere else without putting myself in opposition to His will—barring the case where the spiritual life would become impossible here—and this is a fervent community, so that does not arise.

The only thing to do is to believe Him blindly, and I know in the marrow of my bones that is what He wants, that I should put myself entirely in His hands and trust Him to make me a contemplative, even though my own natural judgment tells me everything seems to be against it. *Because my own judgment is darkness in the sight of God.* That is all there is to it.

And this is the obstacle that has been robbing me of my peace.

Gethsemani—the place and the community—*locus et fratres*—is the spring where I am to drink the waters of life, and if I look somewhere else, it is to a broken cistern as far as I am concerned, because, no matter how excellent it may be in itself, *another place is not God's will for me.*

As soon as I acquiesced completely in this decision, which I did at once, peace came back to my soul, although I feel that God does not trust Himself to me completely—He knows what is in me. But He knows that I want to rest in His will and love His will alone. I believe in His love.

*May 5, 1947, II. 71–72*

# To Kiss It All Good-bye

Vigil of Pentecost. What do I look for tomorrow? Light? No. It is safer to travel in darkness. What I need is the grace to cease making any kind of fuss over anything: travel in darkness and do God's will. He will get me through the obstacles. I will never reach Him by my own efforts, my own wisdom. I give up all my plans, as if I had any in the first place. Forget what other people do; their virtues and their faults are none of my business. Be guided by obedience even if it seems to lead to the ruin of my aspirations. Easier to write it than to do it. I wonder if I mean it, too, to go on in this hopeless muddle of writing and activities and contacts with the world, and trust that that can bring me to God? Yes, that is what I have got to do.

It seems like going around in a circle and saying the same thing over and over again, but it is something that haunts me, and I can't seem to settle it.

I feel in my bones that I will never have any peace until I kiss everything good-bye, even my highest ideals and aspirations. God only tolerates one desire: perfectly doing His will and being annihilated for His glory.

*May 23, 1947, II.76–77*

# My Hands Were Always Empty

Since Easter was early we are already on the threshold of Pentecost. Yesterday, in bright, blazing sun, we planted cabbage seedlings in the garden and, over the way, I could hear them mowing hay in Saint Joseph's field, where probably tomorrow we will all be loading wagons.

Every time I have been in the woods to pray I have loved them more.

At once I remember all the afternoons I had been out in the woods, the dark afternoons in the gullies along the creeks and the rainy afternoons on top of the knobs and the day I sang the *Pater Noster* on one knob and then on another; the day I found the daffodils in an unexpected place, and the other day when I picked them in a place where I knew they would be; and the immense silence of last Good Friday, when I sat on a rotten log in a sheltered corner by a stream with a relic of the Holy Cross. It set the seal on all the silences in which I had found Him without seeming to find anything, and I knew (as I always guessed) that I had every time come home with something tremendous, although my hands were always empty.

*May 7, 1951, II.457–58*

# Resurrection Is Our Destiny

In the night office, St. Ambrose: all *must* rise from the dead. Resurrection is our lot. Life is our destiny whether we want it or not. But to be risen and not want it, to hate life, is the resurrection of judgment. Man is not, and cannot be, a merely ephemeral thing. But if he wills to be evanescent, to remain in what is *not,* he is a living contradiction.

Thunder, lightning and rain all night. Heaviest rain for a long time. Floods in the bottoms. Water bubbling in under the basement wall of the washroom. Novitiate garden flooded in the NW corner. (One day the whole retaining wall will go if this keeps up.) Sound of waters in the valley.

> *My love is*
> *The fragrance of the orchid*
> *And the sound of waters*

says the Haiku on my lovely Zen calendar.

*May 7, 1961, IV.116*

# On Being a Stranger

On being a stranger. I need more awareness of what it involves. And get some such awareness by the invitations I have to refuse.

Being "out of the world" does not mean simply being out of Las Vegas—it means being not on planes, not at the reunions, conferences, etc. Not in Hong Kong today and Lima tomorrow, not in the credit card, expense account, talk circuit where you are paid to be everywhere, and this to make news (because where you are paid to be, there the action is, since the action is that you are paid to be there).

The question is: do I really care? Do I resent being excluded from all this? Inevitably my being grounded in this corner of the woods, unable to move, able only to speak half-surreptitiously to a few who get through to me here, makes me a comic sort of intellectual. Inevitably I am a sort of reform-school kid who is punished by being taken off the street. And one who does not know the latest is not perfectly attuned to the intonations and accents that convey the real message.

Certainly no point in mere resentment of modern society "bla bla."

Nor trying to pretend I am, after all, superior.

Nevertheless, the situation has unique advantages. Much of the real germinating action in the world, the real leavening, is among the immobilized, the outsiders (the vast majority, who have no credit card and never step on a plane), the Negroes, the Latinos, etc. In a way I am on their level. (But I don't have their grapevine!)

*May 8, 1967, VI.231*

# Going On

It is like an English summer day, cool and cloudy, with deep green grass all around the hermitage and trees heavy with foliage. Occasional slow bursts of gentle sunlight that imperceptibly pass by. Shafts of light and great rooms of shadow in the tall tree-church beyond the cedar cross. The path of creek gravel leads into the shadows and beyond them to the monastery, out of sight, down the hill, across fields and a road and a dirty stream. All such things as roads and sewers are far from this place.

Knowing when you do not need any more. Acting just enough. Saying enough. Stopping when there is enough. Some may be wasted, nature is prodigal. Harmony is not bought with parsimoniousness.

Yet stopping is "going on." To cling to something and want more of it, to *use* it more, to squeeze enjoyment out of it. This is to "stop" and not "go on." But to leave it alone at the right time, this is the right stopping, the right going on. To leave a thing alone before you have had anything to do with it, if it is for your use, to leave it without use, is not "stopping," it is not even beginning. Use it to go on.

> *To be great is to go on.*
> *To go on is to be far.*
> *To be far is to return.*

*May 16, 1961, IV.118–19*

# Perplexities and New Births

The sun is rising. All the green trees are full of birds, and their song comes up out of the wet bowers of the orchard. Crows swear pleasantly in the distance, and in the depths of my soul sits God, and between Him, in the depths and the thoughts on the surface of my mind, is the veil of an unresolved problem.

What shall I say this problem is? It is not a conflict of ideas. It is not a dilemma. I do not believe it is a question of choice. Is it a psychological fact? Any interior problem is a psychological fact. Is it a question that I can resolve? No.

This problem is my own personality, in which I do not intend at any time to take an unhealthy interest. But (I speak as one less wise) this problem is my personality or, if you like, the development of my interior life. I am not perplexed either by what I am or what I am not, but by the mode in which I am tending to become what I really will be.

God makes us ask ourselves questions most often when He intends to resolve them. He gives us needs that He alone can satisfy and awakens capacities that He means to fulfill. Any perplexity is liable to be a spiritual gestation, leading to a new birth and a mystical regeneration.

*May 15, 1949, II.311*

# I Am God's Utter Poverty

I am the utter poverty of God. I am His emptiness, littleness, nothingness, lostness. When this is understood, my life in His freedom, the self-emptying of God in me, is the fullness of grace. A love for God that knows no reason because He is the fullness of grace. A love for God that knows no reason because He is God; a love without measure, a love for God as personal. The *Ishvara* appears as personal in order to inspire this love. Love for all, hatred of none, is the fruit and manifestation of love for God— peace and satisfaction. Forgetfulness of worldly pleasure, selfishness, and so on, in the love of God, channeling all passion and emotion into the love of God.

Technology as *Karma*.

What can be done has to be done. The burden of possibility that has to be fulfilled, possibilities which demand so imperatively to be fulfilled that everything else is sacrificed for their fulfillment.

Computer *Karma* in American civilization.

Distinguish work as narcotic (that is, being an operator and all that goes with it) from healthy and free work. But also consider the wrong need for non-action. The *Astavakra Gita* says: "Do not let the fruit of action be your motive and do not be attached to non-action." In other words, do not let your left hand know what your right hand is doing. Work to please God alone.

*May 16, 1968, VII. 102–3*

# When Everything Is Wet

Nothing can spoil this morning. The rain has stopped. The birds sing and starlings pursue a crow across the grey sky. Clouds still hang low over the woods. It's cool.

The whiskey barrels by the woodshed stand or lie in wetness, one of them with wet weeds up the navel, others rolling in the soaked chips of wood and bark.

Someone has sawed a keg in half, and it is one of the most beautiful objects on the property at the moment. An example of *wabi-sabi* (simplicity) that Suzuki talks about. With joy, yesterday, I smelled the charred barrel. How beautiful to see it catch rain.

Yesterday I was bitter for a while, growling to myself. "Yes, we have the Holy Ghost all right—in a cage with His wings clipped." But later, during the Gospel, the "Let not your heart be disturbed" came through into my heart as if especially directed to me and I remembered there was no need to be bitter or to worry, or even to notice what appears to me to be senseless in our life here.

I do not have to react. It is useless. There are much better things to do. And to react is to become implicated—to become a prisoner of the same nonsense that I am compelled to condemn. Do not be compelled.

Here comes a small, shining rabbit. A kingbird gurgles and chortles in the cedars. Everything is wet.

*May 18, 1959, III.281–82*

# A Prayer to the Father

Today, Father, the blue sky praises you. The delicate green and orange flowers of the tulip poplar praise you. The distant blue hills praise you, with the sweet-smelling air that is full of brilliant light. The bickering flycatchers praise you, with the lowing bulls and the quails that whistle over there, and I, too, Father, praise you with these creatures my brothers. You have made us all together and you have placed me here this morning in the midst of them. And here I am.

For a long time I prayed, in the years that are past, and I was in darkness and sorrow and confusion. And no doubt the confusion was my own fault. No doubt my own will was the root of my sorrow, and I regret it, O merciful Father. But whatever may have been my sin, the prayer of Your friends for me and my own prayers were answered, and I am here in this hermitage before You, and here You see me. Here You love me. Here You ask the response of my own love, and of my confidence. Here You ask me to be nothing else than your friend.

To be Your friend is simply to accept your friendship because it is your friendship. And this friendship is Your life, the Spirit of Your Son. You have called me here to be Your son: to be born over again, repeatedly, in Your light, and in knowledge, and in consideration, and gratitude, and poverty, and praise.

*May 20, 1961, IV.120–21*

# The Sea of My Paradise

"You deliver me from the gates of death that I might announce your praises in the gates of the daughter of Sion" (Psalm 9).

Marvelous vision of the hills at 7:45 a.m. The same hills as always, as in the afternoon, but now catching the light in a totally new way, at once very earthly and very ethereal, with delicate cups of shadow and dark ripples and crinkles where I had never seen them, and the whole slightly veiled in mist so that it seemed to be a tropical shore, a newly discovered continent. And a voice in me seemed to be crying, "Look! Look!" For these are the discoveries, and it is for this that I am high on the mast of my ship (have always been), and I know that we are on the right course, for all around is the sea of paradise.

*May 21, 1963, IV.321–22*

# The Climate of My Corner of the Woods

There is a mental ecology, a living balance of spirits, in this corner of the woods. There is a place for many other songs besides those of birds. Of Vallejo, for instance. Or the dry, disconcerting voice of Nicanor Parra. Or there is also Chuang Tzu, whose climate is perhaps most the climate of this hot corner of the woods. A climate in which there is no need for explanations. There is also a Syrian hermit called Philoxenus. There is the clanging prose of Tertullian. There is the deep vegetation of that more ancient forest than mine: the deep forest in which the great birds Isaias and Jeremias sing. When I am most sickened by the things that are done by the country that surrounds this place, I will take out the prophets and sing them in loud Latin across the hills and send their fiery words sailing south over the mountains to the place where they split atoms for bombs in Tennessee.

There is also the nonecology: the destructive unbalance of nature, poisoned and unsettled by bombs, by fallout, by exploitation: the land ruined, the waters contaminated, the soil charged with chemicals, ravaged with machinery, the houses of farmers falling apart because everybody goes to the city and stays there. There is no poverty as great as that of the prosperous, no wretchedness as dismal as affluence. Wealth is poison. There is no misery to compare with that which exists where technology has been a total success. Full bellies have not brought peace and satisfaction but dementia, and, in any case, not all the bellies are full. But the dementia is the same for all.

*May 1965, V.239–40*

# Accepting My Place in Creation

One lovely dawn after another. Such peace! Meditation with fire-flies, mist in the valley, last quarter of the moon, distant owls—gradual inner awakening and centering in peace and in a harmony of love and gratitude. Yesterday I wrote to the man at McGill University who thought all contemplation was a manifestation of narcissistic regression! That is just what it is not. A complete awakening of identity and rapport! It implies an awareness and acceptance of one's place in the whole, first the whole of creation, then the whole plan of Redemption—to find oneself in the great mystery of fulfillment which is the Mystery of Christ. *Consonantia* and not *confusio*.

Jack Ford brought me a couple of loaves of pumpernickel from a Jewish delicatessen in Louisville Monday, and he also gave me some excellent tea, which I iced myself for supper tonight. Twining's Earl Grey. It was superb! And that was about all I had for supper with a can of mandarin oranges. Cool and pleasant. But it is still hot. The sky is cloudy. The birds still sing. Maybe there will be rain tonight.

At Mass I shall pray especially for the Buddhist Vo Tanh Minh, who has been fasting since March in Brooklyn in protest against the fighting in Vietnam. He will probably die, as there is little likelihood of a cease-fire. His calm and peace are completely admirable.

*May 23 and 25, 1965, V.250–51*

# One Last Step

Krishna says in the *Bhagavad Gita:* "By devotion in work He knows me, knows what in truth I am and who I am. Then, having known me in truth, He enters into me."

The states of life. *Brahmacharya:* the life of the student in chastity under his Guru. *Grhastha:* the life of the householder begetting children, practicing Karma Yoga. *Vanaprastha:* the forest life. My present life. A life of privacy and quasi-retirement. Is there one more stage? Yes. *Sanyasa:* total renunciation. Homelessness, begging. The *Sanyasin* lives only on food given to him. He is freed from all ritual obligations. The sacred fire is kindled only within. No household shrine. No temple. He is entirely turned to deliverance, renouncing all activity and attachment, all fear, all greed, all care, without home, without roof, without place, without name, without office, without function, without reputation, without care for reputation, without being known.

*May 16, 1968, VII. 103*

# My Train's Old Song

Early morning. Blessed rain, cooling the air, making the woods wet, where there was fire and danger of burning for weeks, since before Easter. Fire on the lake side, fire over across the creek in a hollow, fires down the valley. Now all is wet. God be praised for the rain.

Fresh green of the valley. Lovely yellow tulips surprised me outside the hermitage. I thought the rabbits had eaten them all but the rain brought them out. A pure and lovely yellow, purer than that of buttercups.

I regret the time I have wasted here this winter working at books. What moments have been lost—moments of realization, lost in the flux of obsession and work. Statements to show, for what?

A train in the valley—that old song.

"Those who have the *dharma* should devote themselves only to its practice. Disputes arise from the desire for conquest and are not in accordance with the Way" (from the *T'an Ching* of Hui Neng).

Unrest, action, protests here and there since atomic testing was renewed. Note the *symbolic* part taken by *milk* in the protest. Other foods (wheat = bread) get as much or more strontium-90 in them. Milk is the American symbol. Mother is full of strontium-90. Mothers protest. Motherhood undermined by the bomb. Sex symbolism of the bomb, and question of genetic effects. The sex life of America, Kinsey report, and H-bomb were contemporary.

There is a plan to launch a Polaris submarine called *The William Penn!!*

*May 1 and 4, 1962, IV.216–17*

# Patiently Exploring Interior Space

Hot, stuffy, misty summer weather.

Now I have got to get my life in order at last without desperation and without compromise. A long succession of wasted opportunities. The need for serious spiritual discipline, especially long periods of meditation. Going on my own, not being held within the limits of accepted practice and custom in the community. I owe it to the community, which has allowed me opportunities for it, more or less, to forge ahead where they do not go. This is certainly implied by the situation in which I have been placed.

I have misused this to a great extent, thinking I was obliged to form a judgment concerning world affairs. That obligation is by no means certain, whereas my obligation to explore "the interior space" is absolutely clear.

From Tertullian: *Malim nullum bonum quam vanum:* "I would rather have nothing than have vanity."

When we face the vanity of our best efforts, their triviality, their involvement in illusion, we become desperate. And then we are tempted to do *anything* as long as it seems to be good. We may abandon a better good with which we have become disillusioned, and embrace a lesser good with a frenzy that prevents us from seeing the greater illusion.

So, through efforts that may seem to be wasted, we must patiently go towards a good that is to be given to the patient and the disillusioned.

*May 29 and 30, 1962, IV.221–22*

# All the Moods of My Place

This morning at four. Great full moon over Nally's hill, pale and clear. A faint mist hanging over the wet grass of the bottoms.

More and more I appreciate the beauty and solemnity of the "Way" up through the woods, past the bull barn, up the stony rise, into the grove of tall, straight oaks and hickories, and around through the pines on top of the hill, to the cottage.

Sunrise. Hidden by pines and cedars on the east side of the house. Saw the red flame of it glaring through the cedars, not like sunrise but like a forest fire. From the window of the front room, then he, the Sun (can hardly be conceived as other than he), shone silently with solemn power through the pine branches.

Now after High Mass the whole valley is glorious with morning light and with the song of birds.

It is essential to experience all the times and moods of this place. No one will know or be able to say *how* essential. Almost the first and most important element of a truly spiritual life, lost in the constant, formal routine of Divine offices under the fluorescent lights in choir—where there is practically no change between night and day.

*May 30, 1961, IV.122*

# The Great Work of Sunrise

The great work of sunrise again today.

The awful solemnity of it. The sacredness. Unbearable without prayer and worship. I mean unbearable if you really put everything else aside and see what is happening! Many, no doubt, are vaguely aware that it is dawn, but they are protected from the solemnity of it by the neutralizing worship of their own society, their own world, in which the sun no longer rises and sets.

Sense of importance, the urgency of seeing, fully aware, experiencing what is here: not what is given by men, by society, but what is given by God and hidden by (even monastic) society. Clear realization that I must begin with these first elements. That it is absurd to inquire after my function in the world, or whether I have one, as long as I am not first of all alive and awake. And if that, and no more, is my job (for it is certainly every man's job), then I am grateful for it. The vanity of all false missions, when no one is sent. All the universal outcry of people who have not been told to cry out, but who are driven to this noise by their fear, their lack of what is right in front of their noses.

*May 31, 1961, IV.123*

# Hang On to the Clear Light!

In our monasteries we have been content to find our ways to a kind of peace, a simple, undisturbed, thoughtful life. And this is certainly good, but is it good enough?

I, for one, realize that now I need more. Not simply to be quiet, somewhat productive, to pray, to read, to cultivate leisure— *otium sanctum*—a holy leisure. There is a need for effort, deepening, change and transformation. Not that I must undertake a special project of self-transformation or that I must "work on myself." In that regard, it would be better to forget it. Just to go for walks, live in peace, let change come quietly and invisibly on the inside.

But I do have a past to break with, an accumulation of inertia, waste, wrong, foolishness, rot, junk, a great need of clarification, of mindfulness, or rather of no mind—a return to genuine practice, right effort, need to push on to the great doubt. Need for the Spirit.

Hang on to the clear light!

*May 30, 1968, VII.113*

# Lost in His Mercy

*(Thomas Merton is ordained a priest on the
Feast of the Ascension, May 26, 1949)*

I was very happy to sing the Gospel—the magnificent triumph of Christ, which is echoed and expressed in the ordination to the priesthood of a thing like myself that He picked up out of the wreckage of the moral universe and brought into His house. It is He Who looks up to heaven, in my own soul full of weakness and infidelity, and cries out, "Father, the hour has come, glorify thy Son, that thy Son may glorify thee." And the context reminds me to whom I belong: "As Thou hast given him power over all flesh, that he may give life everlasting to all whom Thou hast given him." My joy is the great power of Christ. And for that, above all, I am glad of my deep moral poverty, which is always before me these days, but which does not obsess or upset me because it is all lost in His mercy.

*May 26, 1949, II.316*

# Visiting the Brothers

The long yellow side of the monastery faces the sun on a sharp rise with fruit trees and beehives. I climb sweating into the novitiate, put down the water bottle on the cement floor. The bell is ringing. I have some duties in the monastery. When I have accomplished these, I return to the woods. In the choir are the young monks, patient, serene, with very clear eyes, thin, reflective, gentle. For fifteen years I have given them classes, these young ones who come, and grow thin, become more reflective, more silent. But many of them are concerned with questions. Questions of liturgy, questions of psychology, questions of history. Are they the right questions? In the woods there are other questions and other answers, for in the woods the whole world is naked and directly present, with no monastery to veil it.

Chanting the Alleluia in the second mode: strength and solidity of the Latin, seriousness of the second mode, built on the *Re* as though on a sacrament, a presence. One keeps returning to the *Re* as to an inevitable center. *Sol-Re, Fa-Re, Sol-Re, Do-Re.* Many other notes in between, but suddenly one hears only the one note. *Consonantia:* all notes, in their perfect distinctness, are yet blended in one.

In the heat of noon I return through the cornfield, past the barn under the oaks, up the hill, under the pines, to the hot cabin. Larks rise out of the long grass singing. A bumblebee hums under the wide shady eaves.

*May 1965, V.241–42*

# On America in the Sixties

Yesterday I dipped into the manuscript that Julian Miller at Harcourt, Brace & World wanted me to comment on—nuns used as whores by Viet Cong, etc. The correct mythology, which assumes a compound of oversexuality, crude violence, honest bourgeois privatism, native American honesty, a bit of lesbianism for kicks. In other words, a pile of stupid shit. What revolted me was not so much the sex as the attitude—the mixture of superficial objectivity and *Time-Life* self-righteousness—and the suburb sophistication. America as she sees herself. The kind of America that makes Norman Mailer vomit—and me too.

It always gets back to the same thing. I have dutifully done my bit. I have been "open to the world." That is to say, I have undergone my dose of exposure to American society in the '60s—particularly in these last weeks. I love the people I run into, but I pity them for having to live as they do, and I think the world of U.S.A. in 1967 is a world of crass, blind, overstimulated, phony, lying stupidity. The war in Asia slowly gets worse—and almost more inane. The temper of the country is one of blindness, fat, self-satisfied, ruthless, mindless corruption. A lot of people are uneasy about it but helpless to do anything against it. The rest are perfectly content with the rat race as it is, and with its competitive, acquisitive, hurtling, souped-up drive into nowhere. A massively aimless, baseless, shrewd cockiness that simply exalts itself without purpose. The mindless orgasm, in which there is no satisfaction, only spasm.

*May 27, 1967, VI.239*

# United with History's Sacred Currents

Tomorrow Sts. Nereus and Achilleus: I said their office in anticipation in the fresh green woods after work clearing brush, where the fire still smoked. I will always remember their little empty church in Rome, half in the country, on a spring afternoon in 1933.

"The Lord has plucked up proud men by their roots, and planted the lowly peoples." "He hath put down the mighty."

If I were more fully attentive to the word of God I would be much less troubled and disturbed by events of our time: not that I would be indifferent or passive, but I could gain strength of union with the deepest currents of history, the sacred currents, which run opposite to those on the surface a great deal of the time!

"Do not quarrel about a matter that does not concern you; and when sinners judge, do not sit in council with them" (*Ecclesiasticus*).

This especially strikes me: "Be wary, take very great care, because you are walking with your own downfall; when you hear such things, wake up and be vigilant." It seems to me that at the moment I very much need this kind of "attention" and "listening," for I have come to the most serious moments of my life.

*May 11, 1965, V.247–48*

# As Night Descends

I sweep. I spread a blanket in the sun. I cut grass behind the cabin. Soon I will bring the blanket in again and make the bed. The sun is overclouded. Perhaps there will be rain. A bell rings in the monastery. A tractor growls in the valley. Soon I will cut bread, eat supper, say psalms, sit in the back room as the sun sets, as the birds sing outside the window, as silence descends on the valley, as night descends. As night descends on a nation intent upon ruin, upon destruction, blind, deaf to protest, crafty, powerful, unintelligent. It is necessary to be alone, to be not part of this, to be in the exile of silence, to be, in a manner of speaking, a political prisoner. No matter where in the world he may be, no matter what may be his power of protest, or his means of expression, the poet finds himself ultimately where I am. Alone, silent, with the obligation of being very careful not to say what he does not mean, not to let himself be persuaded to say merely what another wants him to say, not to say what his own past work has led others to expect him to say.

The poet has to be free from everyone else, and first of all from himself, because it is through this "self" that he is captured by others. Freedom is found under the dark tree that springs up in the center of the night and of silence, the paradise tree, the *axis mundi,* which is also the Cross.

*May 1965, V.241–42*

# Home

Yesterday, Third Sunday after Easter (already!) is my favorite, or one of them. The Introit and the Alleluias especially. The afternoon was warm and glorious with the new summer, the brand new summer, the wheat already tall and waving in the wind, the great cumulous clouds. And all the things one cannot begin to say about it—the new awareness that I am not the "object" that "they" think I am or even that I think, and that the I which is not-I is All and in everyone, and that the outer I must not assert itself anymore but must be glad to vanish, and yet there is no division between them, as there is no division between the surface of the pond and the rest of it. It is the reflection on the surface that seems to give it another being—and no flatness, etc.

I sit in the cool back room, where words cease to resound, where all meanings are absorbed in the *consonantia* of heat, fragrant pine, quiet wind, birdsong, and one central tonic note that is unheard and unuttered. Not the meditation of books, or of pieties, or of systematic trifles. In the silence of the afternoon all is present and all is inscrutable. One central tonic note to which every other sound ascends or descends, to which every other meaning aspires, in order to find its true fulfillment. To ask when the note will sound is to lose the afternoon: it has sounded, and all things now hum with the resonance of its sounding.

*May 1965, V.242, 247*

The country that is nowhere is the real home.

*May 30, 1968, VII.110*

# The Work of the Cell

Coming home—through Shakertown, Harrodsburg, Perryville, and Lebanon. Beautiful June countryside—deep grass and hay, flowering weeds, tall cumulus clouds, corn a foot high and beautifully green tobacco struggling to begin. The old road between Perryville and Lebanon—winding between small farms and old barns, with wooded knobs nearby—is one I like.

The great joy of the solitary life is not found simply in quiet, in the beauty and peace of nature, song of birds, etc., nor in the peace of one's own heart, but in the awakening and attuning of the heart to the voice of God—to the inexplicable, quite definite inner certitude of one's call to obey Him, to hear Him, to worship Him here, now, today, in silence and alone, and that this is the whole reason for one's existence, this makes one's existence fruitful and gives fruitfulness to all one's other good acts, and is the ransom and purification of one's heart, which has been dead in sin.

It is not simply a question of "existing" alone, but of doing, with joy and understanding, "the work of the cell," which is done in silence and not according to one's own choice or the pressure of necessity, but in obedience to God. But the Voice of God is not "heard" at every moment, and part of the "work of the cell" is attention so that one may not miss any sound of that Voice. When we see how little we listen, and how stubborn and gross our hearts are, we realize how important the work is and how badly prepared we are to do it.

*June 6 and 8, 1965, V.253–54*

# When the Bullfrog Says "Om"

The other day (Thursday)—the *full meaning* of Lauds, said against the background of waking birds and sunrise.

At 2:30—no sounds except sometimes a bullfrog. Some mornings, he says "Om"—some days he is silent. The sounds are not every day the same. The whippoorwill, who begins his mysterious whoop about 3 o'clock, is not always near. Sometimes, like today, he is very far away in Linton's woods or beyond. Sometimes he is close, on Mount Olivet. Yesterday there were two, but both in the distance.

The first chirps of the waking birds: *le point vierge*—the virgin point—of the dawn, a moment of awe and inexpressible innocence, when the Father in silence opens their eyes and they speak to Him, wondering if it is time to "be"? And He tells them, "Yes." Then they one by one wake and begin to sing. First the catbirds and cardinals and some others I do not recognize. Later, song sparrows, wrens, etc. Last of all doves, crows.

With my hair almost on end, and the eyes of my soul wide open, I am present, without knowing it at all, in this unspeakable Paradise, and I behold this secret, this wide-open secret which is there for everyone, free, and no one pays any attention ("One to his farm, another to his merchandise"). Not even monks, shut up under fluorescent lights and face to face with the big books and black notes and with one another, perhaps no longer seeing or hearing anything in the course of festive Lauds.

O paradise of simplicity, self-awareness—and self-forgetfulness —liberty, peace.

*June 5, 1960, IV.7*

# Always Needing to Wake Up

Wonderfully cool. Never saw such a June. Bright blue sky. Birds singing everywhere. Not a cloud. Sunlight falls on this page through the branches of the cedars outside the wall and is not oppressive, but pleasant, like the sun of May or October.

The other day—the novices found a bat in the conference room, and brought him out into the garden in broad daylight in the middle of the morning. I took him inside again and let him hang upside down in the tool closet. The wings are a bit repellant (why?) but the bat himself is a beautiful thing. Clinging blindly to my notebook and trembling all over. His long ears, small eyes, "peaceful expression." (There I go again. Rank subjectivity.)

The battle against inertia. In the life and in myself. This is the great thing. The constant struggle to break through illusion and falsity and come to Christ and freedom. And how often we fail. I am convinced there is something in our long offices and formal prayers which induces inertia and stupor. Am I just? Or is this more subjectivism? Be honest in seeking the answer.

The conviction that I have not even begun to write, to think, to pray, and to live, and that only now am I getting down to waking up. And that, by God's grace, this comes from finally trying, with great difficulty, to be genuinely free and alone, as humbly as I can, in God's sight, without passively accepting all the standards and the formulas which have been adopted by others—or, at least, that I am now exercising a wider choice in my sources of inspiration.

*June 22, 1958, III.206–7*

JUNE 4

# Let Our Power Be Dismantled

I suppose that in some way I have been going through a small spiritual crisis. Nothing new, only the usual crisis and struggle, a little more intensified by the "fiftieth year." Still it is getting to be quite decisive because there are fewer evasions possible. As I go on, the ways of escape are progressively closed, renounced, or otherwise abandoned. I know now that I am really committed to stability here, and that even the thought of *temporary* travel is useless and vain. I know that my contacts with others of like mind by mail, etc., are relatively meaningless, though they may have some *raison d'être*. I know that my writing solves nothing for me personally and that it has created some problems which are still unresolved. I know there is nothing to be solved or settled by any special arrangement within the framework of the community. That my position is definitely ambiguous and my job is to accept this with the smallest possible amount of bad faith.

Reading the little book by Eberhard Arnold on the Bruderhof. I think this (from his statement on his fiftieth birthday) applies well enough to be almost a word of God to me: "Let us pledge to him that all our own power will remain dismantled and will keep on being dismantled among us. Let us pledge that the only thing that will count among us will be the power and authority of God in Jesus Christ through the Holy Spirit; that it will never again be us that count but that God above will rule and govern in Christ and the Holy Spirit."

*June 2, 1964, V.107–8*

# Holding On to Nothing

God is using everything that happens to lead me into solitude. Every creature that enters my life, every instant of my days is designed to touch me with the sense of the world's insufficiency. And that goes for every created thing, including monasteries, including even sensible graces, lights of the mind, ideas, fervor in the will. Everything I touch cauterizes me with a light and healing burn. I can hold on to nothing.

It is useless to get upset over these things that pain me. The pain is the token and pledge of God's love for me. It is the promise of His deep and perfect solitude.

Today I seemed to be very much assured that this solitude is indeed His will for me, and that it is truly He Who is calling me into the desert. Not necessarily a geographical one, but the solitude of His own heart in Which all created joys and light and satisfactions are annihilated and consumed.

Things that should have satisfied me, but did not.

*June 13, 1947, II.83*

JUNE 6

# Receiving an Honor

"It particularly belongs to our profession to seek no honor in this life, but to flee honors. . . . " (*The Rule for Solitaries*, c. 23)

Receiving an honor:

A very small, gold-winged moth came and settled on the back of my hand, and sat there, so light that I could not feel it. I wondered at the beauty and delicacy of this being—so perfectly made, with mottled golden wings. So perfect. I wonder if there is even a name for it. I never saw such a thing before. It would not go away until, needing my hand, I blew it lightly into the woods.

In the afternoon: I knew there was an intruder in the front room of the hermitage, where I could hear movement. I went to see, and it was a Carolina wren which had been thinking of coming in already the day before yesterday. It flew out again, as though it were not welcome!

This experience of solitude is important and most valuable. How badly I have been needing whole days and days in succession out here. At last I am getting a decent perspective again, and there is no question that my desire for solitude has been basically right, and not a delusion. I thank God that I have, by His grace, at least come this far and not made the fatal wrong steps that would have probably led to failure without clarification (for instance, trying to make a go of it as a Carthusian).

*June 5 and 6, 1963, IV.328–29*

# Solitude as My Everyday Mind

Corpus Christi was yesterday. I did not concelebrate. It was a good, cool day. Wrote to Marco Pallis in answer to a good letter of his. John Wu wrote and sent some chapters of his book on Zen.

"Solitude" becomes for me less and less of a specialty, and simply "life" itself. I do not seek to "be a solitary" or anything else, for "being anything" is a distraction. It is enough to be, in an ordinary human mode, with only hunger and sleep, one's cold and warmth, rising and going to bed. Putting on blankets and taking them off (two last night. It is cold for June!). Making coffee and drinking it. Defrosting the refrigerator, reading, meditation, working, praying. I live as my fathers have lived on this earth, until eventually I die. Amen. There is no need to make an assertion of my life, especially to assert it is MINE, though it is doubtless not somebody else's. I must learn to gradually forget program and artifice. I know this, at least in my mind, and want it in my heart, but my other habits of awareness remain strong.

Will say the Mass of St. Alban when I go down today (Day of Recollection). Misty morning. Lots of noise from Boone's cows. Yesterday Father Matthew, with his crazy little tractor, cut the long grass in the field next to the hermitage, and in order to do work that would not require too much concentration, did some texts of St. Maximus on nonviolence, perhaps for the *Catholic Worker*.

*June 22, 1965, V.257–58*

# Lost with the Lost, Desiring Lucidity

One only ceases to be absurd when, realizing that everything is absurd when seen in isolation from everything else, meaning and value are sought only in wholeness. The solitary must, therefore, return to the heart of life and oneness, losing himself, not in the massive illusion, but simply in the root reality, plunging through the center of his own nothingness, and coming out in the All which is the Void and which is, if you like, the Love of God.

One cannot cease to be absurd by dint of metaphysics, or concentration, or meditation, or study, or knowledge: only by experiencing the fact that there is no wall between ourselves and others, in other words, by accepting the absurdity of our own life in terms of the suffering of others: no separating "my" pain, suffering, limitation, lostness, etc., from that of others. As long as a single person is lost, I am lost. To try to save myself by getting free from the mass of the damned (Augustine's *massa damnata*), and becoming good by myself, is to be both damned and absurd—as well as antichrist. Christ descended into hell to show that He willed to be lost with the lost, in a certain sense emptied so that they might be filled and saved, in the realization that now their lostness was not theirs but His. Hence the way one begins to make sense out of life is taking upon oneself the lostness of everyone—and then realizing not that one has done something, or "made sense," but that one has simply entered into the stream of realization. The rest will work out by itself, and we do not know what that might mean.

*June 20, 1966, VI.323–24*

# Something More than Reefers

If we are ever going to have peace again, we will have to hate war for some better reason than that we fear to lose our houses, or our refrigerators, or our cars, or our legs, or our lives. If we are ever to get peace, we have got to desire something more than reefers and anesthetics—but that is all we seem to want: anything to avoid pain.

It is terrifying that the world doesn't wake up to this irony: that at a time when all our desire is nothing but to have pleasant sensations and avoid painful sensations, there should be almost more pain and suffering and brutality and horror, and more *help-lessness* to do anything about it, than there ever was before!

*June 25, 1940, I.233*

Basic: the struggle for lucidity, out of which compassion can at last arise. Then you are free. That is, you are lost: there is no self to save. You simply love. Free of desire for oneself, desiring only lucidity for oneself and others.

*June 20, 1966, VI.323–24*

# Moments of Lucidity Day After Day

The Mass each day purifies and baffles me at the same time. This beautiful mixture of happiness and lucidity and inarticulateness fills me with great health from day to day. I am forced to be simple at the altar.

But in the middle of this beautiful sobriety the indescribably pure light of God fills you with what can only be described as the innocence of childhood.

Day after day I am more and more aware how little I am my everyday self at the altar: this consciousness of innocence is really a sense of replacement. Another has taken over my identity, and this other is a tremendous infancy. And I stand at the altar—excuse the language, these words should not be extraordinary—but I stand at the altar with my eyes washed in the light that is eternity, as if I am one who is agelessly reborn. I am sorry for this language. There are no words I know of simple enough to describe such a thing, except that every day I am a day old, and at the altar I am the Child Who is God. Yet, when it is all over, I have to say, "The light shines in the darkness and the darkness did not comprehend it" (John 1:15), and I have to fall back into my own poor self that cannot receive Him altogether, and I even have to rejoice at being a shell. Well, I have contained some echo of His purity, and it has meant something tremendous for me and for the whole world, so that at my Memento of the living—the prayer of remembering those for whom I pray—which is very long, I swim in seas of joy that almost heave me off my moorings at the altar.

*June 19, 1949, II.326–27*

# The Bitter, Lucid Joys of Solitude

The bitter and lucid joys of solitude. The real desert is this: to face the real limitations of one's own existence and knowledge and not try to manipulate them or disguise them. Not to embellish them with possibilities. Simply to set aside all possibilities other than those which are actually present and real, here and now. And then to choose or not, as one wishes, knowing that no choice is a solution to anything, but merely a step further into a slightly changed context of other, very few, very limited, very meaningless concrete possibilities. To realize that one's whole life, everybody's life, is really like that. In society the possibilities seem infinitely extended. One is in contact with other people, other liberties, other choices, and who knows what the others may suddenly all choose?

In society, in the middle of other people, one can always imagine one will break through into other liberties and other frames of reference. Other worlds. We have trained ourselves to think that we live at every moment amid *unlimited hopes*. There is nothing we cannot have if we try hard enough, or look in the right place for it.

But in solitude, when accurate limitations are seen and accepted, they then vanish, and new dimensions open up. The present is in fact, in itself, unlimited. The only way to grasp it in its unlimitedness is to remove the limitations we place on it by future expectations and hopes and plans, or surmises, or regrets about the past, or attempts to explain something we have experienced (or the revived, warmed-up experience) in order to be able to continue living with it.

*June 19, 1966, VI. 309–10*

# In Solitude for Everybody's Salvation

In the last analysis, what I am looking for in solitude is not happiness or fulfillment but salvation. Not "my own" salvation, but the salvation of everybody. And here is where the game gets serious. I have used the word *revolt* in connection with solitude. Revolt against what? Against a notion of salvation that gets people lost. A notion of salvation that is entirely legal and extrinsic and can be achieved no matter how false, no matter how shriveled and fruitless one's inner life really is. This is the worst ambiguity: the impression that one can be grossly unfaithful to life, to experience, to love, to other people, to one's own deepest self, and yet be "saved" by an act of stubborn conformity, by the will to be correct. In the end, this seems to me to be fatally like the very act by which one is lost: the determination to be "right" at all costs, by dint of hardening one's core around an arbitrary choice of a fixed position. To close in on one's central wrongness with the refusal to admit that it might be wrong. That is one of the reasons why solitude is a dangerous thing: one may use it for that purpose. I don't think I can. I am not that stubborn. I am here in solitude for one thing: to be open, to not be "closed in" on any one choice to the exclusion of all others: to be open to God's will and freedom, to His love, which comes to save me from all in myself that resists Him and says no to Him. This I must do not to justify myself, not to be right, not to be good, but because the whole world of lost people needs this opening by which salvation can get into it through me.

*June 24, 1966, VI.345*

# The Sense That Love Makes

One thing I must admit: a failure of lucidity in regard to love. It is so easy to assume that love is somehow a solution to a problem. Like: life is a problem which is impossible until someone comes along that you can love. Or, man is himself a problem, solved by love. Love is a key to a hidden answer in us. And so on, but is this true? Or is it only what everybody *wants to be true?* Maybe love, like everything else, is in large measure absurd. Does love too *have to make* perfect sense? In what way does it have to?

The sense that love makes, and I think the only sense it makes, is the beloved. The discovery, the revelation of the *absolute value* of the one loved. This is not so much a discovery of meaning as a discovery of goodness. To think of love as an answer or a "solution" is to evade the stark directness of this discovery. The fact that you are you is something of absolute value to me. But if I love in a certain way, this becomes covered over and hidden with all the operations of love, and what happens then is that love takes the place of the beloved. Then love, instead of being a solution (which it is not supposed to be) becomes a problem for which there is no solution. For then love stands in the way between the lovers. It veils the goodness of the beloved. It dresses (or undresses) the beloved as desirable object. Which is all right, too, except that one loves desire instead of the beloved.

The fact that you *are:* that you *are* you. This is all I have left. But it is the whole of love. And nothing can change it.

*June 1966, VI.307*

# John Wu and the Tao Pay a Visit

An indigo bunting flies down and grasps the long, swinging stem of a tiger lily and reaches out, from them, to eat the dry seed on top of a stalk of grass. A Chinese painting!

New tractors each year, and each one makes more noise than the last. The one in the valley now sounds like a big bulldozer. Round and round the alfalfa field, in fury. What thoughts it represents, what fury of man, what restlessness, what avidity, what despair.

Around and around it goes, clacking its despair.

John Wu arrived for a visit.

The great simple spirituality of John Wu, who knows *Tao* and the *Logos* and the Spirit. Flashes of wit and depth in the things he said, with much searching for words and matter, and his complaints that the Holy Ghost had gone to sleep.

For instance—that suffering is the core of existence.

That we monks can laugh in this monastery as men who know nothing worse can befall them.

He made some astute remarks about pragmatism in the "contemplative life" when questioned about what was "dangerous" to monks in America (the questioner wanted him to say something else, perhaps about love of comfort).

*June 15, 16, and 26, 1962, IV.228–29*

# An Old Friend, My Bookend

A touching letter came today from Nora Chadwick—this is one I really love, though I have never actually met her. She is an old retired Cambridge professor in her eighties and an authority on Celtic monasticism. She is busy writing still. All about the old monks. She writes that she is delighted that I am living the same kind of life as the old guys she writes about: that there actually should be something of the sort in the world today. This is important to me. For she knows what monasticism is, and she respects the *reality* of monastic solitude (not the ersatz and the institutionalized forms that have survived today). That there should be men willing to live in real solitude. Seeing it through her eyes, I am deeply moved by the meaning of this strange life. Here I am in the middle of it. I know I have not been truly faithful to it in many ways. I have evaded it. Yet who can say what its real demands are, other than the one who must meet them? And who knows what were the failures and problems of those forgotten people who actually lived as solitaries in the past? How many of them were lonely, and in love?

All I know is that here I am, and the valley is very quiet, the sun is going down, there is no human being around, and as darkness falls I could easily be a completely forgotten person, as if I did not exist for the world at all. (Though there is one who remembers and whom I remember.) The day could easily come when I would be just as invisible as if I never existed, and still be living here on this hill. And I know that I would be perfectly content to do so.

*June 18, 1966, VI.314*

# Needing to Turn a Corner

The realization that I need to turn a corner, to slough off a skin.

The need for moral effort, in the midst of *engourdissement*—the boring—and confusion. There is probably something sick about the mental numbness and anguish.

It is hard to see exactly what is to be left and what is to be thrown overboard.

But once again, at the risk of getting involved in hopeless confusion, I try to face the incomprehensible problem (for me) of writing. Incomprehensible because I am too involved and committed. That is the bad thing. It is so true that I have to continue being a writer that I do not know where to begin to think about not being one. Where to make the divisions. I feel it is useless even to make them, although I know what they are in my own mind. Certainly I can write something, and write, if possible, creatively. But not to preach, not to dogmatize, not to be a pseudo-prophet, not to declare my opinions. And yet it is essential to take a moral stand on some point—like atomic war. Am I so far gone that I can't do this without putting a brazier on my head and running about like Solomon Eagle in the London fire?

Possibly, what is required of some of us, and chiefly of me, is a solitary and personal response in the form of nonacquiescence, but quiet, definite and pure. I am not capable of this purity because I am frankly and simply clinging to life, to my physical life, of course, and to my life as a writer and a personage. To save myself, I have got to lose at least this attachment.

*June 27, 1961, IV.133–34*

# The Speech a Day Makes

Yesterday all day a small gardenia was a great consolation. Since it rained, I stayed in and wrote the review of the "Two Chinese Classics" sent by Paul Sih (*Tao Te Ching* and *Hsiao Ching*).

Shortness of breath, and palpitations of the heart enough to be noticed, quite prolonged. Not that I care. In any event it could be something merely psychological! But I stayed long looking at a goldfinch and walked slowly up through the woods, gazing at the tall straight oaks that are before you reach the turnstile. Everything is beautiful and I am grateful for all of it. And maybe now I begin to be old, and walk slowly, like Victor Hammer.

When the Dalai Lama was young, still a boy, he was lonely in the Potola and would walk on the roof looking through field glasses down upon the houses of his subjects to see if they were having parties and to watch their enjoyment. But they, in turn, would hide themselves so as not to sadden him still more.

Sweet afternoon! Cool breezes and a clear sky! This day will not come again.

The bulls lie under the tree in the corner of their field. Quiet afternoon! The blue hills, the daylilies in the wind.

This day will not come again.

*June 16, 1961, IV.128*

# A Need for Discipline

I am spending the afternoon reading Shantideva in the woods near the hermitage—the oak grove to the southwest. A cool, breezy spot on a hot afternoon.

Thinking deeply of Shantideva and my own need of discipline. What a fool I have been, in the literal and biblical sense of the word: thoughtless, impulsive, lazy, self-interested, yet alien to myself, untrue to myself, following the most stupid fantasies, guided by the most idiotic emotions and needs. Yes, I know, it is partly unavoidable. But I know, too, that, in spite of all contradictions, there is a center and a strength to which I *always* can have access if I really desire it. And the grace to desire it is surely there.

It would do no good to anyone if I just went around talking—no matter how articulately—in this condition. There is still so much to learn, so much deepening to be done, so much to surrender. My real business is something far different from simply giving out words and ideas and "doing things"—even to help others. The best thing I can give to others is to liberate myself from the common delusions and be, for myself and for others, free. Then grace can work in and through me for everyone.

*June 29, 1968, VII. 135*

# Caring for Ourselves

What impresses me most at reading Shantideva is not only his emphasis on solitude, but the idea of solitude as part of the clarification which includes living for others: the dissolution of the self in "belonging to everyone" and regarding everyone's suffering as one's own. This is really incomprehensible unless one shares something of the deep existential Buddhist concept of suffering as bound up with the arbitrary formation of an illusory ego-self. To be "homeless" is to abandon one's attachment to a particular ego—and yet to care for one's own life (in the highest sense) in the service of others. A deep and beautiful idea.

"Be you jealous and afraid of your own self when you see that it is at ease and your fellow is in distress, that it is in high estate and he is brought low, that it is at rest and he is at labor. Make your own self lose its pleasures and bear the sorrow of its fellows."

*June 29, 1968, VII.136*

# What I Fear Most

There has to be a real fear by which one orients his life. What you fear is an indication of what you seek. What do I fear most? Forgetting and ignorance of the inmost truth of my being. To forget who I am, to be lost in what I am not, to fail my own inner truth, to get carried away in what is not true to me, what is outside me, what imposes itself on me from outside. But what is this? It can take manifold forms. I must fear and distrust them all. Yet I cannot help being to some extent influenced by what is outside me, and hence I must accept that influence to some extent. But always in such a way that it increases my awareness, my remembrance, my understanding, instead of diminishing these.

Fear of ignorance in the sense of *avidya:* the ignorance that is based on the acceptance of an illusion about myself. The ignorance that comes from the decision to regard my ego as my full, complete, real self, and to *work to maintain* this illusion *against* the call of secret truth that rises up within me, that is evoked within me by others, by love, by vocation, by providence, by suffering, by God. The ignorance that hardens the shell, that makes the inner core of selfhood determined to resist the call of truth that would dissolve it. The ignorance that hardens in desire and willfulness, or in conformity, or in hate, or in various refusals of people, various determinations to be "right at any price" (the Vietnam War is a clear example of the American people's insistence on refusing to see human truth).

*June 22, 1966, VI.332*

# What Makes Me Tick

Fear of ignorance that comes from clinging to a stupid idea. Fear of ignorance that comes from submersion in the body, in surrender to the need for comfort and consolation. Yet, at the same time, one must not fear the possibility of relative lucidity in all these things, provided they are understood. There is a *little* lucidity in love, a *little* lucidity in alcohol, a *little* lucidity in religion, but there is also the danger of being engulfed more or less easily in all this. My great fear is then the fear of surrendering to sham lucidity and to the "one source" theory of lucidity—clinging to one kind of affirmation and excluding everything else—which means sinking back into ignorance and superstition. One of the worst sources of delusion is, of course, an exclusive attachment to supposed "logic" and reason. Worse still when the logic and reason are centered on what claims to be religious truth. This can be as deep a source of blindness as any in the world, sex included. One always has to distinguish and go beyond: one has to question reason in order to get to the deeper awareness of reality that is built into life itself. What I fear is living in such a way that life becomes opaque and one-sided, centered on one thing only, the illusion of the self. Everything else has to be defined in relation to this kind of ignorance. Once this is understood, you can understand what makes me run—not only run in the sense of escape but run in the sense of tick.

*June 22, 1966, VI.332–33*

# My Task

What runs and what ticks is, however, no longer important. What is important is that life itself should be "lucid" in me (whoever I am). I am nothing but the lucidity that is "in me." To be opaque and dense with opinion, with passion, with need, with hate, with power, is to be not there, to be absent, to nonexist. The labor of convincing myself that this nonexisting is a real presence: this is the source of all falsity and suffering. This is hell on earth and hell in hell. This is the hell I have to keep out of. The price of keeping out of it is that the moment I give in to any of it, I feel the anguish of falsity. But to extinguish the feeling of anguish, in any way whatever short of straight lucidity, is to favor ignorance and nonexistence. This is my central fear and it defines my task in life.

*June 22, 1966, V.333*

# Why Is My Head So Full of Things?

Another of the beautiful cool days we have been having all year. We did not work this afternoon. Plenty of time to pray. Recollected, I am myself for a while, and I consider the weekdays when I am full of business and when I am not myself or my own. Why must I make my head so full of things?

It is the vigil of my great patron and friend and protector St. John the Baptist. "He shall drink no wine nor strong drink" (Luke 1:15): taste none of the pleasures that flatter and intoxicate nature, our own will, our own vanity, our own desires.

I am tired of being my own Providence, of wanting and seeking things for myself, of making decisions for myself, and yet, quite apart from my own will, I am in this complex of things that seem to stand between me and God.

All I want, Jesus, is more and more to abandon everything to You. The more I go on, the more I realize I don't know where I am going. Lead me and take complete control of me.

"Teach me to do thy will, for thou art my God" (Psalm 142).

*June 24, 1947, II.86–87*

# Living in the Tao

I take delight in Mai Mai Sze's *Tao of Painting*, a deep and contemplative book. I am reading it slowly with great profit.

Early mist. Trees of St. Anne's wood barely visible across the valley. A flycatcher, on a fence post, appears in momentary flight, describes a sudden, indecipherable ideogram against the void of mist, and vanishes. On both sides of the house, the gossip of tanagers. The tow lizards that operate on the porch scuttle away when I arrive, however quietly, from outside. But when I come from inside the house, even though I might move brusquely, they are not afraid and stay where they are. To be conscious of both extremes in my solitary life. Consolation and desolation, understanding and obscurity, obedience and protest, freedom and imprisonment.

In one sense I am transcending the community; in another, banned from it. In one sense I am "rewarded," in another punished, kept under restraint. For instance, I cannot go to Asia to seek at their sources some of the things I see to be so vitally important (all the discussions of expression and mystery in brushwork of Chinese calligraphy, painting, poetry, etc.). An "imprisonment" which I accept with total freedom (what I need could be brought to me here!) but nonetheless a confinement. A perfecting of monastic life and a final disillusionment with monastic life! Renunciation of meaningful action and protest in contemporary affairs, awareness that the action itself my be ambiguous, the renunciation of it more clear, a better defined protest.

*June 12, 1965, V.255–56*

# Christ's Heart

Feast of the Sacred Heart, very cool and clear—in the early morning it was more like September than June. Father Lawrence, my undermaster when I was in the novitiate twenty-three years ago, returned from the monastery in Georgia for a while. I could not recognize him—he is much fatter (was very gaunt then). The Feast of the Sacred Heart is for me a day of grace and seriousness. Twenty years ago I was uncomfortable with this concept. Now I see the real meaning of it (quite apart from the externals). It is the *center,* the "heart" of the whole Christian mystery.

There is one more thing: I may be interested in Oriental religions, etc., but there can be no obscuring the essential difference—this personal communion with Christ at the center and heart of all reality, as a source of grace and life. "God is love" may perhaps be clarified if one says that "God is void" and if, in the void, one finds absolute indetermination and hence absolute freedom. (With freedom, the void becomes fullness and $0 = \infty$.) All that is "interesting," but none of it touches on the mystery of personality in God, and His personal love for me. Again, I am void too, and I have freedom, or am a kind of freedom, meaningless unless oriented to Him.

*June 26, 1965, V.259*

# Living in the Only Real City in America

*(Thomas Merton becomes an American citizen on June 26, 1951)*

Octave of Corpus Christi. Once again, the cloister is paved with flowers, the sanctuary white-hot under the floodlights concealed behind the pillars, high in the ceiling: and you look up at the monstrance through a cloud of hot, sweet smoke from the censer, and the sweat runs down into your eyes! I feel as though I had never been anywhere in the world except Gethsemani—as if there were no other place in the world where I had ever really lived. I do not say I love Gethsemani in spite of the heat, or because of the heat. I love Gethsemani: that means burning days and nights in summer, with the sun beating down on the metal roof and the psalms pulsing exultantly through the airless choir while row upon row of us, a hundred and forty singers, sway forward and bow down. And the clouds of smoke go up to God in the sanctuary, and the novices get thin and go home forever.

*June 1952, II.471*

# The Public Vice of War

Comparing the tracts on patience by Tertullian and St. Cyprian. I think I prefer Tertullian—whom Cyprian, in any case, irritated. There is a great vigor in Tertullian's thought, and a greater, more austere, genius in his style. The struggle for him was far greater and his understanding was deeper. Here was a violent man who realized he had to take with complete seriousness the command of Christ to abandon violence. And who saw that it was naturally impossible. When Tertullian reduces all sin to a root of impatience with God, he is not being arbitrary. What he says is very deep. We need to recover these perspectives.

Lanza del Vasto has seen a deep connection between *play* and *war*. Our society, totally devoted to one (everything is a game), necessarily ends in the other. Play is aimless, and multiplies obstacles so that the "aim," which does not exist, may not be obtained by the other player. Getting a ball in a hole.

"War is the great public vice that insists on playing with the blood of men."

War is not caused by hunger or by need. It is the powerful and the rich who make war. The beauty of the grave: it demands a suppression of conscience, and this is done as a matter of "sacrifice" and "duty." To sacrifice conscience, and then "let go" and kill for the exaltation of one's nation, mad with the need for systematic irresponsibility. Reproach them for this, refuse them their outlet, and they will slaughter you.

*June 4 and 5, 1962, IV.223–24*

# Living the Gospel

Question: (1) Can the Gospel commitment, in Gospel terms, be considered enough, or must it be translated also into concrete, contemporary social terms? (2) Is my commitment by religious vows enough, or must it be clarified by a further, more concrete commitment (a) to a *monastic* policy and (b) to a *social* viewpoint for myself and the other monks? (3) Are the commitments of the Church and the Order such today that they necessarily involve one in a "reactionary" social situation? Or is it faith that to follow the Church even in politics necessarily implies going in the direction of justice and truth, despite appearances to the contrary? Or is this question absurd? What are the Church's politics exactly?

A commitment: to the point at least of reading and studying fully these questions, not speculatively, but in order to form my conscience and take such practical actions as I can.

This requires a certain perspective, which necessarily implies a withdrawal "to see better," a stepping back from the machinery of daily monastic life, solitude for study and thought, and more individual development. Part of my vocation!

To discover *all* the social implications of the Gospel not by studying them but by living them, and to unite myself explicitly with those who foresee and work for a social order—a transformation of the world—according to these principles: primacy of the *person* (hence, justice, liberty, against slavery, peace, control of technology, etc.). Primacy of *wisdom* and *love* (hence, against materialism, hedonism, pragmatism, etc.).

*June 5 and 6, 1960, IV.8–9*

# The Sacrifice of Obedience

*Gehorsamopfer*—to offer obedience.

To offer oneself to God as a sacrifice of obedience in faith. This is the crucial point. Too much emphasis on one's own truth, one's own authentic freedom, and one forgets the limitations and restrictions of this "my own." Tendency to take "my own" truth and freedom as unlimited, ultimate, "in my own case." This is a total loss. The paradox that only God's truth is ultimately my truth (there is no one truth for me, another for my neighbor, another for God) and only God's will is my freedom. When they appear to be opposed, am I acting freely?

"Blessed are the pure in heart who leave everything to God now as they did before they ever existed" (Meister Eckhart). This is what I have to get back to. It is coming to the surface again. As Eckhart was my life raft in the hospital, so now also he seems the best link to restore continuity: my obedience to God begetting His love in me (which has never stopped!).

*June 30, 1966, VI.91–92*

# The Cocoon Between What Crawls and What Flies

The sun, the clear morning, the quiet, the barely born butterfly from the cocoon under the bench.

Solitude—when you get saturated with silence and landscape, then you need an interior work, psalms, scripture, meditation. But first the saturation. How much of this is simply restoration of one's normal human balance?

Like waking up, like convalescence after an illness. My life here in solitude is most real because it is most simple. In the monastery it is also real and simple, at least in the novitiate. The more I reach out into "the world," the less simplicity, the more sickness. Our society is gravely ill. This is said so often and I have said it so often, and saying it doesn't seem to help. Knowing it does not seem to help. My concern has been probably sincere but in great part futile. I don't want to turn off into desperation and negativism, but there has to be far greater reserve and caution and *silence* in my looking at the world and my attempts to help us all survive.

Identity. I can see now where the work is to be done. I have been coming here into solitude to find myself, and now I must also lose myself: not simply to rest in the calm, the peace, in the identity that is made up of my experienced relationship with nature in solitude. This is healthier than my "identity" as a writer or a monk, but it is still a false identity, although it has a temporary meaning and validity. It is the cocoon that masks the transition stage between what crawls and what flies.

*June 3 and 4, 1963, IV.326–28*

# My Book into Which Everything Can Go

It is necessary to write a book in which there will be a little less of the first person singular, a little less dramatizing, and fewer resolutions.

Or rather, it is not necessary to write a book. Or anything else. One is free to keep a notebook. That is sufficient.

One may write or not write. Therefore one may write.

Either you look at the universe as a very poor creation out of which no one can make anything, or you look at your own life and your own part in the universe as infinitely rich, full of inexhaustible interest, opening out into infinite further possibilities for study and contemplation and praise. Beyond all and in all is God.

Perhaps the book of life, in the end, is the book of what one has lived, and if one has lived nothing, one is not in the book of life.

And I have always wanted to write about everything.

That does not mean to write a book that covers everything—which would be impossible. But a book into which everything can go. A book with a little of everything that creates itself out of everything. That has its own life. A faithful book. I no longer look at it as a "book."

*July 17, 1956, III.45*

# Awakened by Wisdom

At 5:30, as I was dreaming in a very quiet hospital, the soft voice of the nurse awoke me gently from my dream—and it was like awakening for the first time from all the dreams of my life—as if the Blessed Virgin herself, as if Wisdom had awakened me. We do not hear the soft voice, the gentle voice, the feminine voice, the voice of the Mother: yet she speaks everywhere and in everything. Wisdom cries out in the marketplace: "If anyone is little, let him come to me."

Who is more little than the helpless man, asleep in bed, having entrusted himself gladly to sleep and to night? Him the gentle voice will awaken, all that is sweet in woman will awaken him. Not for conquest or pleasure, but for the far deeper wisdom of love and joy and communion.

My heart is broken for all my sins and the sins of the whole world, for the rottenness of our spirit of gain that defiles wisdom in all beings—to rob and deflower wisdom as if there were only a little pleasure to be had, only a little joy, and it had to be stolen, violently taken and spoiled. When all the while the sweetness of the "Woman," her warmth, her exuberant silence, her acceptance, are infinite, infinite! Deep is the ocean, boundless sweetness, kindness, humility, silence of wisdom that is *not* abstract, disconnected, fleshless. Awakening us gently when we have exhausted ourselves to night and to sleep. O Dawn of Wisdom!

*July 2, 1960, IV.17–18*

# Live in the Present and Where You Are

It is certain that Gethsemani is God's work. Who shall ever be able to say how much depends and has depended in the past on the prayers and sufferings of the men of this house? I am convinced that the fate of America is tied up with the fate of Gethsemani and her foundations. This obscure unit is tremendously important to the whole Church of God.

Can I love God and love the Church if I despise Gethsemani?

What am I heading for? Where am I going? The answer to that one is: I don't need to know. All these troubles come from mistrusting the love of God. Shall I start asking myself all those same old questions all over again? God knows what He wants to do with me. Rest in His tremendous love—to know the savor and sweetness of God's love expressed from moment to moment in all the contacts between Him and your soul—from outside in events, in His signified will and will of good pleasure, from within myself by the flow of actual graces. Rest in that union. It will feed you, fill you with life. There is nothing else you need. He will show you the way to increase it, and, if necessary, He will lead you into perfect solitude in His own good time. Leave it all to Him. Live in the present.

*July 3 and 6, 1947, II.89–90*

# Mercy Within Mercy

The Voice of God is heard in Paradise:

"What was vile has become precious. What is now precious was never vile. I have always known the vile as precious: for what is vile I know not at all.

"What was cruel has become merciful. What is now merciful was never cruel. I have always overshadowed Jonas with my mercy, and cruelty I know not at all. Have you had sight of Me, Jonas, my child? Mercy within mercy within mercy. I have forgiven the universe without end, because I have never known sin.

"What was poor has become infinite. What is infinite was never poor. I have always known poverty as infinite: riches I love not at all. Prisons within prisons within prisons. Do not lay up for yourselves ecstasies upon earth, where time and space corrupt, where the minutes break in and steal. No more lay hold on time, Jonas, my son, lest the rivers bear you away.

"What was fragile has become powerful. I loved what was most frail. I looked upon what was nothing. I touched what was without substance, and within what was not, I am."

There are drops of dew that show like sapphires in the grass as soon as the morning sun appears, and leaves stir behind the hushed flight of an escaping dove.

*July 4, 1952, II.488*

# Sweating It Out

Saying Mass in the secular chapel these days has been very beautiful. Because of the heat, the front doors are left open, and I stand and speak to Christ on the dark altar, and outside the catbirds in the damp trees shout and sing.

I have never sweated so much in my life, even at Gethsemani. The heat has gone unrelieved for three weeks. No air. Nothing is dry. Water comes out of you as soon as anything—even the air itself—touches your skin, and you kneel in choir with sweat rolling down your ribs, and you feel as if you were being smothered by a barber with hot towels, only this barber doesn't leave a hole for you to breathe through.

Out at work the other day we got into some tomato plants that had been overwhelmed by morning glories, and the soil was full of broken bricks. I think it must have been the site of the old monastery. Anyway we did penance that must have been like the days of Dom Benedict. Tides of sweat coming out of you, blinding your face, making your clothes weigh twice their ordinary weight. And yet somehow it is good and satisfying to suffer these things for the world and do some penance we are supposed to do. At night, when we stand in our boiling tunnel of a church, and shout our *Salve* at the lighted window, you feel the whole basilica moving with the exultation of the monks and brothers who are dissolving in their own sweat.

*July 5, 1949, II.334*

# The Daily Monastic Craziness

We have a mechanical monster on the place called a D-4 Traxca-vator, which is enormous and rushes at the earth with a wide open maw and devours everything in sight. It roars terribly, especially when it is hungry. It has been given to the lay-brother novices. They feed it every day, and you can't hear yourself think in the monastery while the brute is at table. It is yellow and has a face like a drawbridge and is marked all over with signs saying it comes from the Wayne Supply Company in Louisville, but really, as I know from secret information, it was born on a raft in Memphis, Tennessee. There the hippopotamus abounds, which this instrument greatly resembles.

We have bought fans. They are exhaust fans. You make a hole in the building and put the fans there, and they draw all the hot air out of the dormitory. Nobody knows what happens after that. My guess is that the hot air that went out through the fan is then replaced by the hot air that comes in through the windows. The fans are not yet running because the lay-brother novices have not yet made the holes in the building. However, they have begun. They have a scaffold up on the roof of the infirmary, and they have been blasting at the gable of that wing with jackhammers, and two frail novices who are very young were posted down on the ground floor near the doorways with artistic signs which read "Falling Bricks." At first one of them was standing on the precise spot where all the falling bricks would land on his head. He was saying the Rosary in an attitude of perfect abandonment.

*July 11, 1949, II.335*

# A Splendor of Light

In Louisville some weeks ago I found the new D. T. Suzuki anthology—really a thorough "Reader," and since reading it, I am almost irresistibly tempted to write him another letter. Poor good old man. I know he must be flooded with mail, as I am, and that he does what I do: puts the letters in a big box and forgets them.

Asked to speak in a "scientific" symposium on "New Knowledge in Human Values," he handled it with consummate wisdom and latent humor, the serious, humble, matter-of-fact humor of emptiness: "If anything new can come out of human values it is from the cup of tea taken by two monks."

Antigone and stoical tropes of St. Eucherius on *contemptus mundi*—the rejection of the world: the beauty of his prose. How the heavens observe the laws of God when they have been once commanded and we, with volumes of laws, do not obey Him.

This morning, the indescribable magnificence of the dawn. Cirrus clouds on the horizon, first glowing with angry and subtle purple fire, then growing into a great mottled curtain of iridescent flame, of what color I don't know. But off to the south, a pile of mottled grey with all kinds of delicate pink highlights in it, like some Oriental porcelain.

St. Eucherius on that sunrise! "Think how much more the splendor of the light will be for us in the future, if it shines upon us so brilliantly now. In what magnificent form will the light shine on eternal things, when it shines so beautifully now on what is passing away!"

*July 24 and 28, 1962, IV.233–34*

# My Community as My Place of Salvation

A cool evening—or cooler than last evening and the one before. I am on the night watch. It is still light, though everyone is in bed. A robin still sings in the garden and tall gold lilies shine in the dusk. While I was anticipating the night office of St. Mary Magdalen, a female tanager captured a grasshopper on the path a few feet away, and, after dinner, as I sat under the broad woodshed roof, a woodchuck came out of the weeds and chewed at leaves five or six feet away from me, not out of tameness but rather out of sheer stupidity. Woodchucks must be shortsighted and depend mostly on hearing, or so I think.

The mystery of my monastic community as my place of salvation and encounter with God. I was talking of this in the conference this afternoon, and it is getting now, at last, into my bones. Though I *can* be solitary, I no longer have to make an issue out of it. And if I *am* solitary, it can be for love of God and a part of community life, not an expression of a stronger psychological or spiritual need. It can be a contribution to the community's life and worship.

*July 21, 1963, IV.342*

# Heat and Zen Quiet

Blazing hot, stuffy air, barely moved by a little breeze here in the woodshed. What a day it is going to be! Even the woods will be an airless furnace. It calls for one of those nature poems, a kerygma of heat such as the Celts never had. (I finished Kenneth Jackson's excellent book, *Early Celtic Nature Poetry,* before Prime as the fierce sun began to burn my field.)

Said a Mass for John Paul, my brother who died in the War, and included Jean-Paul Sartre in it. Two great pigeons have set up shop in the rafters of the woodshed, and with gurgling and cooing and beating of wings make the place more delightful. This morning they were playing some kind of serious game, flying around the gutters and looking at me through cracks between the gutter and the roof.

Meadowlark sitting quietly on a fence post in the dawn sun, his gold vest bright in the light of the east, his black bib tidy, turning his head this way, that way. This is a Zen quietness without comment. Yesterday a very small, chic, black and white butterfly on the whitewashed wall of the house.

*June 23 and 26, July 2, 1964, V.121–23*

# Links in My Life's Chain

A brilliant Saturday. Bright sky and clouds. Not too hot.

Everything I see and experience in Kentucky is to some extent colored and determined by the thoughts and emotions I had when I first came. It cannot be otherwise. So this day, too. It is another day of the time and another link in the chain that began then, and began long before then.

Hawk. First the shadow flying down the sunlit trees. Then the bird overhead, bared tail, spotted wings with sun shining through them. A half circle above the elm, and then he seemed to put his wings in his pocket and flew like a bullet into the grove across the field.

*July 21 and 23, 1962, IV.232, 233*

# On Leaving My Hermitage

What business have I to be sitting around in Jim Wygal's house in Anchorage, listening to records, trying to talk about something? I don't belong in that anymore, still less in the place where I went with Fr. John Loftus and his friend the other night to hear some jazz. At least I have found out by experience that this just does not go. I am dead to it; it is finished long ago. You don't drag a corpse down to Fourth Street and set it up in a chair, at a table, and in polite society.

This just made the reading of Chuang Tzu all the better and more meaningful. Here at the hermitage I am not dead, because this is my life, and I am awake, and breathing, and listening with all that I have got, and sinking to the root. There is no question that I am completely committed to interior solitude. Where—makes no difference. Not a question of "where." Not "tampering with my heart," or with the hearts of others. This is imperative. "The mind is a menace to wisdom." To be one who "though walking on dry land, is as though he were at the bottom of a pool."

The trouble is this being a "writer," and one of the most absurd things I have gotten into is this business of dialogues and retreats. This has to be faced. I can't completely back out now, but certainly no more pushing.

If the days in solitude have taught me this, they are good enough.

*July 4, 1960, IV.18*

# An Inclusive Monastic Life

I am deeply moved by Adamnan's extraordinary life of St. Columba. A poetic work, full of powerful symbols, indescribably rich. Through the Latin (which is deceptive, and strange, too) appears a completely non-Latin genius, and the prophecies and miracles are not signs of authority but signs of life, i.e., not signs of power conferred on a designated representative (juridically)—a "delegated" power from outside of nature—but a sacramental power of a man of God who sees the divine in God's creation. Then the miracles, etc., are words of life spoken in the midst of life, not words breaking into life and silencing it, making it irrelevant, by the decree of an absolute authority (replacing the authority of life which life has from its Creator).

Literature, contemplation, solitude, Latin America, Asia, Zen, Islam, etc. All these things combine in my life. It would be madness to make a "monasticism" by simply excluding them. I would be less a monk. Others have their own way, I have mine. To write to Rafael Squirru. To follow Miguel Grinberg as he goes to San Francisco, then to Argentina, with a letter when needed. To think with these new men. The opening to the south has not been closed. One day to the monastic places in Western Ireland!

*July 10 and 12, 1964, V.125–26*

# Psalms and the Tao

In the evening I began a perpetual Psalter—a necessity—not to say a given quantity any period of time, but just to keep the Psalter going from now on until I die (or can no longer do it). Need for the continuity the Psalter offers—continuity with my own past and with the past of eremitism. The Latin Psalter is for me! It is a deep communion with the Lord and with His saints of my Latin Church. To be in communion with the Saints of my tradition *is* by that fact to be more authentically in communion with those of the Greek, Syriac, etc., traditions, who reach me through my own Fathers.

St. Elias today. He has something to do with it! He is in it!

Great peace for the last couple of days, since the decision that I am to become a full-time hermit. Any day one could write "great peace," but this is a very special and new dimension of peace: a tranquility that is not got by cultivation. It is given, and "not as the world gives do I give unto you." The peace is not "it" but a confrontation with Thou. Martin Buber is certainly right. Confrontation with "Thee" in this word of solitude. All because of this one word, yesterday. All unified in this. One will, one command, one gift. A new creation of heavenly simplicity. I will write little about this, surely. Enough.

"If a man hears Tao in the morning and dies in the evening, his life has not been wasted." I think now I really know what this means.

*July 19 and 20, 1965, V.273–74*

# When My Books Are Read at Me

Here I sit surrounded by bees and I write in this book. The bees are happy and therefore they are silent. They are working in the delicate white flowers of the weeds among which I sit. I am on the east side of the house, where I am not as cool as I thought I was going to be, and I sit on top of the bank that looks down over the beehives and the pond where the ducks used to be and Rohan's Knob in the distance.

In the Chapter Room they are finishing *Seeds of Contemplation,* reading a couple of pages each evening before Compline.

I am glad the book has been written and read. Surely I have said enough about the business of darkness and about the "experimental contact with God in obscurity" to be able to shut up about it and go on to something else for a change. Otherwise it will just get to be mechanical—grinding out the same old song over and over again. But if it had not been read aloud at me, I might have forgotten how often I had said all those things, and gone on saying them again, as if they were discoveries. For I am aware that this often happens in our life. Keeping a journal has taught me that there is not so much new in the interior life as one sometimes thinks. When you reread your journal you find out that your newest discovery is something you found out five years ago. Still, it is true that one penetrates deeper and deeper into the same ideas, the same experiences.

As usual, after one of my books has been read at me, I am left with the wish that I were simpler.

*July 10, 1949, II.333*

# Dawn at the Hermitage

I slept until three and came up here to say the office of psalms—the long way round, by the road. Very thin end of the moon in the morning sky. Crows bothering an owl.

Once again—the office is entirely different in its proper (natural) setting, out from under the fluorescent lights. There at the monastery Lauds is torpor and vacuum. Here it is in harmony with the singing birds under the bright sky. Everything you have on your lips in praising God is there before you—hills, dew, light, birds, growing things: nothing in the liturgy of light is lost.

I saw in the middle of the *Benedicite* the great presence of the sun, which had just risen behind the cedars (same time and place as Trinity Sunday). And now under the pines the sun has made a great golden basilica of fire and water.

Perspective: crows making a racket in the east, dogs making a racket in the south, and yet over all the majestic peace of Sunday. Is that, after all, the true picture of our world?

*July 9, 1961, IV.140*

# Living in Freedom:
# What You Make of Each Day

Today I tried out the schedule that I hope to follow when I am in the hermitage all day: that is, only going down to the monastery to say Mass and have dinner at midday.

Today I went down late, about eleven, and said Mass at 11:30, came back up again after dinner, and that was it. It was a perfect day. Not to run back and forth to the monastery is certainly a blessing. I felt as if a great load had been lifted off me, and in the late afternoon, saying office before supper, I realized that a complete, total and solid peace had settled completely upon me—a happiness without afterthought and without reflection. "All things are yours and you are Christ's—and Christ is God's. If we live, we live unto God. If we die, we die unto God—whether we live or die, we are God's possession." What more could anyone ask? But I don't think, for me, such things could be fully experienced short of this solitude!

How men fear freedom! And how I have learned to fear it myself! I know that in fact, without faith, this would be a different matter, this living alone. But with faith it becomes an eschatological gift. I have never before really seen what it means to live in the new creation and in the Kingdom. Impossible to explain it. If I tried, I would be unfaithful to the grace of it—for I would be setting limits to it. It is limitless, without determination, without definition. It is what you make of it each day, in response to the Holy Spirit!

*July 27 and 28, 1965, V.275–76*

# A New Sweet-Smelling Altar

*(Merton celebrates his first Mass in the front room*
*of his hermitage on July 17, 1967)*

Today, on the patronal feast of my hermitage, Our Lady of Mount Carmel, first Mass here (after nearly seven years). Went over to Athertonville Saturday after dinner to get the altar, sweet-smelling, in Buck Murfield's dark shop. Some of the fields were still under water from the floods of the other day. Saturday was bright and glorious—exceptionally cool weather, lovely white clouds, dry and full of sun, clean, pure. Set up in the hermitage, with ikons over it, the altar is just right.

Mass about 4:30 or 4:45. Said it slowly, even sang some parts (of Gregorian Kyrie, Gloria, Preface, and other bits). It was a beautiful Mass, and I now see that having the altar here is a *great* step forward and a huge help.

Saying Mass up here changes the shape of the day, and eating dinner up here makes it completely leisurely. The best Sunday I can remember in a very long time.

The quiet of the morning, the singing birds, irreplaceable! But the fact of not being able to go anywhere at the moment, when everybody is on planes, means that I am inevitably out of touch with the full reality of my time. Or does it? *Everybody* on planes? Millions go nowhere—and those monks in Asian monasteries, where do they go? Perhaps going nowhere is better. I don't know.

*July 17 and 18, 1967, VI.265–66*

# All That Matters Is the Gift

Lately, without reading St. Louis de Montfort or thinking about him in any special way, I have been giving myself more fully to the love of our Lady, abandoning myself more and more completely to the graces she has obtained for me from God and to her direction of my life by that grace in all the things that are happening.

The Feast of Our Lady of Mount Carmel on the seveneenth was a great day. Since then I have felt like a different person. Much more consciously and peacefully united with God's will. I am more completely determined to abandon all care for my own interests into God's hands through our Lady, even and especially my highest spiritual interests. I am no longer taking care of my own progress and my own sanctity because it is hopeless. I leave it to Mary's direction, to the Living Christ within me, acting in me, controlling all that I do for His love. It is true, for the moment at least, He seems to have a much fuller control.

All that matters is to give *everything,* and the quicker, the better. Fighting, struggling, rebelling, and delaying make it harder, but *not more meritorious.* On the contrary, less. So it is fruitless to multiply difficulties and delays. Give everything and give it in the quickest possible way. All that matters is the gift. That is what pleases God, atones for sin, converts the world, and leads us into the joys of heaven even here on earth.

*July 20, 1947, II.92–93*

# Landscapes of Contemplation

How beautiful it was last evening with a longer interval after supper. The sun was higher than it usually is in that interval, and I saw the country in a light that I usually do not see. The low-slanting rays picked out the foliage of the trees and highlighted a new wheat field against the dark curtain of woods on the knobs that were in shadow. Deep peace. Sheep on the slopes behind the sheep barn. The new trellises in the novitiate garden leaning and sagging. A cardinal singing suddenly in the walnut tree, and piles of fragrant logs all around the woodshed, waiting to be cut in bad weather.

I looked at all this in great tranquility, with my soul and spirit quiet. For me landscape seems to be important for contemplation. Anyway, I have no scruples about loving it.

Didn't St. John of the Cross hide himself in a room up in a church tower where there was one small window through which he could look out at the country?

Benedictine tranquility. *Pax.* That's what I think about. I have more of it perhaps because I am less mixed up today in peculiar tensions of desire and pride that come from fighting the will of God in an obscure way, under the pretext of a greater good.

There is only one way to peace: be reconciled that of yourself you are what you are, and it might not be especially magnificent, what you are! God has His own plan for making something else of you, and it is a plan which you are mostly too dumb to understand.

*July 2, 1948, II.216–17*

# Going My Own Way

In the morning I went out early and finished cutting down and trimming the young pines still bent over since last winter's big blizzards. The bush boundary of my yard, toward the woods, is now clear. This work made my back sore again—so I have to be careful. In the afternoon I went to the farthest end of the soybean field on Linton's farm and took off my shirt to get the sun on my neck and shoulders while I meditated (Hatha and Yoga Vasishta). A quiet and profitable afternoon and God knows I need much more of this! How much precious time and energy I have wasted in the last three years, doing things that have nothing whatever to do with my real purposes and that only frustrate and confuse me. It is a wonder I haven't lost my vocation to solitude by trifling and evasion.

One thing is very clear: all that passes for *aggiornamento* is not necessarily good or healthy. One has to be pretty critical and independent about *all* ideas. And come to one's own conclusions on the basis of one's own frank experience. Both the conservatives and the progressives seem to me to be full of the same kind of intolerance, arrogance, empty-headedness, and to be dominated by different kinds of conformism: in either case the dread of being left out of their reference group. I have to go my own way in terms of needs that to me are fundamental: need to live a life of prayer, need to liberate myself from my own "cares," need for an authentic monastic solitude (not mere privacy), need for a real understanding and use of Asian insights in religion.

*July 3, 1968, VII. 137*

# Letting Go of the Perfect

Very hot. The birds sing and the monks sweat and about 3:15 I stood in the doorway of the grand parlor and looked at a huge pile of Kentucky cumulus cloud out beyond Mount Olivet—with a buzzard lazily going back and forth over the sheep pasture, very high and black against the white mountain of the cloud. Blue shadows on the cloud.

On the Feast of Our Lady of Mount Carmel, our Lady made me happy in many different ways. At prayer—aware of God's purity surrounding my own imperfection with purity and peace. Yet helpless to get myself out of the way so that there could be nothing left but His purity. No other solution but to wait in love and humility and love my imperfection.

All my desires draw me more and more in a direction: to be little, to be nothing, to rejoice in your imperfections, to be glad that you are not worthy of attention, that you are of no account in the universe. This is the only liberation, the only way to solitude.

As long as I continue to take myself seriously, how can I be a saint, a contemplative? As long as I continue to bother about myself, what happiness is possible in life? For the self that I bother about doesn't really exist and never will and never did, except in my own imagination.

*July 18, 1948, II.219*

# A Paradise of Corn Stalks and Silence

How high the corn is this year, and what joy there is in seeing it! The tall crests nodding twelve to fifteen feet above the ground, and all the silk-bearded ears. You come down out of the novitiate, through the door in the wall, over the trestle, and down into this green paradise of stalks and silence. I know the joy and the worship the Indians must have felt, and the Eucharistic rightness of it! How can one *not* feel such things—so that I love the Mayas and Incas as perhaps the most human of peoples, as the ones who did most honor to our continents.

The irreligious mind is simply the *unreal* mind, the zombie, abstracted mind, that does not see the things that grow in the earth and feel glad about them, but only knows prices and figures and statistics. In a world of numbers you can be irreligious, unless the numbers themselves are incarnate in astronomy and music. But, for that, they must have something to do with seasons and with harvests, with the joy of the Neolithic peoples, who for millennia were quiet and human.

*July 26, 1963, IV.346*

# Prayer to Our Lady of Mount Carmel

What was it that I said to you, in the mirror, at Havana?

Were you not perhaps the last one I saw as the steamer left, you standing on your tower with your back to the sea, looking at the university?

I have never forgotten you. You are more to me now than then, when I walked through the streets reciting. I think I have received them, but I do not remember. More importantly, I have received you whom I know and do not know. Whom I love but not enough.

Prayer is what you bring—for prayer is your gift to us rather than what you ask of us. If only I could pray—and yet I can and do pray. Teach me to go to the country beyond words and beyond names. Teach me to pray on this side of the frontier, here where the woods are.

I need to be led by you. I need my heart to be moved by you. I need my soul to be made clean by your prayer. I need my will to be made strong by you. I need the world to be saved by you and changed by you. I need you for all those who suffer, who are in prison, in danger, in sorrow. I need you for all the crazy people. I need your healing hands to work always in my life. I need you to make me, as your Son, a healer, a comforter, a savior. I need you to name the dead. I need you to help the dying cross their particular river. I need you for myself, whether I live or die. I need to be your monk and your son. It is necessary. Amen.

*July 17, 1956, III.46–47*

# Hating No One

I am reading Karl Rahner's essays on grace—at least those available in translation, and I do not have time to struggle with the German. They seem clear and obvious. I sometimes wonder why Rahner is considered so dangerous. Perhaps because he is too clear and not involved in the technical mumbo jumbo that makes others unreadable. In a word: a *readable* theologian is dangerous.

How true it is that the great obligation of the Christian, *especially now*, is to prove himself a disciple of Christ by *hating no one*, that is to say, by condemning no one, rejecting no one. And how true that the impatience that fumes at others and damns them (especially whole classes, races, nations) is a sign of the weakness that is still unliberated, still not tracked by the Blood of Christ, and is still a stranger to the Cross.

*July 22, 1963, IV.342*

# Praying for Civilized Quail

Heavy rain in the morning and then, after a hot steamy afternoon, a violent thunderstorm at supper time—it blew out the bulb of my desk lamp. After the storm and supper—around bedtime—I went out and there were five small, bedraggled, wet quail, picking around in the path by the doorstep and very tame. Must be from the nursery the brothers had at the Steel Building. They don't seem very well prepared for life in the woods: they preferred the path to the grass that would hide them; no mistrust of a human being—did not run away, only got out of the way of my feet or skipped away if I reached for them. They are now out on the wet lawn somewhere. This place is full of foxes—not to mention the kids who shoot anything that moves, in or out of season! I feel very sorry for these quail! But there is also the wild covey of a dozen or so trained by a zealous mother who often lured me along the rose hedge away from where the little ones were hiding in the deep weeds by the gate.

(I hear a mature quail whistling in the field. Perhaps it's that mother gathering in her five "civilized" ones. Hope she tells them a thing or two about *people!*)

*July 17, 1968, VII.146–47*

# The Real Thing

I am very impressed and deeply moved by Ramana Maharshi: not only his life (of which I know only the bare outline) but his doctrine—traditional *Advaita*—or rather, his experience. Whatever may be the deficiencies of the doctrinal elaboration, and the misleading effect of some of the philosophical concepts, this is the basic experience: God is the ultimate "I" Who is the Self of every self! It is this that Christianity too expresses in and through the doctrines of grace, redemption, Incarnation, Trinity. Sons in the Son by grace, we recognize the Father as Him with Whom we are one—not by nature but by His Gift. But the impact of Maharshi's experience awakens in us the real depth of this truth, and the love that springs from it. How powerless most Christian writing and teaching is today, in this respect! How lost, how far off the real target! The words are there, the doctrine is there, but the realization is absent. Maharshi has an inadequate doctrine, perhaps, but the real realization.

*July 23, 1964, V.130–31*

# Facing Death

Does my solitude meet the standard set by my approaching death? No. I'm afraid it does not. That possibility which is most intimate, isolated, my own, cannot be shared or described. I cannot look forward to it as an experience I can analyze and share. It is not something to be understood and enjoyed. (To "understand" and "contemplate" it beforehand is a kind of imposture.) But the solitary life should partake of the seriousness and incommunicability of death. Or should it? Is that too rigid and absolute an ideal? The two go together. Solitude is not death, it is life. It aims not at a living death but at a certain fullness of life. But a fullness that comes from honestly and authentically facing death and accepting it without care, i.e., with faith and trust in God. *Not* with any social justification: not with reliance on an achievement which is approved or at least understood by others. Unfortunately, even in solitude, though I try not to (and sometimes claim not to), I still depend too much, emotionally, on being accepted and approved.

The greatest "comfort" (and a legitimate one, not an invasion) is to be sought precisely in the Psalms, which face death as it is, under the eye of God, and teach us how we may face it. The Psalms bring us at the same time into contact, rather communion, with all those who have seen death and accepted it. Most of all the Lord Himself, who prayed from Psalm 21 on the Cross.

*July 5, 1965, V.264–65*

# Entering the School of My Life

During the night office and morning meditation, seeing that my whole life is a struggle to seek the truth (at least, I want it to be so) and that the truth is found in the reality of my own life as it is given to me, and that it is found by complete consent and acceptance. Not at all by defeat, by mere passive resignation, by mere inert acceptance of evil and falsity (which are nevertheless unavoidable), but by "creative" consent, in my deepest self, to the will of God, which is expressed in my own self and my own life. And indeed there is a sense in which my own deepest self is in God and even expresses Him, as "word." Such is the deep meaning of our Sonship.

Gradually I will come more and more to transcend the limitations of the world and of the society to which I belong—while fully accepting my own little moment in history, such as it is.

To be detached from all systems, and without rancor towards them, but with insight and compassion. To be truly "catholic" is to be able to enter into everybody's problems and joys and be all things to all men.

*July 31, 1961, IV.146*

# Keeping Awake in Obedience
# to Him Who Is Holy

There is a special peace and sense of blessing on Sunday morning, though all mornings are equally quiet here at the hermitage and the same birds always sing. Today the peace is even greater because of the storm and cleansing in the night.

Seeing more and more that my understanding of myself and of my life has always been most inadequate. Now that I want more than ever to see, I realize how difficult it is. Though there is danger, doubtless, in solitude, I realize more than ever that here, in solitude, for me, is confrontation with the Word, and with God, and with the only possibilities that are fully real, or with those that are most real. (There is something real after all in community, but more and more, as I go down there, I have the sense that reality is smothered there and words are substituted for it.) Yet my job and that of the Church remains this: to awaken in myself and in others the sense of real possibility, of truth, of obedience to Him who is Holy, of refusal of pretences and servitudes—without arrogance and hubris and specious idealism. The terrible thing is that our society, which pretends to be Christian, is in fact rejecting the word of God, enabled to do so by the all-pervading, suffocating noise of its own propaganda, able to make itself believe whatever it wants. This is a deluding, fanatical, stupid society. It is under judgment—and what can one say to it? It would be useless to pretend to be perfect, for no one, as far as I can see, is "sent" with any prophetic message. Least of all I.

*July 18 and 19, 1965, V.271–72*

# Praying in the Night

Lord God of this great night: Do You see the woods? Do You hear the rumor of their loneliness? Do You behold their secrecy? Do You remember their solitudes? Do You see that my soul is beginning to dissolve like wax within me?

"O my God, I cry out by day, but you do not answer; by night, but I find no rest."

Do You remember the place by the stream? Do You remember the top of the Vineyard Knob that time in autumn, when the train was in the valley? Do You remember McGinty's hollow? Do You remember the thinly wooded hillside behind Hanekamp's place? Do You remember the time of the forest fire? Do You know what has become of the little poplars we planted in the spring? Do You observe the valley where I marked the trees?

There is no leaf that is not in Your care. There is no cry that was not heard by You before it was uttered. There is no water in the shales that was not hidden there by Your wisdom. There is no concealed spring that was not concealed by You. There is no glen for a lone house that was not planned by You for a lone house. There is no man for that acre of woods that was not made by You for that acre of woods.

There is greater comfort in the substance of silence than in the answer to a question. Eternity is in the present. Eternity is in the palm of the hand. Eternity is a seed of fire whose sudden roots break barriers that keep my heart from being an abyss.

*July 4, 1952, II.487*

# You Are Not Met with Words

The things of Time are in connivance with eternity. The shadows serve You. The beasts sing to You before they pass away. The solid hills shall vanish like a worn-out garment. All things change and die and disappear. Questions arrive, assume their actuality, and also disappear. In this hour I shall cease to ask them and silence shall be my answer. The world that Your love created and that the heat has distorted and that my mind is always misinterpreting shall cease to interfere with our voices.

Minds which are separated pretend to blend in one another's language. The marriage of souls in concepts is mostly an illusion. Thoughts which travel outward bring back reports of You from outward things—but a dialogue with You, uttered through the world, always ends by being a dialogue with my own reflection in the stream of time. With You there is no dialogue unless You choose a mountain and circle it with cloud and print Your words in fire upon the mind of Moses. What was delivered to Moses on tablets of stone, as the fruit of lightning and thunder, is now more thoroughly born in our souls, as quietly as the breath of our own being.

You, Who sleep in my breast, are not met with words, but in the emergence of life within life and of wisdom within wisdom. With You there is no longer any dialogue, any contest, any opposition. You are found in communion! Thou in me and I in Thee and Thou in them and they in me: dispossession within dispossession, dispassion within dispassion, emptiness within emptiness, freedom within freedom. I am alone. Thou art alone. The Father and I are One.

*July 4, 1952, II.487–88*

# The White-Hot Dangerous Presence

My pious Abbé Fillion suggests that, when we are stumped and cannot find out the meaning of a passage of Scripture, we ought to pray to the "sacred author," that is, to whomever it was that served as God's instrument in writing the work. The suggestion appeals to me, for I have a great though confused affection for the writers of the Bible. I feel closer to them than to almost any other writers that I know of. Isaias, Job, Moses, David, Matthew, Mark, Luke, and John are all part of my life. They are always about me. They look over my shoulder, earnest men, belonging to the façade of a medieval cathedral. I feel that they are very concerned about me and that they want me to understand what God told them to write down, that they have always surrounded me with solicitous prayers, and that they love and protect me.

They are more part of my world than most of the people actually living in the world. I "see" them sometimes more really than I see the monks I live with. I know well the burnt faces of the Prophets and the Evangelists, transformed by the white-hot dangerous presence of inspiration, for they looked at God as into a furnace and the Seraphim flew down and purified their lips with fire. They are solemn and dreadful and holy men humbled by the revelation they wrote down. They are my Fathers. They are the "burnt men" in the last line of *The Seven Storey Mountain*. I am more and more possessed by their vision of God's Kingdom, and wonder at the futility of seeking anything on earth but the truth revealed in them and in tradition—the Church's treasure to which she holds the keys.

*August 26, 1949, II.362*

# The Joy That We Are Human

The one point on which I most profoundly disagree with the Karl Barthians is that of "natural theology." Our very creation itself is a beginning of revelation. Making us in His image, God reveals Himself to us, we are already His words to ourselves! Our very creation itself is a vocation to union with Him and, if we persist in honesty and simplicity, our life and the world around us cannot help speaking of Him and of our calling.

The joy that I am *man!* This fact, that I am a man, is a theological truth and mystery. God became man in Christ. In the becoming of what I am, He united me to Himself and made me His epiphany, so that now I am meant to reveal Him, and my very existence as true man depends on this, that by my freedom I obey His light, thus enabling Him to reveal Himself in me. And the first to see this revelation is my own self. I am His mission to myself and through myself to all men. How can I see Him or receive Him if I despise or fear what I am—man? How can I love what I am—man—if I hate man in others?

The mere fact of my manness should be an everlasting joy and delight. To take joy in that which I am made to be by my Creator is to open my heart to restoration by my Redeemer. And it is to taste the firstfruits of redemption and restoration. So pure is the joy of being man that those whose Christian understanding is weak may even take this to be the joy of being something other than man—an angel or something. But God did not become an angel. He became *man*.

*August 12 and 13, 1965, V.279–80*

# The "Way of Perfection" Is to Follow Christ

1. Is it true and salutary to say, as some spiritual writers say, that God is our end but that, in order to attain to our end, we must *first attain perfection,* so that, in practice, our aim is perfection?

2. And is it true, then, that perfection is attained only by a simple-minded concern for "spiritual things" seen as deeply marked off and separate from "temporal things"?

3. And then, are we to look at these "spiritual things" as, in reality, a set of practices which are (allowing, of course, for grace) sure means of attaining to possession of God?

4. This being so, should we then apply ourselves very industriously to the use of these means in order to attain to perfection very quickly and thus gain possession of God?

All of these statements may be perfectly true, though 3 and 4 lend themselves to dangerous misunderstanding, and the other two are already open to much misapprehension. But after all—supposing each of these statements were faultless—the spiritual life would still be something quite different from that!

For we are perfect when we find God or, rather, when God gains possession of us. And, in a sense, from the moment we seek Him, He has already found us. And from the moment He has found us, all that is blessed by His will becomes "spiritual," even though it may be a material thing like eating.

In the end what does the Gospel say? To follow Christ. This is the spiritual life and the way of perfection.

*August 28, 1956, III.74*

# Praising God: The Only Great Thing

It would be so easy and consoling to say, at every moment: "This thing I am doing is regarded by everyone as a sure means of attaining to perfection and to the possession of God." But would the peace and consolation I felt have anything necessarily to do with perfection or the possession of God? Might it not turn out to be the greatest of all illusions? A surrender to the authority of common opinion—"They say." How weak our consciences are! We give in and shut our eyes. We have conformed to "them." We are at peace. "They say" this is perfection.

Much more to the point: the prayer that struggles to get out of myself and reach God, in obscurity, in trial, fighting down the phantoms.

The great thing and the only thing is to adore and praise God.

To seek Him is to adore Him and to say that He alone is God and there is no other.

We must lay down our life for His Truth. We must bear witness to what *is* and the fidelity of God to His promises.

We must believe with our whole heart what God our Father has offered and promised us.

We must leave all things to answer His call to us, and to reply to His grace. When we have done this, we can talk of perfection, but when we have done this, we no longer need to talk of perfection.

*August 28 and 29, 1956, III. 75–76*

# The Present Feast

The grip the *present* has on me. That is the one thing that has grown most noticeably in the spiritual life—nothing much else has. The rest dims as it should. I am getting older. The reality of *now*—the unreality of all the rest. The unreality of ideas and explanations and formulas. I am. The unreality of all the rest. The pigs shriek. Butterflies dance together against the blue sky at the end of the woodshed. The buzz saw stands outside there, half covered with dirty and tattered canvas. The trees are fresh and green in the sun (more rain yesterday). Small clouds, inexpressibly beautiful and silent and eloquent, over the silent woodlands. What a celebration of light, quietness, and glory! This is my feast, sitting here in the straw!

*August 25, 1958, III.214–15*

# The Blessing of an Ordinary Work

The blessing of Prime under the tall pines, in the cool of early morning, behind the hermitage. The blessing of sawing wood, cutting grass, cleaning house, washing dishes. The blessing of a quiet, alert, concentrated, fully "present" meditation. The blessing of God's presence and guidance. I am very aware of the meaning of faith and fidelity, and of the implications of the relationship they establish. This place is marked with the blessed sign of my covenant with Him Who has redeemed me. May I never fail this goodness, this mercy!

A superb passage from Irenaeus (*Adversus haereses,* 4.39):

"If you are the work of God, wait patiently for the hand of your artist who makes all things at an opportune time. . . . Give to Him a pure and supple heart and watch over the form which the artist shapes in you . . . lest, in hardness, you lose the traces of his fingers. By guarding this conformity, you will ascend to perfection. . . . To do this is proper to the kindness of God; to have it done is becoming to human nature. If, therefore, you hand over to Him what is yours, namely, faith in Him and submission, you will see his skill and be a perfect work of God."

*August 25 and 26, 1965, V.284–85*

# Letting Go of All Self-Images

Yesterday a good day of recollection in the woods. Read the part of Dostoevsky's *The Possessed* about the mad Saint Symeon, and something clicked: a strange light on St. Bernard's concept of *fiducia*—"trust"—and one he might perhaps have repudiated, but the root of my problem remains fear of my own solitude—imagined solitude—the fear of rejection, which I nevertheless anticipate—as if it mattered! I should be more bravely real—it is what I need, and one would be surprised at it in me. I think even that my vocation requires it.

Serious need to give the "folly" of God a predominant place in our very serious and insane world! It is perhaps the most valid reply, if not the *only* reply.

The answer of apparent wildness is the providential and divine criticism that is demanded of us, and I have not been nearly as wild as I need to be: it is a reply also to the serious stupidity of our misguided "holiness" here.

I am really a monk when I can let go completely of "being a monk" (self-consciously), and I think I have let go of that long ago. Now I face the terror of being, by the same "letting go," a Christian? And a writer and myself?

How crazy it is to be "yourself" by trying to live up to an image of yourself you have unconsciously created in the minds of others. Better to destroy the image if necessary. But even this is not serious, or to be taken seriously.

*August 20, 1965, III.214*

# The Revelation of Your True Face

The solitary life: now that I really confront it, it is awesome, won-derful, and I see that I have no strength of my own for it. Deep sense of my own poverty and, above all, awareness of the wrongs I have allowed in myself together with this good desire. This is all good. I am glad to be shocked by grace and to wake up in time to see the great seriousness of it. I have been merely playing at this, and the solitary life does not admit of mere play. Contrary to all that is said about it, I do not see how the really solitary life can tolerate illusion and self-deception. It seems to me that solitude rips off all the masks and all the disguises. It does not tolerate lies. Everything but straight and direct affirmation is marked and judged by the silence of the forest. "Let your speech be 'Yea! Yea!'"

The need to *pray*—the need for solid theological food, for the Bible, for monastic tradition. Not experimentation or philosophical dilettantism. The need to be entirely defined by a relationship with and orientation to God my Father, i.e., a life of sonship in which all that distracts from this relationship is seen as fatuous and absurd. How *real* this is! A reality that I must constantly measure up to, it cannot be simply taken for granted. It cannot be lost in distraction. Distractedness here is fatal—it brings one inexorably to the abyss. But no concentration is required, only *being present*. And also work-ing seriously at all that is to be done—the care of the garden of para-dise! By reading, meditation, study, psalmody, manual work, including some fasting, etc. Above all the work of *hope,* not the stupid, relaxed self-pity of *acedia*—engendered by boredom and distractedness.

*August 10, 1965, V.277–78*

# The Freedom of True Prayer

Yesterday when I went down to the monastery to say Mass, all the community, or a large group rather, were out gathering in the potato harvest under a blue late-summer sky, and I remembered the communal beauty of work in this season—the sense of brotherhood and joy when I used to go over with the students to cut tobacco twelve years ago! Or cutting corn in my novitiate. Now that is all done by machine and there is little really common work outdoors. Anyway, I felt lonely seeing them out there.

In the evening: this turned into a beautiful, clear, cool afternoon and evening. After supper I walked outside the gate to the hermitage enclosure and said some psalms, read and meditated a bit looking out over the bottoms and across at the green, cool line of the hills. It all came alive (as it all should be), and I realized then that I had been running the risk, these past few days, of tying myself down with a mental delusion—taking the hermitage too seriously and myself with it—identifying myself with this stupid little cottage as if my whole life were bound up with it. What total absurdity! Looking at the hills and recovering the freedom of true prayer (of which, incidentally, I have had so much in the hermitage, too), I realized that what is important is not the house, not the hermit image, but my own self and my sonship as a child of God. It is good to see that things which are supposed to be media between ourselves and Him so easily get in the way and become obstacles. I am determined not to fool myself with any such nonsense.

*August 28, 1965, V.286–87*

# God Is All That Matters

My first obligation is to be myself and follow God's grace, and not allow myself to become the captive of some idiot idea, whether of hermit life or anything else. What matters is not spirituality, not religion, not perfection, not success or failure at this or that, but simply God, and freedom in His Spirit. All the rest is pure stupidity. How often I saw this last year and before, just coming up for the afternoons—because then I was nonattached, nonidentified, and the hermitage was a kind of nowhere. Now the terrible thing is that it has become a very definite home. But since I am a homeless body, being tied to a home disturbs me. But I am sure with God's grace this will all settle itself, and I can treat the place as any other hole in the wall that is "not mine." Though I must admit that it is full of a lot of books and nonsense. Here is where I think fasting will be important. Simplifying the meals I take here has already been quite a help. All that cooking of rice and cream of wheat, etc., which I won't scruple to use in cold weather.

I am impatient of all desires. May the Holy Spirit bring me to *true* freedom!!

*August 28, 1965, V.287*

# What Do You Need?

What do I need? Hard question to answer.

I need something beyond my capacity to know. If I call it solitude, I mistake it. Silence, a primitive life.

What I need, as far as I can interpret the desire in my heart, is to make a journey to a primitive place, among primitive people, and there die. It is at the same time a going out and a "return." A going somewhere where I have never been or thought of going—a going in which I am led by God, a journey in which I go out of everything I now have. And I feel that, unless I do this, my spiritual life is at an end. Unfortunately this obscure drive is not recognized by theologians and directors. Certainly it is "nature." But is there no grace in it? I do not know. It is an anxious and imperious thing . . . call it "acting out."

But—if you go to Mexico on the strength of that impulse, are you free? Are you not subordinating your spiritual freedom to blind irrationality? Maybe that is the trouble. (The book about the *New Yorker*—Thurber's—oppresses me. Civilization oppresses me, or rather all that is new in it does. The most comforting thing in the book is the sketch on the cover, a boat in one of the Manhattan docks. The only good thing about New York is that you can sail from there to France.)

What do I need? If necessary I can get by with plenty of mornings like this. Seriously, I need silence, thought, solitude to enter into myself to see and touch reality, to live the contemplative life.

*August 18, 1959, III.319*

# Loving the World

I have finished reading the proofs of the *Divine Milieu* by Père Teilhard de Chardin which were sent to me by Harpers.

Certainly the world is to be loved, as he says it. For God loved the world and sent His Son into the world to save it.

Here *the world* means the cosmos, and all is centered on God. All seek Him.

Christianity should make us "more visibly human"—passionately concerned with all the good, that is, that wants to grow in the world *and that cannot grow without our concern.*

The stoic indifference cultivated by a certain type of Christian spirituality is then a diabolical temptation and an emptying of pity, of charity, of interest. A hardening of the heart, a regression and an isolation.

His concern is admirable. And his indignation that "Christians no longer expect anything." It is true. Nothing great. But we expect *everything trivial.*

*Our indifference to the real values in the world justifies our petty attraction to its false values.* When we forget the Parousia and the Kingdom of God *in the world,* we can, we think, safely be businessmen and make money.

Those who love the world in the wrong sense love it for themselves, exploit it for themselves. Those who truly love it develop it, work in it for God, that God may reveal Himself in it.

*August 26, 1960, IV.36–37*

# The Beauty of the Church

I was in Louisville today and had dinner at the Little Sisters of the Poor. The moral beauty of the place, the authentic beauty of Christianity, which has no equal. The beauty of the Church is the charity of her daughters.

The good Mother Superior, whom I shall never forget. Her transparency, unearthliness, simplicity, of no age, a child, a mother, like the Blessed Virgin—as if no name could apply to her, that is, no name known to anyone but God. And yet more real than all the unreal people in the rest of the world.

The old people. The old man playing the piano and the old man dancing. The sweet, dignified Negro lady who had worked for Fr. Greenwell. The old, beat, heavy Negro lady with wisps of white beard, sunk in her dream, her blank expression, slowly coming out of it when spoken to. The lady who had both legs cut off. The little-girl lady who made the speech in the dining room. The old lady with the visor cap on. And the golden wedding couple.

Sweet, good people. Now I have the prayers of the poor, the strong, merciful, invincible prayer of the poor behind me, and in me, changing my whole life and my whole outlook on life.

*August 16, 1960, IV.31–32*

# Tasting the Real

Cool. Cows lowing in the mist. Long but rich night office. "Mary has chosen the better part." My *love* for the great responsories.

A seventeenth-century Carmelite attacked Jean Mabillon, the French Maurist Benedictine, for his criterion of historical judgment. He asserted that long familiarity with charters and manuscripts gave one a quasi-instinctive "taste" by which one could detect fabrications and falsifications. This, said the critic, was pure subjectivism. And the "objectivity" to which he appealed was that of accepted norms. What had always been regarded as genuine was genuine, because this was the tradition of the Church and the work of God. So too, the appeal to "law" sometimes.

Yet who can guarantee that he has developed the right "instinctive" taste for the real? So the accepted view cannot be disregarded. But it need not be blindly received as final.

The Lespedeza hedge we planted ten or fifteen years ago was blooming with delicate, heather-like purple blossoms, and bees were busy in them. An entirely beautiful, transfigured moment of love for God and the need for complete confidence in Him in everything, without reserve, even when almost nothing is understood.

*August 15 and 16, 1963, V.9*

# A Russian Spirit

Soloviev: "The importance of a truth lies, of course, not in the truth itself, but within us, in our inconsistency. By not carrying out a truth to the end, we limit it—and any limitation of a truth provides an expanse for falsehood." *"It is madness not to believe in God; it is the greater madness to believe in Him only in part."*

He says, in effect, that consistency in truth means striving with pure and perfect hope to realize our "positive unconditionality," that is, that we can possess in God the "whole content, the fullness of being, not as a mere fantasy, but as a real actuality." Also, it is on this "inconsistency" that he bases his accusation of the inadequacy of Catholicism—"it does not carry its faith to its logical end." He adds that modern materialism, struggling to overcome a Catholic tradition (and in this struggle, according to Soloviev, it will be successful), is a transition period between the inadequate spirituality of the past and the new, more perfect, spirituality of the future—"Godmanhood."

In this is a tremendous challenge really *to live my monastic life.*

*August 7, 1956, III.63*

# At Peace in Solitude

This morning—grey, cool, peace. The unquestionable realization of the rightness of living in the woods full-time, because it is from God and it is His work. So much could be said! What is immediately perceptible is the *immense* relief, the burden of ambiguity that is lifted, and I am without care—no anxiety about being pulled between my job and my vocation. . . . I feel as if my whole being were an act of thankfulness—even the gut is relaxed and at peace after a good meditation and long study of Irenaeus in Wingren's book, *Man and the Incarnation.* The woods all crackle with guerrilla warfare—the hunters are out for squirrel season (as if there were a squirrel left!). Even this idiot ritual does not make me impatient. In their way, they love the woods too: but I wish their way were less destructive and less a lie.

"I am the Lord thy God who brought you out of the land of Egypt: open thy mouth wide, and I will fill it." Psalm 80 is where I am in my perpetual Psalter, and there is no question that solitude gives a different horizon to the Psalter, precisely because of the light and nourishment one especially needs.

The five days I have had in real solitude have been a revelation, and whatever questions I may have had about it have been answered. Over and over again I see that this life is what I have always hoped it would be and always sought. A life of peace, silence, purpose, meaning. It is not always easy, but calls for a blessed and salutary effort—and a little goes a long way. Everything about it is rewarding.

*August 21 and 25, 1965, V.283*

# Be Here Now

In the afternoon I went out to the old horse barn with the Book of Proverbs and indeed the whole Bible, and I was wandering around in the hayloft, where there is a big gap in the roof. One of the rotting floorboards gave way under me and I nearly fell through. Afterwards I sat and looked out at the hills and the grey clouds and couldn't read anything. When the flies got too bad, I wandered across the bare pasture and sat over by the enclosure wall, perched on the edge of a ruined bathtub that has been placed there for horses to drink out of. A pipe comes through the wall and plenty of water flows into the bathtub from the spring somewhere in the woods, and I couldn't read there either. I just listened to the clean water flowing and looked at the wreckage of the horse barn on top of the bare knoll in front of me and remained drugged with happiness and with prayer.

Presently the two mares and the two colts came over to see me and to take a drink. The colts looked like children with their big grave eyes, very humble, very stupid, and they were tamer than I expected. They came over and nudged me with their soft muzzles and I talked to them a bit.

Later on I saw other interesting things—for instance a dead possum in a trap and a gold butter-and-egg butterfly wavering on the dead possum's back. There are many Rhode Island Reds over in the southwest corner of the enclosure. When I was on retreat for ordination to the priesthood, I galloped to be at work on the roosts we were building for them then.

*August 30, 1949, II.363*

# The Blessing of Scripture on My Vocation

Merely to set down some of the communicable meanings that can be found in a passage of Scripture is not to exhaust the true meaning or value of that passage. Every word that comes from the mouth of God is nourishment that feeds the soul with eternal life. "Man does not live by bread alone, but by every word that proceeds from the mouth of God." Everywhere in Scripture there are doors and windows opened into the same eternity—and the most powerful communication of Scripture is the *insitum verbum*—the engrafted word—the secret, inexpressible seed of contemplation planted in the depths of our soul and awakening it with immediate and inexpressible contact with the Living Word, that we may adore Him in Spirit and in Truth. By the reading of Scripture I am so renewed that all nature seems renewed round me and with me. The sky seems more pure, a cooler blue, the trees a deeper green, light is sharper on the outline of the forest, and the hills and whole world are charged with the glory of God, and I feel fire and music in the earth under my feet.

The blessings of my Cistercian vocation are poured out on me in Scripture and I live again in the lineage of Saint Bernard, and I see that, had I been deeper in Scripture, all temptations to run to some other Order would have lost their meaning, for contemplation is found in faith, not in geography; you dig for it in Scripture but cannot find it by crossing the seas.

*August 8, 1949, II.349–50*

# Taste and See

From moment to moment, I remember with surprise that I am satisfied, even though everything is not yet fulfilled. I lack nothing. *Omnino replete me*—He satisfies me in all things. *Sapientia*—wisdom = *sapor boni*—savoring the good (St. Bernard). To know and taste the secret good that *is present* but is not known to those who, because they are restless and because they are discontent and because they complain, cannot apprehend it. The present good—reality—God. *Gustate et videte*—Taste and see.

It is easy to say of every new idea that one meets, "It is all in St. Bernard." It is very doubtful, for instance, whether Freud is "all in St. Bernard." However, Emmanuel Mounier's "Personalism" is essentially present in St. Bernard. Hence to read Mounier with understanding is most profitable spiritual reading not only because it helps to understand St. Bernard but helps us to use him. We are paralyzed in our individualism and we turn everything to the advantage of sterile self-isolation (self-centered) and we do this in the name of our contemplative calling. What a disaster to build the contemplative life on the negation of communication. That is why there is so much noise in a Trappist monastery. The infernal chatter and hullabaloo, the continual roar of machinery, the crash of objects falling from the hands of distraught contemplatives—all this protests that we hate silence with all our power because, with our wrong motives for seeking it, it is ruining our lives. Yet the fact remains that silence is our life—but a silence which is communion and better communication than words! If only someone could tell us how to find it.

*August 20, 1956, III.70–71*

# Be Content

*(Thomas Merton officially becomes a full-time hermit on the
Feast of St. Bernard, August 20, 1965)*

I believe with Diadochos that, if, at the hour of my death my confidence in God's mercy is perfect, I will pass the frontier without trouble and pass the dreadful array of my sins with compunction and confidence and leave them all behind forever.

Lord, again, I do not doubt my call to holiness, even though I am not faithful. I do not doubt that You will fulfill Your will in me in spite of my cowardice and lack of effort, in spite of all my unconscious and even conscious prevarications. You are God and You have destroyed my sins on the Cross before they were committed. Keep me from sinning again, keep me even from material sin, make me avoid even imperfections, although so often I cannot even guess at them.

Our glory and our hope—we are the body of Christ. Christ loves us and espouses us as His own flesh. Isn't that enough for us? But we do not really believe it. No! Be content, be content. We are the Body of Christ. We have found Him, He has found us. We are in Him, He is in us. There is nothing further to look for, except the deepening of this life we already possess. Be content.

*August 20, 1956, III.70*

# When Words Fail Us

Morning after morning I try to study the sixth chapter of St. John's Gospel and it is too great. I cannot study it. I simply sit still and try to breathe.

There is a small black lizard with a blue, metallic tail scampering up the yellow wall of the Church next to the niche where the Little Flower, with a confidential and rather pathetic look in her eyes, offers me a rose. I am glad of the distraction because now I can breathe again and think a little.

It does no good to use big words to talk about Christ. Since I seem to be incapable of talking about Him in the language of a child, I have reached the point where I can scarcely talk about him at all. All my words fill me with shame.

That is why I am more and more thankful for the Office and for the psalms. Their praise of God is perfect, and God gives it to me to utter as more my own than any language I could think up for myself.

"Lord our God! How admirable is your name through the whole world" (Psalm 8).

When I have the whole Church crying out with me, there is some chance of finding peace in the feeling that God is somehow, after all, receiving praise from my lips.

*August 31, 1949, II.364*

# Practicing Non-violence

Today I realize with urgency the absolute seriousness of my need to study and practice non-violence. Hitherto, I have "liked" non-violence as an idea. I have "approved" it, looked with benignity on it, have praised it, even earnestly.

But I have not practiced it fully. My thoughts and words retaliate. I condemn and resist adversaries when I think I am unjustly treated. I revile them; even treat them with open (but *polite*) contempt to their face.

It is necessary to realize that I am a monk consecrated to God and this restricting non-retaliation merely to *physical* non-retaliation is not enough—on the contrary, it is in some sense a greater evil.

At the same time, the energy wasted in contempt, criticism and resentment is thus diverted from its true function, *insistence on truth*. Hence, loss of clarity, loss of focus, confusion, and finally frustration. So that half the time "I don't know what I am doing" (or thinking).

I need to set myself to the study of non-violence, with thoroughness. The complete, integral *practice* of it in community life. Eventually teaching it to others by word and example. Short of this, the monastic life will remain a mockery in my life.

*August 21, 1962, IV.238–39*

# The Personalism of Emmanuel Mounier

The toughness and integrity of Emmanuel Mounier, and his book *Personalism*, demand careful attention. Maybe of all the men of our time he is the one we need most to understand and imitate. He is clever and hard with words. You cannot be comfortable with his language unless you think along with it, which is not all that easy. Hence he will make almost everyone uncomfortable—assuming that they even listen to him at all.

Mounier says (in showing that the idea of a person must be defined by the power to communicate—and showing how individualism bars communication): "A kind of instinct works within us to deny or diminish the humanity of those around us. . . . [T]he lightest touch of the individual seems sometimes to infect a mortal poison into any contact between man and man" (*Personalism*, p. 18).

Mounier again: "The person only grows in so far as he continually purifies himself from the individual within him. He cannot do that by force of self-attention but, on the contrary, by making himself available."

*August 17 and 19, 1956, III.66, 68–69*

# To Save Your Life, Lose It

Spiritual reading puts us in contact not just with words, with ideas, but with reality—with God.

To seek God is to seek reality. And this must be something more than a flight from images to ideas. The interior life is not merely what is *not* exterior.

Thunder and rain during breakfast. Curtains of mist hanging over the knobs, pigs garrulous in the lush wet grass, and a dove in the cedar tree. Enough for a haiku?

Temptation: to put together a book the way one furnishes an apartment—to surround oneself with things and act as if one had made it all. The Braque on the wall, the T'ang vase, the Persian carpet. A Cistercian should, no doubt, not even know such things. But a Cistercian on the point of going to New York cannot help but think of them. Caught between good and evil, and sometimes not knowing which is which.

Julien Green was always asking himself, can a novelist be a saint, can a novelist save his soul? But perhaps the salvation of his soul and, even more, his sanctification, depends precisely on taking this role. "He that would save his life will lose it."

*August 19, 1956, III.67–68*

# A Prayer for God's Mercy

Lord, have mercy.

Have mercy on my darkness, my weakness, my confusion. Have mercy on my infidelity, my cowardice, my turning about in circles, my wandering, my evasions.

I do not ask for anything but such mercy, always, in everything, mercy.

My life here—a little solidity and very much ashes.

Almost everything is ashes. What I have prized most is ashes. What I have attended to least is, perhaps, a little solid.

Lord, have mercy. Guide me, make me want again to be holy, to be a man of God, even though in desperateness and confusion.

I do not necessarily ask for clarity, a plain way, but only to go according to your love, to follow your mercy, to trust in your mercy.

I want to seek nothing at all, if this is possible. But only to be led without looking and without seeking. For thus to seek is to find.

*August 2, 1960, IV.28*

# Frater Aelred

Chuang Tzu said: "At the present time the whole world is under a delusion and, though I wish to go in a certain direction, how can I succeed in doing so? Knowing that I cannot do so, if I were to force my way, that would be another delusion. Therefore my best course is to let my purpose go and no more pursue it. If I do not pursue it, whom shall I have to share in my sorrow?"

On Monday Frater Aelred left, which was wise and the only solution—he was getting no education here and would only get into complications. So now he is gone and has left no memorial other than a spot of wine on the altar cloth—and the little India rubber eraser on which he carved my name so that with my ink pad I can stamp it on books, etc. I like the way it is done, rough and crude and simple.

*August 5, 1960, IV.25*

# A Blessed Shipwreck in God's Simplicity

I copy out the sentences from Dom Porion's letter, which I spoke of the other day. Speaking of his book on the Holy Trinity—so simple, so deep and so comprehensive—he says:

"It turns out, furthermore, that my book's atmosphere is, of course, no longer my own. I would like my life to be one of continual looking at God, seizing what he is in pure silence. In this light-filled serenity *a person could forever experience a blessed shipwreck.*"

How I sympathize with that sentence! No matter how simple discourse may be, it is never simple enough. No matter how simple thought may be, it is never simple enough. No matter how simple love may be, it is never simple enough. The only thing left is the simplicity of the soul in God or, better, the simplicity of God.

*August 12, 1949, II.353–54*

# I Must Lead a New Life

Always very fine ideas in Romano Guardini on Providence.

For instance, that the will of God is not a "fate" to which we submit, but a creative act in our life producing something absolutely new (or failing to do so), something hitherto unforeseen by the laws and established patterns. Our cooperation (seeking first the Kingdom of God) consists not solely in conforming to laws, but in opening our wills out to this creative act, which must be retrieved in and by us—by the will of God.

This is my big aim—to put everything else aside. I do not want to create merely for and by myself a new life and a new world, but I want God to create them in and through me. This is central and fundamental—and with this one can never be a mere Marxian communist.

I must lead a new life and a new world must come into being. But not by *my* plans and *my* agitation.

*August 3, 1958, III.211*

# The Flow of Events

Inexorably life moves on toward crisis and mystery.

One must not be too quickly preoccupied with professing definitively what is true and what is false. Not that true and false do not matter. But if at every instant one wants to grasp the whole and perfect truth of a situation, particularly a concrete and limited situation in history or in politics, one only deceives and blinds himself. Such judgments are only rarely and fleetingly possible, and sometimes, when we think we see what is most significant, it has very little meaning at all.

So it is possible that the moment of my death may turn out to be, from a human and "economic" point of view, the most meaningless of all.

Meanwhile, I do not have to stop the flow of events in order to understand them. On the contrary, I must move with them or else what I think I understand will be no more than an image in my own mind.

So, the flow of events: Terry Phillips with a wrecking bar smashing the plaster off the walls of the room in the old guest house where, twenty years ago, I first came on retreat, that moonlit night in Lent! Terry—our youngest postulant—was not even born then.

*August 16 and 19, 1961, IV.152–53*

# Brother Mathias to the End

Brother Mathias received Extreme Unction—the sacrament of the sick and dying—after None, sitting in a brown chair at the head of the choir. He is dying of cancer. Again, the *mystery of the present.* Wasted and changed by illness, he is still Brother Mathias, in fact, more Brother Mathias than ever—his life is crowned by his patience and goodness in his suffering, so that this will be the definitive Brother Mathias—and I am sure he no longer knows anything about this and has lost sight of himself. He just suffers, and the days go by. How strange it would be to say he received the Sacrament "with great faith." Which, of course, is true. How true to say he received it with the earnestness and depth of feeling which we know in him and which is his very self to us. He received it as Brother Mathias—as one loved by Christ, and chosen by him. This is the real heart of the mystery, so obvious and simple. The presence of Divine Mercy in the midst of us, in Christ.

*August 25, 1958, III.215*

# In Your Kindness Dispose Me to Your Pleasure

August ending beautifully—bright days, relatively cool. Wonderful vista opened up at the end of the novitiate garden where I got Frater Gerard to cut down the walnut tree that was doing poorly and hiding the valley, woods and knobs into the bargain. Now a problem—the young beech tree that I put there myself. I suppose I must have the sense to transplant it.

Some annoyances, but they hardly matter. Bulldozer on that dam built ten years ago across the road, and now beginning to fall apart. A lot of banging in the new waterworks. I think all the mosquitoes are coming from the new reservoir—never so many in the dormitory as last year! An awful lot of idiot letters. And so on.

"Do You Yourself in kindness dispose of me, my thoughts and actions, according to Your good pleasure, so that Your will may always be done by me and in me and concerning me" (St. Anselm).

*August 31 and September 1, 1963, V.14*

# With My Writing Pad in Purgatory

This morning, under a cobalt blue sky, summer having abruptly ended, I am beginning the book of Job. It is not warm enough to sit for long in the shade of the cedars. The woods are crisply outlined in the sun and the clamor of distant crows is sharp in the air that no longer sizzles with locusts. And Job moves me deeply. This year, more than ever, it has a special poignancy.

I now know that all my own poems about the world's suffering have been inadequate: they have not solved anything. They have only camouflaged the problem. And it seems to me that the urge to write a real poem about suffering and sin is only another temptation, because, after all, I do not really understand.

Sometimes I feel that I would like to stop writing, precisely as a gesture of defiance. In any case, I hope to stop publishing for a time, for I believe it has now become impossible for me to stop writing altogether. Perhaps I shall continue writing on my deathbed, and even take some asbestos paper with me in order to go on writing in purgatory. Except that I hope our Lady will arrange some miraculous victory over my sins that will make purgatory unnecessary.

*September 1, 1949 II.364–65*

# A Compassionate Transparency

And yet it seems to be that writing, far from being an obstacle to spiritual perfection in my own life, has become one of the conditions on which my perfection will depend. If I am to be a saint— and there is nothing else that I can think of desiring to be—it seems that I must get there by writing books in a Trappist monastery. If I am to be a saint, I have not only to be a monk, which is what all monks must do to become saints, but I must also put down on paper what I have become. It may sound simple, but it is not an easy vocation.

To be as good a monk as I can be, and to remain myself, and to write about it: to put myself down on paper, in such a situation, with the most complete simplicity and integrity, masking nothing, confusing no issue: this is very hard because I am all mixed up in illusions and attachments. These, too, will have to be put down. But without exaggeration, repetition, useless emphasis. To be frank without being boring: it is a kind of crucifixion. Not a very dramatic or painful one. But it requires much honesty that is beyond my nature. It must come somehow from the Holy Spirit.

A complete and holy transparency: living, praying and writing in the light of the Holy Spirit, losing myself entirely by becoming public property just as Jesus is public property in the Mass. Perhaps this is an important aspect of my priesthood—my living of my Mass: to become as plain as a Host in the hands of everybody. Perhaps it is this, after all, that is to be my way to solitude. One of the strangest ways so far devised, but it is the way of the Word of God.

*September 1, 1949, I.365–66*

# A Visit from My Good Teacher

Mark and Dorothy Van Doren were here yesterday on their way back to Illinois—long enough to walk to the cow barn and back and for me to show Mark the novitiate.

I was happy to have him stand in these rooms, so wise a person, and lean against the bookshelf in the scriptorium and talk about some things that had come up when he was at the Hampton Institute the day before. The English professor there complained that his students had no preparation to read Shakespeare, and Mark said that everyone is prepared to read Shakespeare by the time they are eighteen. They have been born, they have had fathers, mothers, they have been loved, feared, hated, been jealous, etc.

At the cow barn we looked at brushfires being lit along the hillside of St. Bernard's field, and Mark talked about his love for fires and I talked of mine. We decided that everybody loves fires and that those who admit it are not pyromaniacs but just love fires reasonably.

When I talked a moment about Bulgakov, Mark quoted the wonderful lines at the end of Dante where he sees in Christ the face of man and the Face of God and they are one face. "But to explain it is as hard as to square the circle," Mark said.

They were pleased that both their sons had married Jews this summer, and I too.

*September 29, 1957, III.122*

# Swimming

A dream last night that was in many ways beautiful and moving—a hieratic dream.

I am invited to a party. I meet some of the women going to the party, but there is an estrangement. I am alone by the waterfront of a small town. A man says that for five dollars I can get across on a yacht to where I want to go. I have five dollars and more than five dollars, hundreds of dollars, and also francs. I am conscious of my clerical garb. The yacht is a small schooner, a workaday schooner, and no yacht. It does not move from shore—we make it move a little by pushing it from inside. Then I am swimming ahead in the beautiful water, magic water from the depths of which comes a wonderful life to which I am entitled, a life and strength that I fear. I know that by diving into this water I can find something marvelous, but that it is not fitting or right for me to dive, as I am going to the further shore, with the strength that has come from the water, immortality.

Then in the summerhouse on the other side, where I have arrived, first of all I play with the dog, and then the child brings me two pieces of buttered white bread that I am to eat on arrival.

*September 12, 1961, III.161–62*

S E P T E M B E R   5

# Beauty's Holiness

You flowers and trees, you hills and streams, you fields, flocks and wild birds, you books, you poems, and you people, I am unutterably alone in the midst of you. The irrational hunger that sometimes gets into the depth of my will tries to swing my deepest self away from God and direct it to your love. I try to touch you with the deep fire that is in the center of my heart, but I cannot touch you without defiling both you and myself, and I am abashed, solitary and helpless, surrounded by a beauty that can never belong to me.

But this sadness generates within me an unspeakable reverence for the holiness of created things, for they are pure and perfect and they belong to God and are mirrors of His beauty. He is mirrored in all things like sunlight in clean water: but if I try to drink the light that is in the water, I only shatter the reflection.

And so I live alone and chaste in the midst of the holy beauty of all created things, knowing that nothing I can see or hear or touch will ever belong to me, ashamed of my absurd need to give myself away to any one of them or to all of them. The silly, hopeless passion to give myself away to any beauty eats out my heart. It is an unworthy desire, but I cannot avoid it. It is in the hearts of us all, and we have to bear with it, suffer its demands with patience, until we die and go to heaven, where all things will belong to us in their highest causes.

*September 14, 1949, II.368–69*

# Called into Silence

You have called me into this silence to be grateful for what silence I have, and to use it by desiring more.

Prayer should not only draw God down to us: it should lift us up to Him. It should not only rest in His reflection (which the soul, still resting in the house of the body, finds within itself). It should rise out of the body and seek to leave this life in order to rest in Him. This is true solitude, unimaginably different from any other solitude of body or of soul. But it is hard to find under the pressure of desires that make us heavy and anchor us to earth when we are immersed in the active life of a community.

Heaven and earth are full of Thy glory. Full of Thy mercy. And I who am nothing have been placed here in silence to behold it and to praise Thee!

*September 3, 1952, III. 15*

# God's Lucid Afternoon

Out here in the woods I can think of nothing except God, and it is not so much that I think of Him either. I am as aware of Him as of the sun and the clouds and the blue sky and the thin cedar trees.

Engulfed in the simple lucid actuality which is the afternoon: I mean God's afternoon, this sacramental moment of time when the shadows will get longer and longer, and one small bird sings quietly in the cedars, and one car goes by in the remote distance and the oak leaves move in the wind.

High up in the summer sky I watch the silent flight of a vulture, and the day goes by in prayer. This solitude confirms my call to solitude. The more I am in it, the more I love it. One day it will possess me entirely and no man will ever see me again.

*September 15, 1952, III. 16*

# The Need for New Directions

I believe that I have the right and the duty to try to go on to a more pure and simple and primitive form of life. I believe that I have the right to appeal to a higher superior for permission to make this trial. I can ask and wait and see what happens. On the one hand, I have to be really sincere about looking for a simpler, poorer, more solitary life, more abandoned to Providence. On the other hand, there are all the things that enter into this and spoil this: desire of liberty, desire to be out from under a stupid form of authority, desire to travel—to go to a more beautiful and primitive country. All these things are there, unfortunately, and they are strong.

The one thing necessary is a true interior and spiritual life, true growth, on my own, in depth, in a new direction. Whatever new direction God opens up for me. My job is to press forward, to grow interiorly, to pray, to break away from attachments and to defy fears, to grow in faith, which has its own solitude, to seek an entirely new perspective and new dimension in my life. To open up new horizons at *any* cost. To desire this and let the Holy Spirit take care of the rest. But really to desire this and *work* for it.

*September 21 and 22, 1959, III.331*

# To Absorb, to Digest, to Remember

Heavy rain after a long dry spell. (I think perhaps I register all the rain in this book—my journal—solicitude for rain and freshness, as if dying in a desert.)

Sorrow. Sorrow for sin. No more fooling about this sorrow in silence. Mourning. Grief.

Importance of being able to rethink thoughts that were fundamental to men of other ages, or *are* fundamental to men in other countries. For me, especially: contemporary Latin America—Greek Patristic period—Mt. Athos—Confucian China—T'ang dynasty—Pre-Socratic Greece. Despair of ever beginning to know and understand, to communicate with these pasts and these distances, yet sense of obligation to do so, to live them and combine them in myself, to absorb, to digest, to "remember." *Memoria.* Have not yet begun. How will I ever begin to appreciate their problems, reformulate the questions they tried to answer? Is it even necessary? Is it sane? For me it is an expression of love for man and for God. An expression without which my contemplative life would be useless.

And to share this with my own contemporaries.

*September 8 and 9, 1960, IV.42–43*

# Clarity and Redemption

How much I need clarity. I live in great darkness and weakness, occasionally getting some smell of the fresh air where light is outside my cellar.

The center of the problem: my own pride, the pride of others, the pride of my monastery. I enter into dialogue with the pride of others, and it is my own pride that speaks. Hence I have to see their pride and not my own.

Fury after Prime, or brief spasm of it, resentment, clearly seen. And the realization that the whole thing can someday break off like a cliff and fall into the sea, if I don't learn to not identify myself with my own angry, righteous and spiteful image.

Moving words of Karl Barth preached on Good Friday, 1948, in Hungary at Debrecen, the great Calvinist center:

"For in His meekness, which we remember today, He achieved the mightiest of all deeds ever fulfilled on earth. In His own person He restored and re-established the violated law of God and the shattered law of man. In this meekness the grace of God appeared in His person, and the obedient man, at peace with God and in whom God has pleasure, was revealed. In this meekness of His, Jesus Christ, nailed to the cross as a criminal, created order in the realm of creation, the order in which man can live eternally as the redeemed, converted child of God" (*Against the Stream*).

*September 18 and 23, 1960, IV.50–51*

# Seeing Deerness

Magenta mist outside the windows. A cock crows over at Boone's. Last evening, when the moon was rising, saw the warm, burning, soft red of a doe in the field. It was still light enough, so I got the field glasses and watched her. Presently a stag came out, then I saw a second doe and, briefly, another stag. They were not afraid. Looked at me from time to time. I watched their beautiful running, grazing. Everything, every movement, was completely lovely, but there is a kind of gaucheness about them sometimes that makes them even lovelier. The thing that struck me most: one sees, looking at them directly in movement, just what the cave painters saw— something that I have never seen in a photograph. It is an awe-inspiring thing—the *Mantu* or "spirit" shown in the running of the deer, the "deerness" that sums up everything and is saved and marvelous. A contemplative intuition! Yet perfectly ordinary, everyday seeing. The deer reveals to me something essential in myself! Something beyond the trivialities of my everyday being and my individuality. The stag is much darker, a mouse grey or rather a warm grey-brown, like a flying squirrel. I could sense the softness of their coat and longed to touch them.

*September 6, 1965, V.291*

# Prayer to the Martyr of My French Hometown

Through the merits of thy martyr, O Lord, through thy martyr Saint Antonin in whose town I knew Thee, whose sanctuary I did not enter, though, as a child—through the great merit of thy ancient martyr, O Lord, bring me to the fullness of truth, to a great love and union with the truth, to a great fortitude with which to embrace and suffer reality, which is, in fact, my joy.

Thy martyr, O Christ, has a deep green river, and a limestone bridge of unequal arches, reflected in the water.

Thy martyr, O Christ, has cliffs and woods and, as I understand, he no longer has a train.

Sometimes, O Lord, I pray best to the saints and best of all to this one, O my Lord, this martyr who had a clarinet, a gramophone (I was reproved for putting my head in the horn). The people of thy town, O Lord! they have not changed. The Germans probably did not come. Wine barrels, berets, *tabliers, l'accent du Midi,* singing in the stinking dark streets, walking quietly, walking slowly.

Thy martyr's town, O Lord, walks at the pace of ox carts.

Some charitable, some uncharitable, all of the houses smell of the same kind of cooking and of rabbits stewed in wine. How could I forget the people of thy martyr, laughing at table?

Or the dark-skinned girl at the Hôtel L'Enfant who told me: "Arnold Bennett slept here."

*September 2, 1956, III.79*

# Returning to the World

In a sense, a very true and salutary sense, coming to the hermitage has been a "return to the world," not a return to the cities, but a return to direct and humble contact with God's world, His creation, the world of poor men who work. Andy Boone is more physically my neighbor than the monastery. It is his sawmill I hear, not the monastery machines. His rooster crows in my morning, his cows low in the evening.

I do not have the official "space"—sanctified, juridically defined, hedged in with elaborate customs—of the monastery as my milieu. To be out of that is a great blessing. It is a space rich with delusions and with the tyranny of willful fabrication. My space is the world created and redeemed by God. God is in this true world, not "only" and restrictively a prisoner in the monastery. It is crucially important for the monastery to abandon the myth of itself as a purely sacred space—it is a disaster for its real "sacredness." Curiously, the move to the hermitage is getting out in rumors. Though the situation is partly understood and partly not, it is interpreted with shock as my "leaving the monastery." This is true. The general reproach is then that I am not clinging, in spite of reason, grace and everything else, to something God no longer wills for me—clinging to it just because society expects me to do so! My life is a salutary scandal, and that is another proof of the reality of my vocation, I believe. Here I see my task is to get rid of the last vestiges of a pharisaical division between the sacred and the secular, to see that the *whole* world is reconciled to God in Christ.

*September 11, 1965, V.293–94*

# And Now for Something a Little Different

Yesterday was a fabulous day. Stephen Spender's wife, Natasha, blew in with a girl from the Coast, Margot Dennis—driving across the continent. They stayed for High Mass and spent most of the day here. At first we were very decorous and intelligent walking up and down the front avenue talking about Zen, Freud, music, John of the Cross, and the Dark Night of the Soul. Then it went down a notch, became more familiar, and amusing, as we went out to St. Bernard's lake and ate sandwiches and fruitcake and talked about monasteries and abbots, bishops and popes, Corn Island, Mexico, God knows what. This was very charming and maybe I began to be less scared. Finally we went to Dom Frederic's lake and went swimming, which was the most enjoyable of all. Margot, once dipped into the water, became completely transformed into a Naiad-like creature, smiling a primitive smile through hanging wet hair. We sunbathed a bit, then finally they trundled off to Cincinnati with their immense load of luggage.

It is hard to remember when I have ever so completely enjoyed anything. Of course, it had a devastating effect in the form of distractions, but I don't care. Except of course I had better make a mental note to be very careful in the future when I am going to see more of women with intelligence. I am obviously utterly starved for that kind of conversation. Everything was really as it ought to be—except that the swimming was an act of disobedience, which may or may not be justified by appeal to a higher rule. I leave that to the mercy of God.

*September 6, 1958, III.326*

# Just This

This beautiful day, with the quiet sun shining on the bronze paint of the Garden Virgin and on the marigolds and the weeds and the hills. Crickets everywhere. Nothing moving in the garden but the wind, a butterfly, and my pen.

Fair day of recollection in the new novitiate chapel, and I was happy in it and accepted its imperfections, and accepted everything. That is all that is needed. When you accept what you have, you see all you have received is more than enough and you are overwhelmed. I desire other things because I fear to be content with what I have—I fear it is inglorious. In the last few days I have seen what matters is to be humble enough to admit I am content with just this. Leave the rest to God.

*September 7, 1958, III.216*

# A Child and His Candy

I fear the ignorance and power of the United States. And the fact that it has quite suddenly become one of the most decadent societies on the face of the earth. The body of a great, dead, candied child. Yet not dead: full of immense, uncontrolled power. Crazy.

If somebody doesn't understand the United States pretty soon —and communicate some of that understanding to the United States—the results will be terrible. It is no accident that the United States endowed the world with the Bomb.

The mixture of immaturity, size, apparent indulgence and depravity, with occasional spasms of guilt, power, self-hate, pugnacity, lapsing into wildness and then apathy, hopped up and wild-eyed, inarticulate and wanting to be popular. You need a doctor, Uncle!

The exasperation of the other nations of the world who know the United States thinks them *jealous*—for what they don't want and yet what fascinates them. Exasperation that such fools should be momentarily kings of the world. Exasperation at them for missing their great chance—this everyone finds unforgivable, including America itself. And yet what held the United States back was a spasm of that vestigial organ called conscience. Unfortunately not a sufficiently educated conscience. The conscience of a ten-year-old boy, unsure of his parents' standards—not knowing where approval or disapproval might come from!

*September 9, 1961, IV.160–61*

# Discovering America

Last time I was in town—we had to drop something at the G.E. plant—Appliance Park. We came at the enormous place from the wrong side and had to drive miles all around it. Surrounded by open fields with nothing whatever in them, not even thistles, marked "Property of General Electric. No Trespassing." The buildings were huge and go on forever and ever, out in the midst of their own wilderness. Stopped by guards, we signed in at the appropriate gate and promptly got lost in the maze of empty streets between the buildings. Finally came out right. What struck me most was the immense seriousness of the place—as if at last I had found what America takes seriously. Not churches, not libraries. Not even movies, but THIS! This is it. The manufacture of refrigerators, of washing machines, of tape recorders, of light fixtures. This is the real thing. *This* is America.

*September 26, 1958, III.218–19*

# Love Is Our Measure

The measure of our identity, of our being (the two are the same), is the amount of our love for God. The more we love earthly things, reputation, importance, pleasures, ease, and success, the less we love God. Our identity is dissipated among things that have no value, and we are drowned and *die* in trying to live in the material things we would like to possess, or in the projects we would like to complete to objectify the work of our own wills. Then, when we come to die, we find we have squandered all our love (that is, our being) on things of nothingness, and that we are nothing, we are death. But then, most of all, in the terrifying light of pure Being and perfect Love, we see the hatefulness of nothingness, of death. But if we have loved Him, and lost ourselves in Him, we find ourselves in Him, and live forever in joy.

But tribulation detaches us from the things of nothingness in which we spend ourselves and die. Therefore, tribulation gives us life, and we love it, not out of love for death, but out of love for life.

Let me then withdraw all my love from scattered, vain things—the desire to be read and praised as a writer, or to be a successful teacher, praised by my students, or to live in ease in some beautiful place—and place it all in Thee, where it will take root and live, instead of being spent in barrenness.

My life is measured by my love of God, and that, in turn, is measured by my love for the least of His children. And that love is not an abstract benevolence: it must mean sharing their tribulation.

*September 3, 1941, I.398–99*

# The Interminable Beauty of Human Beings

In the pile of things I have lying around waiting to be read, I picked out today the mimeographed conference by Jacques Maritain (in December 1964) to the Little Brothers of Jesus on their vocation.

Jacques emphasizes the *microsignes*—the microsigns—of a Christian love that acts without awareness and is received without special or detailed awareness—the human and unconscious "aura" of a contemplative love that is simply there. How does one dare to undertake this? This idea of *presence* in and to the world is fundamental: "There are no longer walls, but the demands of a constantly purified love for one's fellow being which protects and shelters their contemplation of love."

The importance of a *purely immanent activity* (the contemplative does not do nothing). This can be a basis for an incomparably deep understanding of another's suffering.

"The human being down here in the darkness of his fleshly state is as mysterious as the saints in heaven in the light of their glory. There are in him inexhaustible treasures, constellations without end of sweetness and beauty which ask to be recognized and which usually escape completely the futility of our regard. Love brings a remedy for that. One must vanquish this futility and undertake seriously to recognize the innumerable universes that one's fellow being carries within him. This is the business of contemplative love and the sweetness of its regard."

*September 20, 1966, VI.137–38*

# Love Best Shown by Deeds

Yesterday, having received a note from Ethel Kennedy (wife of the attorney general and sister-in-law of the president), I wrote her an explicit statement of objection to the resumption of nuclear testing. At least this much I can do. Yet there is something very unsatisfactory, something not quite true, about this whole moral question. This idea that it is important to take a "stand" as an individual. As if by mere gestures and statements one could satisfy conscience. And as if the satisfaction of one's conscience (emphasis on *satisfaction*) was the great thing. It can become a mere substitute for responsibility and for love.

Mao Tse Tung said there would be no love until the Revolution had triumphed. There is a grain of truth in this—in this very great and misleading lie. Yet that one grain is what I lack.

Confucius said: "The higher type of man is not like a vessel which is designed for some special use." He was wiser than we monks are.

*September 5, 1961, IV.158*

# The Slighter Gestures of Dissent

"For what, in that world of gigantic horror, was tolerable except the slighter gestures of dissent?" So says E. M. Forster, discussing his satisfaction on reading the early T. S. Eliot during World War I.

We tend to think massive protest is all that is valid today. But the massive is also manipulated and doctored. It is false. The genuine dissent remains individual. At least that is my option. In my view it is saner and nobler to take the kind of view E. M. Forster takes, not line up with the manipulated group. But to the group that looks like defeat. It looks like futility.

What is likely to be wrong is the failure of action. This kind of dissent may never be anything but words, attitudes, ideas.

On the other side, what seems to be "action" on the mass scale may be nothing more than a parade—or an organized disaster. A big, blown-up expression of a puny idea which, by its very emptiness, leads to a cataclysm of destructiveness. This is the gigantic horror against which even the slightest idea is of great value.

*September 10, 1960, IV.44*

# Karl Barth's Dream

Karl Barth had a dream about Mozart. (Mozart a Catholic and Barth is piqued by the fact that Mozart did not like Protestantism, for he said it was "all in the head" and that they didn't know the meaning of *Agnus Dei qui tollis peccata mundi*.) Well, Barth dreamt he had to "examine" Mozart in Dogma. He wanted to make it as favorable as possible, and in his questions he alluded pointedly to Mozart's "Masses." But Mozart did not answer a word.

I am tempted to write Barth a letter about his moving dream, which of course concerns his own salvation.

He says that for years he has played Mozart every morning before going to work on dogma himself. (Just think! Dogma is his daily work!!)

The Mozart in himself is perhaps in some way the better, hidden, sophianic fact that grasps the "center" of cosmic music and is saved by love (yes, *Eros!*). The other, the theologian, is seemingly more occupied with love, but it is a stern, actually more cerebral, *agape* . . . a love that is not in us, only in God.

I remember my own dream about "Protestants." (They are perhaps my *aggressive* side.)

Barth seeks perhaps to be saved by the Mozart in him.

*September 22, 1960, IV.49–50*

# Holiness and the Daily Round

Last night, at moonrise (the moon is full) a doe was out in the field again. She has become quite used to me. I walked about saying Compline in front of the hermitage and she was not disturbed, even came down the field *towards* me! I only hope this tameness is wisely confined to one association: with the white hermitage and the monk in black and white, without a rifle.

There is no question that I really feel I am living a saner and better life in the hermitage. I would not exchange this for anything, even though for four days a snake was living in the jakes. (I finally persuaded him to go elsewhere, I hope!) In spite of the hornets, the noise of the machines in the field, the dogs and hunters, etc. All this is plain ordinary reality without any need of ideology or explanation. It *is.* That is enough. In the monastery everything has to be justified because everything is very seriously under question. Here only *I* am under question, and it is right for me to face the doubt which is my own empirical self, myself as question, knowing that in myself I also have Christ as answer.

For the rest—I love the night silence, the early meditation and the moon, the reading and the breakfast coffee (or good tea!), sawing wood after sunrise, washing up, tired, as the sun begins to grow warm and the Atlanta plane goes over. Afternoon meditation slow—then work on the book (*Conjectures*)—office in the late afternoon, quiet supper, reading, walking, looking at the hills, the silence, the moon, the does, darkness, prayer, bed.

*September 10, 1965, V.292–93*

# Only Faith Is to Be Taken Seriously

A magnificent line from Karl Barth: "Everyone who has to contend with unbelief should be advised that he ought not to take his own unbelief too seriously. Only faith is to be taken seriously, and if we have faith as a grain of mustard seed, that suffices for the devil to have lost his game (*Dogmatics in Outline*)." What stupendous implications in that!

Always the old trouble, that the devil and our nature try to persuade us that, before we can begin to believe, we must be perfect in everything. Faith is not important as it is "in us." Our faith is "in God," and with even a very little of it, God is in us. "To believe is the freedom to trust in Him quite alone" (and to be independent of any other reliance) and to rely on Him in everything that concerns us.

*September 30, 1963, V.20*

# Just Another Day

Today is the anniversary of the death of the holy staretz Sylvan, at St. Panteleimon on Mount Athos—September 11, 1938. Or rather, on their calendar, September 25th. But this sudden confusion of perspectives makes me wonder about *all* days. Who says this is September 11th? Well, we do. We have elected to call this September 11th. Actually it is just "a day." A rainy, grey one, with crows busy over the woods there and a cold wind in the grasses and blue jays behind me by the church. Rare cars on the road, going where? We have chosen to call this "a day." In order to imitate God's day on which everything is already complete, or in order to imagine that our days are leading somewhere? Like that car that passed going south toward the distillery. (But will it turn either right or left before reaching the distillery? Where then? As if anyone had to know. If we do not assume it is *known* by someone, we will grow anxious.)

Staretz Sylvan did not want to die in the infirmary because they would put him in a room with a clock, which would disturb his prayer.

*September 11, 1960, IV.44–45*

# Writing to Think and Live and Pray

It is a bright afternoon: what am I going to do? I am going to work with my mind and with my pen, while the sky is clear, and while the soft white clouds are small and sharply defined in it. I am not going to bury myself in books and note-taking. I am not going to lose myself in this jungle and come out drunk and bewildered, feeling that bewilderment is a sign that I have done something. I am not going to write as one driven by compulsions but freely, because I am a writer, and because for me to write is to think and to live and also, in some degree, even to pray.

This time is given to me by God that I may live in it. It is not given to make something out of it, but given me to be stored away in eternity as my own.

But for this afternoon to be my own in eternity, it must be my own this afternoon, and I must possess myself in it, not be possessed by books and by ideas not my own, and by a compulsion to produce what nobody needs. But simply to glorify God by accepting His gift and His work. To work for Him is to work that I myself may live.

How else shall I study Boris Pasternak, whose central idea is the sacredness of life?

*September 27, 1958, III.219*

# What a September Day Should Be

Czeslaw Milosz was here yesterday. Same face as on the new French book (*Une Autre Europe*) but considerably aged. I am enthusiastic about the Polish poets he has gathered into an anthology. A great deal of irony, depth, sophistication, intelligence, and compassion. This seems to me to be very real and human. I react to it as I do to most Latin American verse: as something belonging to my world. (I can hardly say this for most American or English poetry except Stevie Smith and Peter Levi.)

Everything that a September day should be—brilliant blue sky, kind sun, cool wind in the pines. But I have to wear white gloves because I cannot go near the woods without getting more poison ivy. I seem to have become extraordinarily sensitive, and if I am within fifteen or twenty or thirty feet of it, I seem to get more. On my face, too, but I shall go with face bare. If necessary I shall make myself a mask out of a little bag with holes in it and come into solitude looking sinister like a Ku Kluxer. Tiny, delicate fishbones of clouds in the sky. Harps of sound in the sweet trees. Long shadows on the grass. The distant bottomland flat and level and brown, ploughed and harrowed. The hills.

*September 10 and 12, 1964, V.142–43*

# Coming Home to the Monastery

Coming back from the hospital to the monastery (last evening) was never better. Sense of recovery, of returning to something good and sane, principally the quiet here.

Coming home—cool evening, grey sky, dark hills. I felt again, once more, a renewal of the first intuition, the awareness of belonging where these rocky hills are, that I belong to this parcel of land with pine trees and woods and fields, and that this is my place.

Bright, cool afternoon. Lavender flowers on the soybeans in the field below the novitiate. As I came into the woods a covey of young quail started up out of the long grass and I was very happy—for I had worried about them. I hope the hunters keep away from there this fall.

A very fine, penetrating essay by Ivan Illich on missionary poverty, not clinging to one's own culture and background. I must rethink all this in the light of my own vocation, for I have not been good at that kind of poverty. On the other hand, my studies, etc., are useful for the community and for what I write. But I must be careful to distinguish where I am "not poor." My greatest failures are perhaps in poverty.

A cool wind moves all the leaves in the forest and blows joyously and freely all through the house.

*September 6, 1962, IV.244–45*

# I Speak Out as One Not Wise

The "Letter to Pablo Antonio Cuadra Concerning Giants" that I wrote last week is bitter and unjust. It lacks perspective. It cannot do much good to anyone in its present shape, and yet I have mailed it off to him and it may get published (though only in Nicaragua) before I have time to make any serious changes.

How did it get to be so violent and unfair?

The root is my own fear, my own desperate desire to survive even if only as a voice uttering an angry protest, while the waters of death close over the whole continent.

Why am I so willing to believe that the country will be destroyed? It is certainly possible, and in some sense it may even be likely. But this is a case where, in spite of evidence, one must continue to hope. One must not give in to defeatism and despair, just as one must hope for life in a mortal illness which has been declared incurable.

This is the point. This weakness and petulancy rooted in egoism, and which I have in common with other intellectuals in this country. Even after years in the monastery I have not toughened up and got the kind of fiber that is bred only in humility and self-forgetfulness. Or rather, though I had begun to get it, this writing job and my awareness of myself as a personage with definite opinions and with a voice has kept me sensitive and afraid on a level on which most monks long ago became indifferent. Yet also it is not good to be indifferent to the fate of the world on a simply human level.

So I am concerned, humanly, politically, yet not wisely.

*September 19, 1961, IV.162–63*

# Clinging to the Invisible God

Can I hope that I am now in a new area, traveling more securely, and that my commitment to the hermit life will be something more than a comic gesture? Is the whole thing just a fantastic private comedy? I question myself and my whole life very seriously. The real absurdity of it all! The unreality of so much of it. I mean especially the *unreality* of years I look back on when, being Master of Students, for example, my job gave an appearance of substance and consistency, but actually I was floating in a kind of void! I think I enjoyed it to a great extent, but, if I had been more fully aware, I would probably have not been able to cope with it.

In a word, what I see is this: that, while I imagined I was functioning fairly successfully, I was living a sort of patched-up, crazy existence, a series of rather hopeless improvisations, a life of unreality in many ways. Always underlain by a certain solid silence and presence, a faith, a clinging to the Invisible God. This clinging (perhaps rather His holding on to me) has been in the end the only thing that has made sense. The rest has been absurdity. What is more, there is no essential change in sight. I will probably go on like this for the rest of my life. Here "I" am: this patchwork, this bundle of questions and doubts and obsessions, this gravitation to silence and to the woods and to love. This incoherence!

There is no longer anything to pride myself in, least of all "being a monk" or being anything—a writer or anything.

*September 5, 1966, VI.125*

# The Mystical Body of Friends

These are the most beautiful days of the year, except for days in May.

Sun every day now, and very bright sky, clear, dark blue. The leaves of the trees change, though not all change into bright colors, as in the North. The sweet gums do well, though—there are some small ones coming up in the novitiate woods. Some good poplars in the wood of the former pig lot we are clearing (thinning out) along the Bardstown road.

Then on Friday Mark Van Doren's autobiography came and I have begun it, getting with him as far now as the army in World War I and the Negroes. The world of Illinois and his childhood is very much the same as the world all around us, and yet I suddenly find it hard to believe in such peace and security.

Thursday afternoon Reverend Father gave me a letter from Boris Pasternak. The letter was brief but cordial and confirmed my intuition of the deep and fundamental understanding that exists between us. And this is the thing I have been growing to see is most important. *Everything* hangs on the possibility of such understanding, which forms our interior bond, which is the only basis of true peace and community. External, juridical, doctrinal, etc., bonds can never achieve this. And this bond exists between me and countless people like Pasternak everywhere in the world (genuine people like Pasternak are never "countless"), and my vocation is intimately bound up with this bond and this understanding, for the sake of which also I have to be solitary and not waste my spirit in pretenses that do not come anywhere near this reality or have anything to do with it.

*October 12, 1958, III.223–24*

# Dialogue in the Kingdom of God

Two letters have arrived from Pasternak. My letter and "Prometheus" got through to him and apparently quite easily. He commented on "Prometheus," saying that he liked especially sections IV and VII, and that the last had some "fine individual Christosophic touches." I was very pleased. Will write to him again. He keeps insisting that his early work is "worthless." His heart is evidently in *Doctor Zhivago,* to which he does not refer by the full name. Only as "Dr Zh" or "the book published by Pantheon."

Talking to Frater Lawrence about it, I remarked on the strange and marvelous fact of this apparently easy and natural communication between a monk in a strictly guarded Trappist monastery and a suspect poet behind the Iron Curtain. I am in closer contact with Pasternak than I am with people in Louisville or Bardstown or even in my own monastery—and have more in common with him.

And all this while our two countries, deeply hostile to one another, have nothing to communicate between themselves—and yet spend millions trying to communicate with the moon!

The simple and human dialogue with Pasternak and a few others like him is to me worth thousands of sermons and radio speeches. It is to me the true Kingdom of God, which is still so clearly, and evidently, "in the midst of us."

*October 18, 1958, III.224*

# St. Benedict's Sanity

There is nothing whatever of the ghetto spirit in the Rule of St. Benedict.

That is the wonderful thing about the Rule and the saint. The freshness, the liberty, the spontaneity, the broadness, the sanity and the healthiness of early Benedictine life.

But closed in on itself, interpreting interpretations of interpretations, the monastery becomes a ghetto.

Reforms that concentrate too excessively on a return to *strictness* do not in fact break the spell. They tend to increase the danger of spiritual suffocation. On the other hand, fresh air is not the air of the world.

Just to break out of the ghetto and walk down the boulevard is no solution. The world has its own stink, too—perfume and corruption.

The fresh air we need is the air of the Holy Spirit "breathing where He pleases," which means that the windows must be open and we must expect Him to come from any direction.

The error is to lock the windows and doors in order to keep the Holy Spirit within our house. The very action of locking doors and windows is fatal.

*October 27, 1957, III.130–31*

# Needing the Angels and the Saints

*(The Seven Storey Mountain is officially published on October 4, 1948)*

I see more and more the fruitfulness of this life here with its struggles, its long hours of silence, the sun, the woods, the presence of invisible grace and help. It has to be a creative and humiliating life, a life of search and obedience, simple, direct, requiring strength (I don't have it, but it is "given"). There are moments of frightening disruption, then recovery. I am only just beginning to know what life really is—away from all the veils, cushions, and evasions of the common life. Yet I see my great need for the common life. Seriously, last night at supper, a deep awareness that I need the saints and angels with me in my loneliness (cf. Jacques Maritain on the Heavenly Church). Read Maritain's beautiful biographical note on Vera Oumansoff. This is the real dimension of Christian community. What could be more beautiful or more real? There is much of this in the monastery, in spite of everything.

The picture of Galla Placidia in Herbert Read's *Icon and Idea*. Byzantine medallion of her, her son and daughter. A most lovely and fascinating picture. The children are beautiful but dull. She is full of life and character. A fascinating face. How is it that this face is so contemporary to me, so ready to speak to me? As if she were someone I had always known. I can imagine it is Mother, perhaps, I see in her; there is some resemblance, the same kind of features. Anyway I am moved by the picture.

*October 6, 1965, V.301*

# Learning the Tempo of Solitude

I was finally right in the heart of Isaac of Stella—the translation of his "island loneliness" in the metaphysic of being and nothingness of the Sexagesima sermons (Sermon XIV). Hit very hard by a lot of ambiguities of expression, but an unquestionably deep and austere intuition, and very modern. But deeply mystical. Profound implications for my own prayer and solitude opened up. (Prayer of Christ on the Cross!)

I find more and more the power—the dangerous power—of solitude working on me. The easiness of wide error. The power of one's own inner ambivalence, the pull of inner contradiction. How little I know myself really. How weak and tepid I am. I need to work hard, and I don't know how—hence I work at the wrong things. I see that the first two months I got off to a nearly false start with too much excited reading of too many things, and my life has been grossly overstimulated for a solitary (in community, all right). Especially I worked too hard, too obsessively on the book, too frantic a pace for a solitary (again, in community solitude seems crowded and hopped up to me).

Everything has meaning, dire meanings, in solitude. And one can easily lose it all in following the habits one has brought out of common life (the daily round). One has to start over and receive (in meekness) a new awareness of work, time, prayer, oneself. A new tempo—it has to be in one's very system (and it is not in mine, I see).

And what I do not have I must pray for and wait for.

*October 25 and 30, 1965, V.309–10*

# Praying Through the Noise

The offices at night have been fine. I have slept more and have a clearer head to attend to the Word of God.

Yet it is surprising that I do not lose more sleep, as there is a bulldozer *working day and night* in the corn fields, in the bottom-lands, and I sleep next to the window right over those fields. What are they doing? Can't they be content to let the creek wind the way it always did? Does it have to be straight? Really, we monks are madmen, bitten by an awful folly, an obsession with useless and expensive improvements.

To the east, then, the bulldozer day and night. The noise never stops. To the west, the dehydrator. The noise stops perhaps at midnight. A layman drives the bulldozer, our brothers work at the dehydrator.

To the northwest—a pump, day and night. Never stops. There is nothing making any noise to the south, but then to the south the monks' property soon comes to an end, and there are only lay people whose lives are generally quiet. They only speak. We make "signs," but drown everything in the noise of our machines. One would think our real reason for making "signs" might be that it is not always easy to be heard.

*October 19, 1961, IV.170–71*

# America, the World's Mad Abbot

Clarity in the early morning studying William of Conches on Plato's *Timaeus*. The dark, the silence. Then, clarity at Mass, exactly at dawn. The sun is now rising at seven and I am clothed in dawn light as I stand at the altar (the first rays of the sun add the only warmth in the chapel). Then after, the day is warm.

The United States is now spending more each year on armaments than was spent in any year before 1942 for the *entire national budget*.

People demand that the government "interfere" in nothing, just pour money into the armament industry and provide a strong police for "security." But stay out of everything else! No interference in medicine, mental health, education, etc., etc. Never was a country at once shrewder and less wise—shrewd in nonessentials and lunatic in essentials.

I have no doubt the world feels toward America the way many monks feel toward an abbot who wants to exercise total power, to receive unquestioning obedience on the basis of slogans about which he himself ceased thinking twenty-five years ago, and who above all wants to be loved, so that he may never, at any time, to himself, seem to be exercising power, or loving it. Nobody denies him the power he has: few give him the love that he needs in order to be safe and content. And therefore he uses his power, from time to time, in unpredictable, arbitrary, and absurd ways in which he defends his own ends and makes everybody miserable.

*October 20, 1962, IV.259*

# A Different Sense of Time

Last night I slept in the monastery, because spiritual direction ran late and my shoulder also was hurting, so that I wanted the traction which is fixed up on my bed in the novitiate dorm. Sleeping at the hermitage gives one a totally different sense of time—measured by the phases of the moon (whether or not one will need the flashlight, etc.). This in itself is important. The whole day has different dimensions. And so for office in choir, its artificiality impresses me more and more. Not that it is not a "good thing." Not that there is not a great will to do good and praise God there. But the whole décor of habits and stalls and stained glass seems unreal when you have been praying the psalms among pine trees. The thing I most appreciate about the monastery is the electric light. The lamplight of the hermitage is primitive and mysterious, but the lamp smokes and one cannot read well by it. Which is all right since it means more meditation. Yet I like and need to sit here with a book open and really read, take notes, study.

As to the brethren, it is good to be with them and to see them (even though I know them enough to recognize their tensions and troubles), but I can tell that a feeling of loneliness for them would probably be a deception—or a *reflex*. One can love them and still live apart from them without explanation.

*October 19, 1964, V.158*

# God's Mustard Seed in Me

The Henry Corbin book on Ibn al'Arabi is in ways tremendous. The plays and changes on the theme of the divine compassion, on the "sympathy" of the spirit and God, on God seeking to manifest Himself in the spirit that responds to a "Name" which is meant to embody its life. Compare the medieval Cistercians with their births of Christ in us. Need for compassion and tenderness towards the infinite fragility of the divine life in us, which is *real* and not an idea or an image (as in our conception of God as "object").

This could and should lead me more and more to a new turning, a new attitude, an inner change, a liberation from all futile concerns to let Him emerge in His mystery and compassion within me. Yielding to the inexplicable demand of His presence in weakness. To be very careful and timid now about those innumerable self-affirmations that tend to destroy His weakness and littleness in me—fortunately indestructible. This mustard seed, His kingdom in me. The struggle of the very small to survive and change my self-affirmations.

*October 3, 1961, IV.167*

# Godlikeness Begins at Home

Brilliant and gorgeous day, bright sun, breeze making all the leaves and high brown grass shine. Singing of the wind in the cedars. Exultant day, in which a puddle in the pig lot shines like precious silver.

Finally I am coming to the conclusion that my highest ambition is to be what I already am. That I will never fulfill my obligation to surpass myself unless I first accept myself—and, if I accept myself fully in the right way, I will already have surpassed myself. For it is the unaccepted self that stands in my way—and will continue to do so as long as it is not accepted. When it has been accepted, it is my own stepping-stone to what is above me. Because this is the way man was made by God—and original sin was the effort to surpass oneself by being "like God," i.e., unlike oneself. But our Godlikeness begins at home. We must become like ourselves, and stop living "beside ourselves."

*October 2, 1958, III.220–21*

# Witnessing to the Personal

A day of spiritual fires, quiet fires, warm skies. Pink beasts in the field (pigs).

Angry kingfisher rattles over the foul creek and swings upward, to head for the clean lake.

Everything adds up to these two points:

A. My instinct to regard as an evil and as an oversimplification the thought of "losing oneself" in total identification with (submersion in) any group as such—this instinct against such is correct, it is good. To be a man of the church I have to be fully myself—and fully responsible and free before God—not a "unit" or a mere "number."

B. My vocation and task in this world is to keep alive all that is usefully individual and personal in me, to be a "contemplative" in the full sense—and to share it with others—to remain as a witness of the nobility of the private person and his primacy over the group.

*October 2 and 7, 1958, III.221–22*

# Farewell to My Woodchuck

Late yesterday afternoon Brother Dunstan came up with typed copies of the book *Barth's Dream* (*Conjectures*)—much bigger than I expected. Then it rained (quietly) most of the night and it is cooler. I said Mass (of St. Anselm) for all my friends in England and Anglican friends everywhere. There is a woodchuck which has dug a new hole outside my jakes, and I watch him furnishing it with dead leaves for the winter.

Evening. A turning point in the weather. The heavy rain clouds broke up a bit in the morning. There were patches of sun, a few short showers late in the afternoon. It is turning cold. I noticed that my woodchuck had buried himself completely, covering up the entrance to his hole, and had gone to sleep for the winter in his bed of leaves. I wish him a happy sleep! And today is very autumn-like—cold clouds flying, trees half bare, wet leaves lying around everywhere, the broad valley beautiful and lovely. The wonderful, mysterious, lonely sense of an autumn evening.

*October 20 and 23, 1965, V.307–8*

# Truth and Silence

Dan Berrigan arrived by surprise Tuesday—I was not expecting him until the end of the week. We concelebrated twice—once in the regular present rite, and today, with a new Mass he found somewhere which is very fine and simple. I don't know how "legal" we were. It was a very moving, simple English text (Canon and all). I think it was composed by Anglicans and has been used by them. Contrast to the Mass, old style, that I said for Jacques Maritain when he visited last week. That was very sober, austere, solemn, intense. This Mass very open, simple, even casual, but very moving and real. Somehow I think the new is really better—and is very far from anything we will be permitted here for a long time. I have nothing against the old.

A dark October morning with clouds. Extraordinary purple in the north over the pines. Ruins of gnats on the table under the lamp. Albert Camus's preface to *L'Étranger—The Stranger*—has things to say on truth and silence which have deep monastic implications. I must refuse all declarations and affirmations of what I do not fully and actually know, experience, believe *myself.* Not making statements that are expected of me, simply because they are expected, whether by the monastery (or monastic life) or by the peace movement, or by various literary orthodoxies and anti-orthodoxies or routine rebellions. If I renounce all this, there will be precious little left to say. But above all (as Jacques Maritain and I agreed) to steer clear of the futilities of "Post-Conciliar" theological wrangling and image making.

*October 13 and 14, 1966, VI.149–50*

OCTOBER 14

# Something in My Core Needs Revealing

Dawn. Cold. Mist in the valley. The rampart line of hills is always new every day.

There has been much self-searching, some futile, some disquieting. It may be excessive, but there is something in the core of my being that needs to be revealed. I wonder if I can face it? Is it futile even to try? "Let sleeping dogs lie, leave things as they are, etc." I will try to do whatever God wills. Jeremias 20:14–18 (Cursed be the day on which I was born, etc.). Lines I do not experience nor understand. I hope to God I do not have to experience them. Reading them is enough. I have the Vulgate and Luther's German (which is much more graphic and concrete). Importance of obedient meditation. God will take care of the rest.

*October 11, 1965, V.302*

# Walking on Water

Whether we live or die, we are the Lord's. Life and death alike can be offered up as penance. I can make reparations for my impiety by living as perfectly as I can the Rule and Spirit of St. Benedict—obedience, humility, work, prayer, simplicity, the love of Christ.

The light of truth burns without a flicker in the depths of a house that is shaken with storms of passion and of fear. "You will not fear the terror of the night." And so I go on trying to walk on the waters of the breakdown. Worse than ever before and better than ever before. It is always painful and reassuring when he who I am not is visibly destroyed by the hand of God in order that the simplicity in the depths of me, which *is* His image, may be set free to serve Him in peace. Sometimes in the midst of all this I am tremendously happy, and I have never in my life begun to be so grateful for His mercy.

And no more professional spirituality! Terrifically purged of ideas about prayer, and of all desire to preach them, as if I *had* something!

*October 22, 1952, III.22*

# An Autumn Dream

Last night I took an hour out of my sleep and made a two-hour meditation before retiring, instead of one. As a consequence this morning's meditation was much more serious and my reading has been more sober and fruitful. It was a good inspiration, and I will do it again once in a while. (Not habitually, for it would be just another routine.) During the night I dreamt I was in a strange city with some other monk(?), and we had to go to some place at the center and begin a journey. A waitress in the lunchroom left to come with us and show us the way. I remember the warmth of her presence sitting in the car with me. I spoke of streets like "Page" and "Sky" which I found on a map, but she had another and shorter way. All along, it was a case of her *knowing* the way and of my not knowing it.

> *Whose house is not built now shall build no more,*
> *Who now is lonely long shall be alone,*
> *shall lie awake, and read, long letters write,*
> *and restlessly, among the drifting leaves*
> *of avenues shall wander, to and fro.*

Rilke's autumn poem ("Autumn Day"). Beautiful and close to home.

*October 19, 1965, V.306–7*

# Plato's Music, Gandhi's Truth

After the night office. The superb moral and positive beauty of Plato's *Phaedo.* One does not have to *agree* with Plato, but one must hear him. Not to listen to such a voice is unpardonable, it like listening to conscience or to nature. I repent, and I love this great poem, this "music." It is purifying music of which I have great need.

And Gandhi—how I need to understand and practice nonviolence in every way. It is because my life is not firmly based on the truth that I am morally in confusion and captivity—under the half truths and prejudices that rule others and rule me through them.

"A person who realizes a particular evil of his time and finds that it overwhelms him dives deep in his own breast for inspiration and, when he gets it, he presents it to others" (Gandhi).

Moved and delighted by the line of the Book of Wisdom about ships (14:1–7), especially the one ". . . so that even if a man lacks skill he may put to sea." Profound implications, especially for me at this moment. The necessity of risk and its place in the context of Providence and wisdom. A desire for gain plans the vessel (not necessarily reproved here); wisdom builds it; Providence guides it; and the navigator needs not long experience but trust and good sense.

*October 10, 12, and 13, 1960, IV.57*

# What We Most Need

The anchor in the window of the Old Zion Church, before it burned in 1924 or 1925: this is the earliest symbol of which I remember being conscious. I was struck by it, aged perhaps seven or eight, but could not see why it was in a church window. Perhaps I did not know what it was. Yet I had seen the symbol somewhere in crossing the ocean (and I desired to be a sailor). Anyway, there was an anchor in the window and I was aware of it. I have forgotten almost every other detail of the church, except perhaps the eagle on whose outspread wings the Bible rested, and even of this I am not sure. Was there really such an eagle? Whether or not, it is relevant that the anchor is a symbol of hope; hope is what I most need. And the world needs most.

Letter from the Fellowship of Reconciliation. They want to reprint "The Root of War" as a pamphlet. Convinced again that I must set everything aside to work for the abolition of war. Primarily, of course, by prayer. I remain a contemplative, but as for writing, contacts, letters, that kind of effort: here it seems to me everything should yield first place to the struggle against war.

*October 30, 1961, IV.175–76*

# The Technological Society

I am reading Jacques Ellul's book *The Technological Society*. Great, full of firecrackers. A fine, provocative book and one that really makes sense. Good to read while the Second Vatican Council is busy with Schema 13 (as it is). One cannot see what is involved in the question of "The Church and the Modern World" without reading a book like this. I wonder if the Council Fathers are aware of all the implications of a technological society? Those who can only resist it may be wrong, but those who want to go along with all its intemperances are hardly right. Or do they know that this might be what they were wanting?

Gentle whistles of a bluebird and, in the mist, a SAC plane swoops huge and low over the ridges where Edelin's valley is and where the final hermitages are to be. I wonder if it carries bombs. Most probably. They all do, I am told. The technological society! I will go out and split some logs and gather a basket of pinecones.

*October 30, 1964, V. 159–60*

# Going Beyond My Boundaries

A wonderful letter from Pasternak to Kurt Wolff, in German, was forwarded to me from Pantheon. Most of it concerned with his reaction to my letters and to my "perfect" understanding of all that was most important to him in his work. "The aptness of his understanding and the clarity of his insights is beyond belief." And he picked out especially my reaction to his Hamlet poem and the business about the Red Sea and the Blessed Virgin, and about God-manhood.

That I have been able to give the consolation of understanding and appreciating what he most wanted to say is also to me a great consolation.

Later in the letter, a most important point, and one which came back to me this morning after my Mass:

"One cannot remain immobile where the political and aesthetic customs and potentialities are so conspicuous and compelling: one must take another step."

I agree with this perfectly, and I see that this is the very heart of my own personal vocation.

I must—in my writing, in my prayer, in my life—take this further step and go beyond my limitations and the limitations of thought, art and religion of our time. And this requires effort and suffering. I simply cannot sit down and *accept* my limitations—that is impossible. But I must take care most of all not to be content with merely fanciful transcendence—going beyond my limitations in thought and imagination only. It must be a real transcendence.

*October 31, 1958, III.227–28*

# Night Is Coming

Though I am nearly forty-eight, and it is doubtless time to feel a change of climate in my physical being, which begins to dispose itself for its end some one of these years, it is useless to interpret every little sign or suggestion of change as something of great significance. This is a temptation I yield to. I am still too young mentally to be in the least patient of any sign of age. My impatience is felt as an upheaval of resentment, disgust, depression. Yet I am joyful. I like life. I am happy with it. I have nothing to complain of. But a little of the chill, a little of the darkness, the sense of void in the midst of myself, and I say to my body: "Okay, all right then, *die,* you idiot!" But it is not really trying to die, it just wants to slow down.

This war scare aggravates it, this sense of death and desperation running through my whole society with all its bombs and its money and its death wish. The colossal sense of failure in the midst of success that is characteristic of America (but that America cannot really face). I have a comfortable sense of success, which I know to be more or less meaningless, yet I want to make my will now—as a writer. Go on, fool! Forget it! You may write another twenty books, who knows? In any case, does it matter? Is this relevant? On the contrary, now is the time I must learn to stop taking satisfaction in what I have done, or being depressed because the night will come and my work will come to an end. Now is the time to give what I have to others and not reflect on it. I wish I had learned the knack of it, of giving without question or care. I have not, but perhaps I still have time to try.

*October 2, 1962, IV.253*

# The Birds Don't Know They Have Names

The warblers are coming through now. Very hard to identify them all, even with field glasses and a bird book. (Have seen at least one that is definitely not in the bird book.) Watching one which I took to be a Tennessee warbler. A beautiful, neat, prim little thing —seeing this beautiful thing which people do not usually see, looking into this world of birds, which is not concerned with us or with our problems, I felt very close to God or felt religious anyway. Watching those birds was as food for meditation, or as mystical reading. Perhaps better.

Also the beautiful, unidentified red flower or fruit I found on a bud yesterday. These things say so much more than words.

Mark Van Doren, when he was here, said, "The birds don't know they have names."

Watching them I thought: who cares what they are called? But do I have the courage not to care? Why not be like Adam, in a new world of my own, and call them by my own names?

That would still mean that I thought the names were important.

No name and no word to identify the beauty and reality of those birds today is the gift of God to me in letting me see them.

(And that name—God—is not a name! It is like a letter X or Y. Yahweh is a better name—it finally means Nameless One.)

*October 5, 1957, III. 123–24*

# Being Alive and Awake

I got up to the hermitage about nightfall. Wonderful silence, saying Compline gently and slowly with a candle burning before the icon of our Lady. A deep sense of peace and truth, that this was the way things are supposed to be, that I was in my right mind for a change (around the community I am seldom in my right mind). Total absence of care and agitation. Slept wonderfully well, even though there was a great pandemonium of dogs in the woods when I got up about 12:20 and went out to pee off the edge of the porch.

I thought I could hear the bell for Vigils at the monastery and didn't. However, I woke up soon after that and lit the fire and said Lauds quietly, slowly, thoughtfully, sitting on the floor. I felt very much alive, and real, and awake, surrounded by silence and penetrated by truth. Wonderful smell of predawn woods and fields in the cold night!

*October 13, 1964, V.154*

# One Must Be Careful of Words

My need for genuine interior freedom is now urgent. Yet this is something I am helpless to enter except through the Cross, and I must try to see and accept the Cross of conflict—to renounce myself by renouncing "my" answers and by restraining my urge to answer, to *reply,* in order that I may silently respond, or obey. In this kind of obedience there is never a full understanding of what one has to do—this does not become clear until the work has been done.

Victor Frankl's point that in the camps the prisoners who wanted to keep human had to take on their suffering itself as a task (individually and together) in order to give it meaning.

I have used a lot of existentialist terms. I can already see how nauseated I will be with them when they become vulgar currency (commitment, authenticity, etc.), and they are already vulgar. I am nauseated by the Secular City syndrome. But forget it—in a year there will be another nausea. What is the use of being in the silence of true words and letting in this noise? Yet I do not quite see how to manage the situation. With patience, it will arrange itself.

For me—the betrayal I have to look out for is that which would consist simply in attaching myself to "a cause" that happens to be operating at this time, and getting involved, and letting myself be carried along with it, simply making appropriate noises from time to time, at a distance.

*End of 1965, V.342–43*

# Grateful for Life

Brilliant, windy day—cold. It is fall. It is the kind of day in October that Pop used to talk about. I thought about my grandfather as I came up through the hollow, with the sun on the bare persimmon trees, and a song in my mouth. All songs are, as it were, one's last. I have been grateful for life.

Many strange things I remember: for instance, if I had only stayed with the cross-country team, at Columbia, until the end of the season, I would have had my "letter." Why think of that?

Great clouds of seed fly in the wind from the poplar tree.

The new magazine, *Ramparts,* had two impressive pictures of Brother Antoninus in a black and white Dominican habit, among birch trees. I know he often feels as I do. I must write to him and say, "Courage! We are honest men!"

Deep pessimism in a letter from E. I. Watkin. I cannot say there is much hope to be seen among politicians and military men.

*October 23, 1962, IV.260*

# Waiting for God

Now is the time to see what great strength comes out of silence—and not without struggle.

Obedience to God means, first of all, *waiting,* having to wait, *sustine Dominum*—waiting for the Lord. The first thing then is to accept the fact that one will have to *wait.* Otherwise obedience is undermined by an implicit condition that destroys it.

To say that I am a child of God is to say, before everything else, that I grow. That I begin. A child who does not grow becomes a monster. The idea "Child of God" is therefore one of living growth, becoming, possibility, risk, and joy in the negotiation of risk. In this God is pleased: that His child grows in wisdom and grace.

God is the Father who fights to defend and rescue His child. The life of the Child of God is not in the "development of spirituality" but in obedience to the Good Shepherd who seeks him, knowing he is lost. It is in solitude that we recognize, with a shock, how lost we have been, and that now we are found, rescued, recovering conscience, returning to ourselves, to Truth, carried by Him who has sought and found us.

*End of 1965, V.334*

# Always Beginning Again

It is not complicated to lead the spiritual life. But it is difficult. We are blind and subject to a thousand illusions. We must expect to be making mistakes all the time. We must be content to fail repeatedly and to begin again to try to deny ourselves for the love of God.

It is when we are angry at our own mistakes that we tend most of all to deny ourselves for love of ourselves. We want to shake off the hateful thing that has humbled us. In our rush to escape the humiliation of our mistakes, we run headfirst into the opposite error, seeking comfort and compensation. And so we spend our lives running back and forth from one attachment to another.

If that is all our self-denial amounts to, our mistakes will never help us.

The thing to do, when you have made a mistake, is not to give up doing what you were doing and start something altogether new, but to start over again with the thing you began badly and try, for the love of God, to do it well.

*October 7, 1949, II.372*

# Taking Sides

The train whistle in the valley reminds me of the first day I came here—the first day we worked, on a grey afternoon like this, in St. Edmund's field. And my gratitude. It is the same gratitude and the same vocation. What has died in my spirit and my vocation here lately has come back to life. I feel at last that I can grow and move forward, and that all life has not been stamped out of my heart.

I opened Isaias at the forty-ninth chapter and read from verso 7 to the end: the marvelous liberation from Babylon and the return.

I have little desire, at the moment, to read anything but the Prophets.

"The gravest moral problems are found at the political level" (Tresmontant). Never was this more true than in our time. Hence the importance of political decisions and of taking sides in crucial and "prophetic" affairs which are moral touchstones and in which Christians are often in large numbers on the side of the unjust and the tyrant.

Problem of atomic bomb. How many Christians have taken a serious and effective stand against atomic warfare? How many theologians have striven to *justify* it?

*October 6 and 25, 1959, III.335–37*

# Writing Before the World Burns

In choir the less I worried about the singing, the more I was possessed by Love. There is a lesson in that about being poor. You have got to be all the time cooperating with Love in this house, and Love sets a fast pace even at the beginning and, if you don't keep up, you'll get dropped. And yet, any speed is too slow for Love—and no speed is too fast for you if you will only let Love drag you off your feet—after that you will have to sail the whole way. But our instinct is to get off and start walking. . . .

I want to be poor. I want to be solitary. This business burns me. "My strength is dried up like a potsherd" (Psalm 21:16). I am all dried up with desire and I can only think of one thing—staying in the fire that burns me.

Sooner or later the world must burn, and all things in it—all the books, the cloister together with the brothel, Fra Angelico together with the Lucky Strike ads. Sooner or later it will all be consumed by fire and nobody will be left, for by that time the last man in the universe will have discovered the bomb capable of destroying the universe and will have been unable to resist the temptation to throw the thing and get it over with.

And here I sit writing a diary.

But Love laughs at the end of the world because Love is the door to eternity, and he who loves is playing on the doorstep of eternity, and before anything can happen, Love will have drawn him over the sill and closed the door, and he won't bother about the world burning because he will know nothing but Love.

*October 3 and 10, 1948, II.234–36*

# Prayer Is All I Have Left

If everything centers on my obligation to respond to God's call in solitude, this does not mean simply putting everything out of my mind and living as if only God and I existed. This is impossible anyway. It means rather *learning* from what contacts and conflicts I still have how deep a solitude is required of me. This means *now* the difficult realization that I have relied too much on the support and approval of others—and yet I do need others. I must now painfully rectify this. That is to say that there is a sense in which *some* of God's answers must come to me from others, even from those with whom I disagree, even from those who do not understand my way of life. Yet it would be disastrous to seek merely to placate these people—the mere willingness to do so would make me deaf to whatever real message they might have. To do this job rightly is beyond my power. Prayer is all I have left—and patient, humble (if possible) obedience to God's will. One thing is certain: I do not possess my answers ready at hand in myself. (It almost seems an axiom that a solitary should be one who has his own answers. . . .) But I cannot simply seek them from others either. The problem is in learning to go for some time, perhaps for long periods, with no answer!!

*End of 1965, V.347–48*

# The Smell of Night Under Cold Stars

These nights I have spontaneously been remembering the days when I first came to Gethsemani twenty-three years ago: the stars, the cold, the smell of night, the wonder, the *Verlassenheit*—abandonment (which is something else than despondency)—and above all the melody of the *Rorate Coeli*. That entire first Advent bore in it all the stamp of my vocation's particular character. The solitude inhabited and pervaded by the cold and mystery and woods and Latin liturgy. It is surprising how far we have got from that cold and the woods and the stars since those days.

My fiftieth year is ending and, if I am not ripe now, I never will be. It is the *kairos,* say the stars, says Orion, says Aldebaran, says the sickle moon rising behind the dark tall cedar cross. And I remember the words I said to Father Philotheus at St. Bonaventure's, which may have been in part a cliché, but they were sincere and I know at the time that I really meant them. And they were unpremeditated: that "I want to give God everything." Until now I really have not, I think. Or perhaps in a way I have tried to. Certainly not too hard! I cannot say my life in the monastery has been useless, or a failure. Nor can I say where or how it has had a meaning. Nor will I probably find where and how the hermitage has a meaning. It is enough that there is the same anguish and certitude, the same sense of walking on water, as when I first came to the monastery.

*October 31, 1964, V.160*

# Virgin Time .

Marco Pallis on grace in Buddhism: "The word 'grace' corresponds to a whole dimension of spiritual experience; it is unthinkable that this should be absent from one of the great religions of the world.

"The function of grace . . . is to condition man's homecoming to the center itself . . . which provides the incentive to start on the Way and the energy to face and overcome its many and various obstacles. Likewise grace is the welcoming hand into the center when man finds himself at long last on the brink of the great divide where all familiar human landmarks have disappeared" ("Is There Room for 'Grace' in Buddhism?").

*November 6, 1968, VII.260*

The contemplative life must provide an area, a space of liberty, of silence, in which possibilities are allowed to surface and new choices—beyond routine choice—become manifest. It should create a new experience of time, not as stopgap, stillness, but as *temps vierge*—virginal time—not a blank to be filled or an untouched space to be conquered and violated, but a space which can enjoy its own potentiality and hopes—and its own presence to itself. One's *own* time. But not dominated by one's own ego and its demands. Hence, open to others—*compassionate* time, rooted in the sense of common illusion and in criticism of it.

*November 7, 1968, VII.262*

# Praying for the Dead

Abbé Jules Monchanin was convinced of the great importance of his prayer for "all the dead of India" as part of his mission to India, as part of the "convergence" of all mankind upon the Christ of the Day of Judgment.

Louis Massignon and Charles de Foucauld were both converted to Christianity by the witness of Islam to the one living God. Someone wrote of Foucauld (and his devotion to the dead of Islam): "For a mystic the souls of the dead count as much as those of the living; and his particular vocation was to sanctify the eternal Islam—for that which has been is forever—in helping to give a saint to Christianity." And again: "Asceticism is not a solitary luxury preparing us for God but the most profound act of mercy: that which heals broken hearts by its own breaks and wounds" (Massignon, *Opera Minora* III).

*November 17, 1964, V.166–67*

# The Importance of Self-Effacement

Necessity of the Bible. More and more of it.

A book like Guillet's *Thèmes bibliques* fantastically rich and useful. Every line has something in it you do not want to miss. Opens up new roads in the Old Testament.

Extraordinary richness and delicacy of the varied Old Testament concepts of sin—very existential concepts, not at all mere moralism! For instance, sin as a "failure" to contact God. *Peccavi tibi.* "I have failed Thee—I have failed to reach Thee." And all that follows from that!

Importance of reading and thinking and keeping silent. Self-effacement, not in order to be left looking at oneself but to be "found in Christ" and lost to the rest.

Yet—not by refusing to take an interest in anything vital.

Politics vital—even for monks. But in this, due place and with right measure.

To live in a monastery as if the world had stopped turning in 1905—a fatal illusion.

*November 12, 1957, III.135*

# Afraid of Mystery

This morning I was preparing for Mass in the woods, as usual. It was cold but the sun came up and melted the frost. It was quiet, except for the crows. I sat on an old chair under the skinny cedars, with my feet in the brown, frosty grass, and reflected on the errors of my monastic life. They are many and I am in the midst of them. I have never seen so many mistakes and illusions. It should be enough for me that God loves me. For His love is greater than anything else. It is the beginning and end of all. By it and for it all things were created. Yet, outside His love, I am tempted to erect a cold house of my own devising—a house that is small enough to contain my own self, and that is easier to understand than His incomprehensible love and His providence. Why is it we must be afraid of Mystery, as if the Mystery of God's love were not infinitely simple and infinitely clear? Why do we run away from Him into the dark, which, to us, is light? There is the other mystery of sin, which no one understands. Yet we act as if we understood sin and as if we were really aware of the love of God when we have never deeply experienced the meaning of either one.

*November 7, 1952, III.23*

# Kinships

In the afternoon, lots of pretty little myrtle warblers were playing and diving for insects in the low pine branches over my head, so close I could almost touch them. I was awed at their loveliness, their quick flight, their hissings and chirpings, the yellow spot on the back revealed in flight, etc. Sense of total kinship with them as if they and I were of the same nature, and as if that nature were nothing but love. And what else but love keeps us all together in being?

I am more and more convinced that Romans 9–11 (the chapters on the election of Israel) are the key to everything today. This is the point where we have to look, and press, and search, and listen to the word. For here we enter the understanding of Scripture, the wholeness of revelation and of the Church. Vatican II is still short of this awareness, it seems to me. The Chapter on the Jews has been woefully inadequate. It was naturally cautious, I will not say to the point of infidelity, but it was obtuse. It went nowhere. And in its inadequacy it is itself a providential sign, a "word." So we must look harder and further into this mystery. A "contemplation" that is wide of this is simply a waste of time, vanity and vexation of spirit.

*November 4, 1964, V.162*

# My Zen

Praying this morning during meditation to learn to read the meaning of events.

First of all, the meaning of what I myself do and bring upon myself and then the meaning of what all mankind does and brings upon itself. In the middle is this monastery—what it does and brings upon itself.

Before one knows the meaning of what happens, he must be able to see what happens. Most men do not even do that—they trust the newspapers to tell them.

My Zen is the slow swinging tops of sixteen pine trees.

One long thin pole of a tree fifty feet high swings in a wider arc than all the others and swings even when they are still.

Hundreds of little elms springing up out of the dry ground under the pines.

My watch lies among the oak leaves. My tee shirt hangs on the barbed wire fence, and the wind sings in the bare wood.

*November 21 and 25, 1958, III.231–32*

# Working for Peace

I must pray more and more for courage, as I certainly have neither the courage nor the strength to follow the path that is certainly my duty now.

With the fears and rages that possess so many confused people, if I say things that seem to threaten their interests or conflict with obsessions, then I will surely get it.

It is shocking that so many are convinced that the Communists are about to invade or destroy America: "Christians" who think the only remedy is to destroy them first. Who thinks seriously of disarming? For whom is it more than a pious wish, beyond the bounds of practicality?

I need patience to listen, to learn, to try to understand, and courage to take all the consequences and be really faithful. This alone is a full-time job. I dread it, but it must be done, and I don't quite know how. To save my soul by trying to be one of those who spoke and worked for peace, not for madness and destruction.

*November 12, 1961, IV.179*

# The Gift of Fatherhood

On the night watch, hurrying by, I pushed open the door of the novice's scriptorium and flashed the light over all the empty desks. It was as if the empty room was wholly full of their hearts and their love, as if their goodness had made the place wholly good and rich in love. The loveliness of humanity which God has taken to Himself in love, and the wonder of each individual person among them. This is of final and eternal significance. To have been appointed by God to be their father, to have received them from God as my children, to have loved them and been loved by them with such simplicity and sincerity, without nonsense or flattery or sentimentality: this is completely wonderful and is a revelation, a *parousia* of the Lord of History.

From this kind of love necessarily springs hope, hope even for political action, for here, paradoxically, hope is most necessary. Hope is always most necessary precisely when everything, spiritually, seems hopeless. And this is precisely in the confusion of politics. Hope against hope that man can gradually disarm and cease preparing for destruction and learn at last that he *must* live at peace with his brother. Never have we been less disposed to do this. It must be learned, it must be done, and everything else is secondary to this supremely urgent need of man.

*November 27, 1961, IV.183*

# Living in the Face of Death

Our great dignity is tested by death—I mean our freedom. When the "parting of the ways" comes—to set one's foot gladly on the way that leads out of this world. This is a great gift of ourselves, not to death but to life. For he who knows how to die not only lives longer in this life (as if it matters) but lives eternally because of his freedom.

Never has man's helplessness in the face of death been more pitiable than in this age when he can do everything except escape death. If he were unable to escape so many other things, man would face death better.

But our power has only strengthened our illusion that we can cling to life without taking away our unconscious fear of death. We are always holding death at arm's length, unconsciously trying to think ourselves out of its presence. This generates an intolerable tension that makes us all the more quickly its victims. It is he who does not fear death who is more ready not to escape it, and, when the time comes, he faces it well.

So he who faces death can be happy in this life and in the next, and he who does not face it has no happiness in either. This is a central and fundamental reality of life, whether one is or is not a "believer"—for this "facing" of death implies already a faith and an uprightness of heart and the presence of Christ, whether one thinks of it or not. (I do not refer to the desperateness of the tough guy, but only to the sincerity of an honest and sober and sensitive person, assuming responsibility for his whole life in gladness and freedom.)

*November 25, 1958, III.232*

# Emblems in a Season of Fury

Jim Douglass sent a letter with a clipping in it about a pacifist who burned himself to death in front of the Pentagon—it must have been All Souls' Day! It was a protest against the Vietnam War. They will probably try to write him off as a nut, but he seems to have been a perfectly responsible person, a Quaker, very dedicated. What can one say of such a thing? Since I do not know the man, I do not know that his motives were necessarily wrong and confused—all I can say is that objectively it is a terrible thing. Certainly it is an awful sign, and perhaps there had to be such a sign. Certainly the sign was powerful because incontestable and final in itself (and how frightful!). It broke through the undifferentiated, uninterpretable noises, and it certainly must have hit many people hard. But in three days it becomes again contestable and in ten it is forgotten.

I went out on the porch before dawn to think of these things, and of the words of Ezekiel (22:30): "And I sought among them for a man that might set up a hedge and stand in the gap before me in favor of the land that I might not destroy it, and I found none." And while I was standing there, quails began to whistle all over the field and in the wood. I had not heard any for weeks and thought sure they were all dead, for there have been hunters everywhere. No, there they are! Signs of life, of gentleness, of helplessness, of providence, of love. They just keep on existing and loving and making more quails and whistling in the bushes.

*November 7, 1965, V.313*

# The Struggle to Keep Awake

A long and good letter from Jaime Andrade from Quito. He speaks at length about my idea for a foundation in Quito and says I would be caught in the middle between an extremely reactionary clergy and ruling class and a red intelligentsia and would be fired at from both sides, which I think is true. And that is going to be necessarily a part of anything loving and useful I may do—because I cannot produce anything good if I identify myself too closely either with the Reds or with Capitalism. The vocation of a very good writer and spiritual man today lies neither with the one or the other, but beyond both. Heartily agree with Czeslaw Milosz's conclusions at the end of his very fine book *The Captive Mind*.

What matters is *not to line up with the winning side* but to be a true and revolutionary poet.

The struggle to keep awake on this island of Lotus Eaters.

*November 13, 1958, III.231*

# The Coming Kingdom

Have mercy on our blindness and our poverty.

Our inability to grasp the infinite riches of God's mercy and His Kingdom. Immense sorrow for those who seek to alleviate man's misery by an earthly parody of the Kingdom. The vicious lie of communist messianism, which can still appeal to the hearts of so many great men. Pablo Neruda—wonderful poet—his faith in that lie breaks my heart. He and his poetry will, of course, be destroyed by what he has chosen to serve, for there is really in him nothing in common with Stalinism.

Inability above all of Christians, of priests, to realize the objective immensity and power of the Kingdom that is established, in mystery, and of the great unknown liturgy that goes up to God from the darkness of the world in which the Kingdom is denied. Its citizens perhaps do not even know for sure of what Kingdom they are citizens, yet they suffer for God, and the Word triumphs in them, and through them man will once again be, in Christ, the perfect ikon of God. (Man is, already, in Christ, that ikon, but even we, who should know it best and be overwhelmed by it, are constantly forgetting.)

Subjective faith, personal spontaneity, ascetic goodwill, devotion to duty—these are not enough. Yet they, too, are necessary. But they are only the beginning.

*November 26, 1957, III.143*

NOVEMBER 13

# A Decisive Clarity

Tomorrow is the last Sunday after Pentecost. "Let he who is in Judea flee to the hills." Always the same deep awe and compunction at this Gospel. It has been with me every year since my conversion, and its repetition has not robbed it of significance or turned it into a dead, routine affair. On the contrary, I see more and more how central this is in my life.

Yesterday afternoon at the hermitage, surely a decisive clarity came. That I must definitely commit myself to opposition to, and noncooperation with, nuclear war. This includes refusing to vote for those who favor the policy of deterrence, and going forward in trying to make this kind of position and its obligation increasingly clear. Not that I did not mean this before—but never so wholly and so definitely.

Last evening, a note from Louis Massignon about fasting for the Algerians recently slaughtered in Paris. I have often skipped breakfast but this time skipped my evening meal. Very good. Slept better, much more clarity at the night office and meditation. Also my Mass—too dark to read the Epistle and Gospel without light but, after the Offertory, only the dawn light. Splendor of the first, dim, holy light of the day. Much meaning.

*November 25, 1961, IV.182*

# Truth Is Formed in Silence, Work, and Suffering

We talk of God when He has gone far from us. (We are far from Him and His nearness remains to accuse us!) We live as if God existed for our sakes, figuring that we exist for Him. We use grace as if it were matter handed over to form according to our pleasure. We use the truth of God as material for the fabrication of idols. We forget that we are the matter and His grace is the form imposed upon us by His wisdom. Does the clay understand the work of the potter? Does it not allow itself to be formed into a vessel of election?

The truth is formed in silence and work and suffering—with which we *become* true. But we interfere with God's work by talking too much about ourselves—even telling Him what we ought to do—advising Him how to make us perfect and listening for His voice to answer us with approval. We soon grow impatient and turn aside from the silence that disturbs us (the silence in which His work can best be done), and we invent the answer and the approval which will never come.

Silence, then, is the adoration of His truth. Work is the expression of our humility, and suffering is born of the love that seeks one thing alone: that God's will be done.

*November 12, 1952, III.24*

# Feast of Joy and Anguish

Feast of the Dedication of Gethsemani's Church. This always turns out to be a feast of anguish, as well as one of joy.

Nothing could be more beautiful, nothing could make me happier than the hymn *Urbs Jerusalem*—and to sing certain verses of that hymn in the evening looking at the sacramental flames of candles upon the wall where the building was touched and blessed by Christ and made into a sacrament of Himself.

"They shall stand forever within the sacred walls." I, too, "will stand forever," placed in a permanent position. I am glad, I am truly happy, I am really grateful to God, for it means eternal salvation.

And yet it raises again the unanswerable question: "What on earth am I doing here?" I have answered it a million times. "I belong here," and this is no answer. In the end, there is no answer like that. Any vocation is a mystery, and juggling with words does not make it any clearer.

It is a contradiction and must remain a contradiction.

*November 15, 1957, III.137*

# Through Faith and Fire

*(Merton is baptized a Roman Catholic at Corpus Christi Church in New York City on November 16, 1938)*

The chief thing that struck me today before the Blessed Sacrament: I have put my fingers too much in the running of my own life.

I put myself in God's hands, and take myself out again to read just everything to suit my own judgment. On that condition I abandon myself to Him.

Consequence? We seek the good and behold we find disturbance. We say "Peace! Peace!" and there is not Peace!

Jesus, I put myself in Your hands. I rest in Your wisdom, which has arranged all things for me. I promise to stop jumping out of Your arms to try and walk on my own feet, forgetting that I am no longer on the ground, or near it!

Now, at last, let me begin to live by faith. "Seek first, therefore, the kingdom of God."

*November 16, 1947, II.134*

# The Key to Peace

In the night, a rumpled thin skin of cloud over the sky, not totally darkening the moon. It has become thicker as the morning wears on. There is a feeling of snow in the air. Streaks of pale, lurid light over the dark hills in the south.

The SAC plane sailed low over the valley just after the bell for the Consecration at the conventual Mass, and an hour later another one went over even nearer, almost over the monastery. Enormous, perfect, ominous, great swooping weight, grey, full of Hiroshimas and the "key to peace."

How full the days are, full of quiet, ordered, occupied (sawing wood, sweeping, reading, taking notes, meditating, praying, tending to the fire, or just looking at the valley). Only here do I feel fully human. And only what is authentically human is fit to be offered to God.

It is good to know how cold it is, and not by looking at a thermometer. And to wear heavy clothes, and cut logs for the fire. I like washing in the small basin with the warm water left over from making coffee. And then walking down in the moonlight to say Mass, with the leaves growling under my feet. Not pulled at, not tense, nor waiting for what is to descend on me next, not looking for a place quiet enough to read in. Life here seems real.

*November 24, 1964, V.169*

# The Unaccountable Truth

*Gelassenheit*—letting go—not being encumbered by systems, words, projects. And yet being free *in* systems, projects. Not trying to get away from all action, all speech, but free, unencumbering *Gelassen* in this or that action. Error of self-conscious contemplatives: to get hung up on a certain kind of non-action which is an imprisonment, a stupor, the opposite of *Gelassenheit*. Actually quietism is incompatible with true inner freedom. The burden of this stupid and enforced "quiet"—the self sitting heavily on its own head.

Still thinking of K.C., who wrote from Cincinnati. From a certain point of view my letter to her was a scandal. I was in effect saying, "Don't listen for the voice of God, He will not speak to you." Yet this had to be said. Today, for a certain type of person, to "listen" is to be in a position where hearing is impossible—or deceptive. It is the wrong kind of listening: listening for a limited message, an objective sound, a sensible meaning. Actually one decides one's life by responding to a word that is *not* well defined, easily explicable, safely accounted for. One decides to love in the face of an unaccountable void, and from the void comes an unaccountable truth. By this truth one's existence is sustained in peace—until the truth is too firmly grasped and too clearly accounted for. Then one is relying on words, i.e., on one's own understanding and one's own ingenuity in interpreting existence and its "signs." Then one is lost and has to be found once again in the patient Void.

*November 13, 1966, VI.160–61*

# Being a Teacher

Finishing William of Conches's *Philosophia Mundi*. Beautiful little chapter on the Teacher. I was very moved by it. I usually ignore this element in my own vocation, but obviously I am a writer, a student, and a teacher, as well as a contemplative of sorts, and my solitude, etc., is that of a writer and teacher, not a pure hermit. And the great thing is, or should be, love of truth. I know there is nothing more precious than the bond of charity created by communicating and sharing the truth. This really is my whole life.

Yesterday Aidan Nally came up to me by the woodshed and said, "Father, it seems the wars have ceased."

Later I conjectured he was referring to the cessation of atmospheric nuclear testing announced by Kennedy.

Today (a blacker day than usual and there have been many) Aidan Nally met me out by the greenhouse just before dinner and uttered some prophecies of doom according to something he had seen on TV. None of it was clear. Probably the Russians trying to make up for their loss of face over Cuba. Something on Germany? Berlin?

The problem is not to lose one's sense of perspective and seriousness. It is always "the end" and each time it gets closer. The students at the Oxford Union drank up their best wine in the Cuban crisis. They will not have any for this one, whatever it is—if it is a crisis, and not something imagined by Aidan. But Aidan's imagination is as good as any paper—only a little foggy.

*November 13 and 17, 1962, IV.264–66*

# Another Lost Customer

Reading Mabillon's wise and delightful book on monastic studies. Among other things, this beautiful quotation from Seneca: "If you will give yourself to study, you will ease every burden of life, you will neither wish for night to come or the light to fail; neither shall you be worried or preoccupied with other things."

Warm sun, quiet morning. Pigs bang the lids of their feeding troughs. Frater Placid madly at the honeysuckle. I sit on the very low bench under the cedars, outside the wall. Frater John of the Cross told a story about Brother Clement and "his men" trying to "capture" Brother Colman and a local farmer to whom Colman was selling pigs. They thought the farmer was stealing pigs because Brother Colman, zealous for poverty, did not put on the lights. One brother rushed upon Brother Colman in the dark crying, "This one's all for me!" Nobody was hurt, but the farmer was paralyzed and speechless for five minutes. He said he would never come here to buy pigs again.

*November 10, 1958, III.229–30*

# Fireworks

Riches! The comet. I went out and, though there was mist, I saw it as it first began to appear. Later it became more definite and quite bright (what I am seeing is the reflection of the comet's tail, for it is now past the sun). A most beautiful and moving thing, this great spear pointing down to the horizon where the sun will not appear yet for an hour and a half. As I watched, under the oaks, with acorns dropping around me, the bell rang in the Church for the Preface and the Consecration. Three meteorites flashed across the sky in fifteen minutes. Two army transports growled and blinked across the comet's path, and the stag cried out in the dark field behind my hedge. Riches! I recited Psalm 18, "The heavens proclaim," with joy.

*November 5, 1965, V.312–13*

# God in Search of Humanity

At the heart of Abraham Heschel's splendid book, *God in Search of Man,* is the consistent emphasis on the importance of time, of the event in revealed religion, Biblical, prophetic religion.

Event, not process. The unique event, not repeated.

The realm of the event is the realm of the person. Liberation from the process by decisions, by free act, unique, irreplaceable. The encounter with God.

Heschel: "An event is a happening that cannot be reduced to a part of a process."

"To speak of events is to imply that there are happenings in the world that are beyond the reach of our explanation."

See early chapter of St. John—the encounter of the Apostles and of John with Jesus. Emphasis on the words to *see,* to *find,* and the naming of names, the designations of persons.

And Jacob's dream and his awakening: "This is the house of God." It became *so* by reason of the encounter, the ladder.

By virtue of great events—relived and remembered—the past becomes present and one transcends the process.

"Such understanding of time is not peculiar to historians. It is shared unknowingly by all men and is essential to civilized living."

*November 15, 1960, IV.66*

NOVEMBER 23

# Suspended by God's Mercy

The annual retreat is ending. I was very deeply moved by Fr. Phelan's conference on the Sacred Heart. Great depth of theology in clear and simple terms. It showed me how there really is an abyss of light in the things the simplest faithful believe and love, and that sometimes seem trite to the intellectuals. Indeed, perhaps it is the simplest and most popular truths that are also the deepest after all.

For my own part, I think much has been done to me in the course of this retreat—in emptiness and helplessness and humiliation. Aware that I might crack up at any moment, I find, nevertheless, that when I pray, I pray better than ever. I mean that I no longer have any special degree of prayer. Simple vocal prayer, and especially the office and the psalms, seems to have acquired a depth and simplicity I never knew in *any* prayer. I have nothing but faith and the love of God and confidence in the simple means He has given me for reaching Him. Suspended entirely from His mercy, I am content for anything to happen.

*November 29, 1952, III.25*

## Sitting for a Portrait

Lovely, cold, lonely afternoon, winter afternoon, rich winter silence and loneliness and fullness into which I entered nearly twenty years ago! These afternoons contain all the inexplicable meaning of my vocation.

Victor Hammer came over. Brought the beginning of the woodcut for *Hagia Sophia* and some proofs of his new thing on *Mnemosyne,* which is excellent. (I finally apprehend the simple thing that Fiedler is getting at: that the work of art is to be seen—not imagined, worked over intellectually by the viewer. Central is the experience of seeing.)

Victor worked on a sketch for a portrait of me, and this (contrary to what one might say according prejudice) makes at least some sense. The patient, human work of sitting and talking and being understood on paper. How different from the camera! I am incurably camera shy! The awful instantaneous snapshot of pose, of falsity, eternalized. Like the pessimistic, anguished view of judgment that so many mad Christians have—the cruel candid shot of you when you have just done something transient but hateful. As if this could be truth. Judgment really a patient, organic, long-suffering understanding of the man's whole life, of *everything* in it, all in context.

*November 17, 1961, IV.179*

# Experiences of Seeing

At Mass, which was all before sunrise and without lights, the quality, the "spirituality" of the predawn light on the altar was extraordinary. Silence in the chapel and that pure, pearl light! What could be a more beautiful liturgical sign than to have such light as witness of the Mystery?

Wild grey kitten among the dead leaves in the garden, fleeing to the hole in the wall. Sun on the building work, the waterhouse. Dead leaves.

Hawk on the way up to the hermitage, over the cedars in the low bushy place where the quails were (*were!!*). He circled four or five times, spreading his tail, which shone rusty in the light, and he flashed silver like the dove in the psalm, when sun caught him under the wings.

*November 25, 26, and 27, 1962, IV. 267–69*

# The Community Is My Mother

Our Lady of Gethsemani. Mary is, in a certain sense, the community which is my Mother. It is her love that has brought us here and keeps the community together. It is her love I have known out under the cedars, and working in the fields and singing in choir. It is her love that has made me desire solitude, and she will fulfill that desire. She is my solitude and she is here. It seems I have to keep finding it out over and over again.

Maybe this time it is the end. I hope I have stopped asking questions. I have begged her for the grace to finish the course here and die as a holy monk in the monastery or in a solitude closely dependent on the monastery. I feel great peace and my heart has never been so free, so poor and empty.

*November 29, 1952, III.2*

# One Small Miracle in a Day of Noise

A lovely afternoon but full of noise. Reading after dinner—snatches from the *Dhammapada*—I thought of this clear sky and how it must be like Mexican sky.

And now, noise everywhere. Hammers all over the roof of the east wing—the buzz saw cutting hickory for the smokehouses. Novices kicking pigs. A huge road-grader sent by the politicians, roaring up and down significantly on the day before elections. ("Get out the vote," says the Abbot. "Show them that we have power!")

Sick of writing, sick of letters, sick of self-expression.

Silence and solitude and peace.

Even if everything else is noise, I can be silent within my own house.

Every time I go to Chapter such ties as bind me to Gethsemani are weakened still more.

Read a little about the Indians who make lacquer at Patzcuaro. The Night of All Souls is a great night on the Island of Juntzio (Sibylle Akers's photographs of the Indian women sitting with candles on the graves, with food).

Hurray! The buzz saw has broken down!

*November 2, 1959, III.338–39*

# An American Mysticism

At midnight I woke up, and there was a great noise of wind and storm. Rain was rolling over the roof of the hermitage heavy as a freight train. The porch was covered with water and there was a lot of lightning. Now at dawn the sky is clean and all is cold again (yesterday warm). Yesterday I read some article on psychedelics. There is a regular fury of drug-mysticism in this country. I am in a way appalled. Mysticism has finally arrived in a characteristic American mode. One feels that this is certainly it. The definitive turn in the road taken by American religion. The turn I myself will not take (don't need to!). This leaves my own road quieter and more untroubled, I hope. Certainly the great thing, as I see it now, is to get out of all the traffic: peace movement traffic, political traffic, Church traffic. All of it! Big peace protest in Washington (against Vietnam War) today. I am fasting and praying for them, and offering no hosannas of my own.

*November 27, 1965, V.318–19*

# The Sin of Idolatry

The Christian faith enables, or should enable, a man to stand back from society and its institutions and realize that they all stand under the inscrutable judgment of God and that, therefore, we can never give an unreserved assent to the policies, the programs and the organizations of men, or to "official" interpretations of the historic process. To do so is idolatry, the same kind of idolatry that was refused by the early martyrs who would not burn incense to the emperor.

The policies of men contain within themselves the judgment and doom of God upon their society, and when the Church identifies her policies with theirs, she too is judged with them—for she has in this been unfaithful and is not truly "the Church." The *power* of "the Church" (who is not "the Church" if she is rich and powerful) contains the judgment that "begins at the house of God."

*November 30, 1964, V.171*

# On the Threshold of a Hard Winter

All day it has been deceptively like spring. Not only because of light and cool-warm air (warm with a slightly biting March-like wind) but because I fasted and it felt like Lent. Then in the evening (I had my meal about four instead of supper at five) it was suddenly much lighter, as though it were March.

At noon, when I was not eating, I was out by St. Bernard's lake (which is surprisingly low) and the sky, hills, trees, kept taking on an air of clarity and freshness that took me back to springs twenty years ago when Lents were hard and I was new in the monastery.

Strange feeling! Recapturing the freshness of those days when my whole monastic life was ahead of me, when all was still open: but now it is all behind me, and the years have closed in upon their silly, unsatisfactory history, one by one. But the air is like spring and fresh as ever. And I was amazed at it. Had to stop to gaze and wonder: loblolly pines we planted ten or fifteen years ago are twenty feet high. The first tower shines in the sun like new— though it was up ten years ago (with what hopes, on my part!). Flashing water of the lake. A blue jay flying down as bright as metal. I went over to the wood where the Jonathan Daniel sculptures are now, and read some selections from Origen. And again stood amazed at the quiet, the bright sun, the spring-like light. The sharp outline of the pasture. Knolls, the brightness of bare trees in the hopeful sun. And yet it is not spring. We are on the threshold of a hard winter.

*November 25, 1967, VII.15*

# Advent Weather

It is beautiful Advent weather, greyish and cold, with clouds of light snow howling across the valley, and I see it is really winter. I put some bread out for the birds.

I feel closer to my beginning than ever, and perhaps I am near my end. The Advent hymns sound as they first did, as if they were the nearest things to me that ever were, as if they had been decisive in shaping my heart and my life, as if I had received their form, as if there could never be any other melodies so deeply connatural to me. They are myself, words and melody and everything. So also the *Rorate Coeli* that brought me here to pray for peace. I have not prayed for it well enough, or been pure enough in heart, or wise enough. And today, before the Blessed Sacrament, I was ashamed of my impertinences and the deep infidelities of my life, rooted in weakness and confusion.

Yesterday, I celebrated my Mass for the new generation, the new poets, the fighters for peace, and my novices. There is in many of them a peculiar quality of truth that older squares have driven out of themselves in days of rigidity and secure right thinking. May God keep us from being "right thinking" men, who think, that is, with their own police (and since the police don't think, neither do these others).

*December 9, 1962, IV.272–73*

# Love Born Out of Prayer in Seclusion

"Love comes from prayer and prayer from remaining in seclusion" (Isaac of Syria). Certainly the break in my more solitary routine (going down to the monastery earlier without the long meditation, spending most of the day there, ceremonies, lectures, etc.) has created a kind of confusion, disturbance and laxity. Solitude is not something to play with from time to time. And yet of course I still need a good part of the common life, and will always need to maintain very definite contacts. But it is hard and confusing to be uprooted from peace every time you begin barely to get into it— or rather, not to be able to sink completely into unity and simplicity. There is peace too in community, of course, but it has a different and more active rhythm.

Yet, in this solitude there must be, with the fiery substance of the eternal prophets, also the terse anger and irony and humor of the Latin American poets with whom I am united in bonds of warmth and empathy, for instance, the Peruvian Blanca Varela (I must translate her, a poem or two), or Jorge Eduardo Eielson!

At last there is light again. First there were some stars here and there, when I first got up at 2:15. Then a surprise—in an unexpected corner of woods, the thin last slice of leftover moon. The sun came up at 8:05 (our time here is unnatural, as we are on Eastern standard). Then there was the extraordinary purity and stillness and calm of that moment of surprise and renewal. Peace of the woods and the valley, but then somewhere a heifer salutes the morning with enthusiastic lowing.

*December 29, 1964, V.184–85*

# A Brush with the Angel of Death

How often in the last years I have thought of death. It has been present to me and I have "understood" it, and known that I must die. Yet last night, only for a moment, in passing, and so to speak without grimness or drama, I momentarily experienced the fact that I, this self, will soon simply not exist. A flash of "not-thereness," of being dead. Without fear or grief, without anything. Just not there. And this I supposed is one of the first tastes of the fruits of solitude. So the angel passed along, thinking aloud to himself, doing his business, and barely taking note of me. But taking note of me nevertheless. We recognized one another. And of course the other thing is that this "I" is not "I," and I am not this body, this "self," and I am not just my individual nature. But yet I might as well be, so firmly am I rooted in it and identified with it—with this that will cease utterly to exist, in its natural individuality.

In the hermitage—I see how quickly I can fall apart. I talk to myself, I dance around the hermitage, I sing. This is all very well but it is not serious, it is a manifestation of weakness, of dizziness. And again I feel within this individual self the nearness of disintegration. (Yet I also realize that this exterior self can fall apart and be reintegrated too. This is like losing dry skin that peels off while the new skin forms underneath.)

*December 4, 1964, V.173–74*

# My Old Life Slowly Breaks Loose

Last evening at supper I began Jacques Ellul's *L'Illusion politique.* It is some comfort to find someone who agrees with my position. I must be resolutely non-political, provided I remain ready to speak out when it is needed. However, I think this book, too, may turn out insufficient and naïve (philosophically weak perhaps, I am not far into it). But he is basically right in attacking the modern super-stition that "what has no political value has no value at all"—"A man who does not read the newspapers is not a man." And to be apolitical is to be excommunicated as a sorcerer. That the deepest communion of man with man is in political declarations.

What is primary? God's revelation of Himself to me *in Christ* and my response in faith. In the concrete, this means for me my present life of solitude, acceptance of its true perspectives and demands, and the work of slow orientation that goes on. Each day, a little, I realize that my old life is breaking loose and will eventually fall, in pieces, gradually. What then? My solitude is not like the German poet Rilke's: ordered to a poetic explosion. Nor is it a mere deepening of religious consciousness. What is it then? What has been so far only a theological conception, or an image, has to be sought and loved: "Union with God!" So mysterious that in the end man would perhaps do anything to evade it, once he realizes it means the *end* of his own Ego self-realization, once for all. Am I ready? Of course not. Yet the course of my life is set in this direction.

*December 5 and 7, 1965, V.322*

# Resolve to Die in Christ

"Resolve to die rather than abandon this life-giving search." Read slowly, in the lamplight, early cold morning. Simeon the New Theologian is a man of burning words indeed. In the comfort of the monastery it is easier to neglect him as an extremist. "To have no thought of oneself for any earthly end, but to have one's whole mind centered on Christ. What measure, think you, will this procure of heavenly good, and of angelic condition?" (*Catechism*, II).

How clearly I see and experience this morning the difference and distance between my own inertia, weakness, sensitivity, stupidity, and the love of Christ, which instantly pulls all things in me together so that there is no longer any uncertainty or misdirection or lassitude. What a shame and dishonor to Christ if I let my life be such a mess of trivialities and silly concerns (that are in reality only a mask for despair!).

I will not easily forget the thin sickle of old moon rising this morning just before dawn, when I went down to say Mass. Cold sky, hard brightness of stars through the pines, snow and frost, exaltation on the bright darkness of morning. In the cold of Advent I recapture the lostness and wonder of the first days when I came here twenty-three years ago, abandoned to God, with everything left behind. I have not felt this for a long time here. Breaking off and living (to a great extent) in the woods brings me back face to face with the loneliness and poverty of the cold hills and the Kentucky winter—incomparable, and the reality of my own life!

*December 1, 1964, V.172*

# This Precious Poverty

I think more and more in terms of self-emptying and self-forgetfulness—but not in order merely to drown in a communal superstition and hopelessness. To renounce myself to serve truth and patiently to minister to individuals who, one by one, come needing help. To see their need, and try to minister to it, and not worry about results, or rewards. Ecce!—*Behold!*

Evening: rain, silence, joy.

I am certain that where the Lord sees the small point of poverty and extenuation and helplessness to which the monk is reduced, the solitary and the man of tears, then He *must* come down and be born there in this anguish, and make it constantly a point of infinite joy, a seed of peace in the world. And this is, and always has been, my mission. There is for me no truth and no sense in anything that conceals from me this precious poverty, this seed of tears and joy. I have a right to speak to others in so far as I speak to the same truth in them, and assuage their doubts, and make them strong in this small point of exhaustion in which the Lord becomes their wisdom and their life everlasting. What do the Psalms say but this?

"Be firm, you will see the help of the Lord upon you!"

How deep is this truth, how tremendously important!

*December 25, 1962, IV.280–81*

# One Prays to Pray

In the hermitage, one must pray or go to seed. The pretense of prayer will not suffice. Just sitting will not suffice. It has to be real—yet what can one do? Solitude puts your back to the wall (or your face to it!) and this is good. One prays to pray. And the reality of death. John Donne's poems and Lancelot Andrewes.

Then it becomes very important to remember that the quality of one's night depends on the thoughts of the day, on the sanity of the day. I bring there the sins of the day into the light and darkness of truth to be adored without disguise—then I want to fly back to the disguises. Who ever said that the solitary life is one of pretense and deception? As if pretense were easy in solitude!!! It is easier in the community, for there one can have the support of a common illusion or a common agreement in forms that take the place of truth. One can pretend in the solitude of an afternoon walk, but the night destroys all pretences: one is reduced to nothing and compelled to begin laboriously the long return to truth.

Tonight it is cold again and, as I came up in the dark, a few small snowflakes were flying in the beam of the flashlight. The end of an oak log was still burning with small flames in the fireplace. Came up with candles, and sugar for coffee, and a jar to urinate in so that I won't have to go out in the snow in the middle of the night. What greater comforts could a man want?

*December 5, 1964, V.175–76*

# The Old Man in a Thousand Wrappings

Evening: The heart is deceitful above all things
The heart is deep and full of windings
The old man is covered up in a thousand wrappings.
(Lancelot Andrewes, *Preces*)

True sad words, and I would not have felt the truth of them so much if I had not had so much solitude these days, with rain coming down on the roof and hiding the valley. Rain in the night, the nuisance of water in the buckets. Or cutting wood behind the house, and a faint smell of hickory smoke from the chimney—while I taste and see that I am deceitful and that most of my troubles are rooted in my own bitterness. Is this what solitude is for? Then it is good, but I must pray for the strength to bear it! (The heart is deceitful and does not want this—but God is greater than my heart!)

I will acknowledge my faults, O Lord.
O who will give scourges to my mind
That they spare not my sins?

*December 3, 1964, V.173*

# The Complexity of Our Real "I"

When I got up it was about thirty degrees on the porch and now at dawn it is down to twenty-one. These are the coldest hours—meditation, *lectio* (spiritual reading), and hot tea with lemon and a good fire. I am reading Paul Evdokimov's *La Femme et le salut du monde* (*Woman and the Salvation of the World*)—after tea—and then Rilke's *Duino Elegies*.

"The cross is made up of our weaknesses and failures, it is constructed by our ego and above all by our profound gloom and unspeakable and culpable ugliness, in short, by all the complexity that is at this time the real I."

I experience the truth of this very real and exact insight of Evdokimov. Still, in regard to the Catholic Peace Fellowship—about which nothing is settled—I see how much there was that was inauthentic (i.e., false, spurious) in my own initial enthusiasm for identification with peace activities, *The Catholic Worker,* etc. It was in reality selfish and naïve at the same time. And I did not foresee that necessarily they and I could hardly go along forever in agreement, living in totally different circumstances. Yet I do agree with their ideal in general—not with all its particular implementations. One could go on analyzing interminably. I must accept this result of my own inner contradictions and trust God to bring a solution in which His will may be done by me and all of them too. And I don't know what to do next—hence I must be content not to act at all, when I would very much like to settle everything in a big sweep.

*December 2, 1965, V.320–21*

# Dying and Being Reborn in Christ

*(Thomas Merton enters Gethsemani on December 10, 1941;*
*he dies by accident while attending a monastic conference*
*in Bangkok, Thailand, on December 10, 1968)*

I come into solitude to die and love. I come here to be created by the Spirit in Christ.

I am called here to grow. "Death" is a critical point of growth, or transition to a new mode of being; to a *maturity* and fruitfulness that I do not know (they are in Christ and in His Kingdom). The child in the womb does not know what will come after birth. He must be born in order to live. I am here to learn to face death as my birth.

This solitude—a refuge under His wings, a place to hide myself in His Name, therefore, a sanctuary where the grace of Baptism remains a conscious, living, active reality valid not only for me but for the whole Church. Here, planted as a seed in the cosmos, I will be a Christ seed, and bring fruit for other men. Death and rising in Christ.

I need to be "confirmed" in my vocation by the Spirit (speaking through the Church, i.e., the abbot and the community). This ordains me to be the person I am and to have the particular place and function I have, to be myself in the sense of choosing to tend toward what God wants me to be, and to orient my whole life to being the person He loves. (We are all "loved in general," but we have to personally accept a special love of God for ourselves.)

*December 1, 1965, V.333–34*

# Wanting to Start Over

While I was saying Mass, at my Communion, I heard the bells ring for an agony—one of the monks is dying—and guessed they were for Brother Gerard (they rang for *thee!*), and he died about an hour later. Another of the old brothers, the past dying.

A distant relative sent an old snapshot taken when he and his wife visited Douglaston—where I lived with my grandparents—thirty years ago. It shows them with Bonnemaman and myself—and the back porch of the house, and the birch tree. There is Bonnemaman as I remember her—within two years of her dying. And there am I: it shakes me! I am the young rugby player, the lad from Cambridge, vigorous, light, vain, alive, obviously making a joke of some sort. The thing shakes me. I can see that that was a different body from the one I have now—one entirely young and healthy, one that did not know sickness, weakness, anguish, tension, fatigue—a body totally assured of itself and with care, perfectly relaxed, ready for enjoyment. What a change since that day! If I were wiser, I would not mind, but I am not so sure I am wiser. I have been through more, I have endured a lot of things, perhaps fruitlessly. I do not entirely think that—but it is possible. What shakes me is that—I wish I were that rugby player, vain, vigorous, etc., and could start over again! And yet how absurd. What would I ever do? Those were, no matter how you look at it, better times! There were things we had not heard of—Auschwitz, the Bomb, etc. (Yet it was all beginning, nevertheless.)

*December 21, 1965, V.325–26*

# A Simple Benedictine Life

Benedictine life is perfectly simple—it is the Gospel pure and simple—it liberates us from ourselves by enabling us to give ourselves entirely to God.

I give myself completely to God. He draws me more and more to that. I cannot know what lies ahead for me, for us, but more and more I realize God wants me to put myself in His hands, and let Him take me through the things that are to come, and I must learn to trust Him without fear, or questions, or hesitations, or withdrawal.

Yesterday, in the infirmary, old Brother Gregory lay dying.

And today it was very beautiful, warmish with the sun out and little neat clouds high up in the sky and the brown dirt piled high on top of Brother Gregory, who turns out to have been Swiss. And one day here a bull got playful and tossed him over a stone wall and that was why he always limped.

I asked Reverend Father what made Brother so saintly, and he said, "He was always working, never idle. When he was out tending the cows in the pasture, he would come back with a bucket of blackberries. He couldn't be idle." I might have known what kind of answer I would get!

*December 14, 16, and 18, 1947, II.145–47*

# All My Fathers

*(Thomas Merton becomes a postulant at Gethsemani
on December 13, 1941)*

In the cemetery I looked up at the sky and thought of the great sea of graces that was flowing down on Gethsemani as her hundredth year was ending. All the crosses stood up and spoke to me for fair this time. It was as if the earth were shaking under my feet and as if the jubilant dead were just about to sit up and sing.

And I got some taste of how much there is to be glad for in the world because of Gethsemani. Not that I am looking for any such taste anymore: only how to serve God better and belong more completely to Him.

Father Amadeus was speaking today of the need for a concrete spiritual ideal. What strikes me is the need of something absolutely concrete and definite—poverty, humility: not something abstract, off in the heavens, but here, at Gethsemani. Not for other people first, but for myself first. To make it a real ideal you work for, not just one you occasionally think and preach about. To ask God somehow to make me the quietest and meekest and most unobtrusive man in the whole house, the *poorest* man, the one with nothing. I am right at the other end of the pole from that—but in the circumstances God has given me to work with, there are still graces—and all the Fathers of Gethsemani, whom I love, will all pray for me.

*December 20, 1948, II.256–57*

# Arriving at the Place God Destined for Me

Yesterday, went down to the monastery only for my own Mass and dinner. Cooked supper at the hermitage, in fact, cooked too much rice, having miscalculated, and sat half an hour consuming it, with tea. But it was a splendid supper (looking out at the hills in the clear evening light). After that, washing dishes—the bowl, the pot, the cup, the knife (for oleo), the spoon—looked up and saw a jet like a small rapid jewel traveling north between the moon and the evening star—the moon being nearly full. Then I went out for a little walk down to my gate (about a hundred yards) and looked out over the valley. Incredibly beautiful and peaceful. Blue hills, blue sky, woods, empty fields, lights going on in the Abbey, to the right, through the screen of trees, hidden from the hermitage. And out there, light on the three farms I can see. One at Newton's and two others out there in the hills behind Gethsemani station.

Everything that the Fathers say about the solitary life is exactly true. The temptations and the joys, above all, the tears and the ineffable peace and happiness. The happiness that is so pure because it is simply not one's own making, but sheer mercy and gift! And the sense of having arrived at last in the place destined for me by God, and for which I was brought here twenty-three years ago!

*December 16, 1964, V.179–80*

# Love Is the Only Answer

"My responsibility is to be in all reality a peacemaker in the world, an apostle, to bring people to truth, to make my whole life a true and effective witness to God's truth."

Moving words of Albert Einstein (with whom I agree that Gandhi has been in reality the most effective and trustworthy political thinker of our time): "We must revolutionize our thinking, revolutionize our actions, and must have the courage to revolutionize our relations among the nations of the world. Clichés of yesterday will no longer do. . . . To bring this home to men all over the world is the most important and fateful function intellectuals have ever had to shoulder. Will they have enough courage to overcome their own nationalities to the extent that is necessary to induce the peoples of the world to change their deep-rooted national traditions in a most radical fashion?"

Love is the only answer. But medieval talk about love does nothing. What does love mean today? What is its place in the enormous dimensions of the modern world? We have to love in a new way and with a new attitude, and I suppose perhaps the first thing to do is admit that I do not know the meaning of love in *any* context—ancient or new.

*December 27, 1957, III.149–50*

# Transfiguring the Ordinary

Yesterday I selected poems for a paperback collection, to be issued by New Directions. Saw that my best ones were the early ones, and that I cannot go back to that.

The fervor of those days was special and young. It can inspire me to seek a new and different kind of fervor, which is older and deeper. This I must find. But I cannot go back to the earlier fervor or to the asceticism that accompanied it. The new fervor will be rooted not in asceticism but in humanism. What has begun now must grow but must never seek to become spectacular or draw attention to itself—which is what I unconsciously did in those days, proclaiming that I was a poet and a mystic. Both are probably true, but not deep enough, because then it was too conscious. I have to write and speak not as an individual who has cut himself off from the world and wants the world to know it, but as the person who has lost himself in the service of the vast wisdom of God's plan to reveal Himself in the world and in man. How much greater, deeper, nobler, truer, and more hidden. A mysticism that appears no longer transcendent but ordinary.

*December 11, 1958, III.237–38*

# In the Company of Friends

Bob Lax's circus book—*Circus of the Sun*—is a tremendous poem, an Isaias-like prophecy that has a quality you just don't find in poetry today. A completely unique simplicity and purity of love that is not afraid to express itself. The circus as symbol and sacrament, cosmos, and church—the mystery of the primitive world, of paradise in which men have wonderful and happy skills, which they exercise freely as at play. Also a sacrament of the *eschaton*—the last things—our heavenly Jerusalem. The importance of human love in the circus—for doing things well. It is one of the few poems that has anything whatever to say. I want to write an article about it.

Victor and Carolyn Hammer came over yesterday. We ate sandwiches in the jeep, in a sunny field near the shallow lake, drank coffee, ate apples and ginger. I lost a filling from a tooth. He came back to see the chapel—I have hopes that he will make a tabernacle for us and candlesticks. He looked at the chapel without inspiration, and said, "This is an awful place." A prophetic utterance, quite unlike the words of Jacob used as Introit for the Feast of the Dedication of a Church. But he offered to lend us one of his painted crucifixes—one of those he did for Kolbsheim.

He gave me one of his little Japanese knives. I cleaned up the room in its honor.

Went out alone to get three large trees and a small one in the wasteland along by Andy Boone's.

A sunny, happy day, yesterday.

*December 20, 1959, III.360–61*

# Praying for a Wise Heart

This morning I was praying much for a wise heart. I think the gift of this Christmas has been the real discovery of Julian of Norwich. I have long been around her and hovered at her door and known that she was one of my best friends, and just because I was so sure of her wise friendship, I did not make haste to seek what I now find.

She seems to me a true theologian with a greater clarity and organization and depth even than St. Teresa of Avila. I mean she really elaborates the content of revelation as deeply experienced. It is first experienced, then thought, and the thought deepens again into life, so that all her life the content of her vision was penetrating her through and through.

One of the central convictions is her eschatological orientation to the central, dynamic secret act "by which all shall be made well" at the last day, the "*great deed*" ordained by our Lord from without beginning.

*Especially the first paradox*—she must "believe" and accept the doctrine that there are some damned, yet *also* the "word" of Christ shall be "saved in all things" and "all manner of thing shall be well." The heart of her theology is this apparent contradiction in which she must remain steadfastly. I believe that this "wise heart" that I have prayed for is precisely this—to stay in this hope and this contradiction, fixed on the certainty of the "great deed," which alone gives the Christian and spiritual life its true, full dimension.

*December 27, 1961, IV.189–90*

# In the End, Grace Alone

I have to admit the truth that the particular frustrations of this life here are first of all not intrinsic to monasticism as such, and not essential to my own "way" by any means. They are the product of social background and involvement in the economic and cultural pattern of the country (unavoidable). We are much more involved than we think, and my assessments of the Abbot are based mostly on this: that he is through and through a businessman, and indeed even prides himself on his practicality and shrewdness, and yet he "gets away" with this by a formal unworldliness in certain spheres —discouraging correspondence, visits, recreations, etc. (He resents my involvement in the intellectual world. My frustrations are to some extent those of all intellectuals in a society of businessmen and squares.)

The great fault of my own spirituality is a negativism which is related to bourgeois sterility. What Jean-Paul Sartre calls "right-wing existentialism." Regarding *angst* as an ordinary, universal element in all life. . . (maybe this is to some extent true, however). Projecting my own frustrations and incapacities on the whole world. The fact remains that I here suffer from the sterility of my culture, and its general impotence. The optimism I reject is the optimism that denies this sterility. But where is the real optimism I should have as a Christian?

"The simplicity of the adult," says Emmanuel Mounier, "is won by long effort, without miracles." Grace alone, the grace of the heights, sets the final grace upon the rejuvenation of the new man!

*December, 26, 1963, V. 50*

# Prayer Is Always First

White smoke rising up the valley, against the light, slowly taking animal forms, with a dark background of wooded hills behind. Menacing and peaceful, probably brush fires, maybe a house, probably not a house. Cold, quiet morning, watch ticks on the desk. Produce nothing.

Perhaps I am stronger than I think. Perhaps I am afraid of my own strength and turn it against myself to make myself weak. Perhaps I am most afraid of the strength of God in me.

It is simply time that I must pray intently for the needs of the whole world and not be concerned with other, seemingly "more effective" forms of action. For me, prayer comes first, the other forms of action follow, if they have their place. And they no doubt do to some extent. Prayer (yesterday's Mass) for Latin America, all of America, for this hemisphere—sorrow for the dolts, for the idiot civilization that is going down to ruin and dragging everything with it.

*December 13, 1960, IV.73*

# Christmas Frenzies

Quiet, early morning, dark. Distress and confusion of this year. What will it bring? Yet I think the foolish business about bomb shelters, with all its enormous stupidities—down to the plastic burial suit for $50.00—has got people "roused," as the saying goes, and there is a lot of protest. The sane ones have been too passive, and they are beginning to be forced to react. But perhaps it is too late.

Life is madder and madder, except that the woods and fields are always a relief. Bright sun on the big sycamore by the mill yesterday and light snow underfoot. And silence. Silence now also, and the night.

I still haven't ploughed through all the pile of Christmas mail, not all of it. It appalls me. I haven't read enough of the things I should be reading and want to read: Clement, Gregory of Nyssa. Then again I have worked myself into an equivocal and silly position with *curiositas*. By now that should be familiar. Yet one *must* speak and act now. But I pray I may someday learn how rightly. I feel there is not much time left for one to be learning the most important things, and I will have to trust to God for all that I lack and will continue to lack.

*December 31, 1961, IV.190*

# The Unknown Power of the Cross

Yesterday, day of recollection, realized again above all my need for profound and total humility—especially in any work I may do for peace. Humility is more important than zeal. Descent into nothingness and dependence on God. Otherwise I am just fighting the world with its own weapons and there the world is unbeatable. Indeed it does not even have to fight back, for I will exhaust myself and that will be the end of my stupid efforts.

To seek strength in God, especially in the Passion of Christ.

The mysterious, unknown power of the Cross. Preachers of the Cross hide its power and distort its meaning by their own image of the Crucified.

The crucifixion is literally the destruction of the "Image" of God.

An "image" is presented and then taken away from man (and restored if man follows into the night). There is no adequate image. Preachers preserve an image, often a very faulty one. Meaning of the stress on the Resurrection here.

But to descend into the Night of the Passion, the Night of Christ's death, baptism in His sufferings, without image.

*December 11, 1961, IV.184–85*

# Suspended over Nothingness and Yet in Life

A charming letter from Eleanor Shipley Duckett, who, on return-ing to Smith College from England (Cambridge), found some notes I had sent and is making them her "Advent reading." I am very attracted to her. She is a sweet person. She wrote part of her letter in Latin. Though I have so far not had much contact with her (it began when the University of Michigan Press sent proofs of her *Carolingian Portraits*), I feel we can be very good friends, that this friendship can be really precious to us both—with the autumn quality of detachment that comes from the sense that we are coming to the end of our lives (she must be quite older than I, in her sixties, I presume). This sense of being suspended over noth-ingness and yet in life, of being a fragile thing, a flame that may blow out and yet burns brightly, adds an inexpressible sweetness to the gift of life, for one sees it entirely and purely as a gift. A gift that one must treasure in great fidelity with a truly pure heart.

*December 15, 1962, IV.275–76*

# Raised from the Dead

Issac of Stella's Easter sermon—deep, deep intuition of faith as a resurrection because it is an act of obedience to God considered as supreme life. What matters is the act of submission to infinite life, to the authority of Creative and Redemptive Life, the Living God. Faith is this submission. The interior surrender of faith cannot have its full meaning except as an act of *obedience,* i.e., self-commitment in submission to God's truth in its power to give life, and *to command one to live.*

Hence Faith is not simply an act of choice, an option for a certain solution to the problem of existence, etc. It is a birth to a higher life, by obedience to the Giver of life, *obedience to the source of life.*

*To believe is to consent to a creative command that raises us from the dead.*

*December 5, 1960, IV.72*

# I Heard and Believed

I am finally reading Vladimir Lossky's fine book *La Vision de Dieu,* which reminds me that the best thing that has come out of the Second Vatican Council is the Declaration on Ecumenism, particularly on oriental theology. If it were a matter of choosing between "contemplation" and "eschatology," there is no question that I am, and would always be, committed entirely to the latter. Here in the hermitage, returning necessarily to beginnings, I know where my beginning was, having the Name and the Godhead of Christ preached in Corpus Christi Church. I heard and believed. And I believe that He has called me freely, out of pure mercy, to His love and salvation, and that at the end (to which all is directed by Him) I shall see Him after I have put off my body in death and have risen together with Him. And that at the last day "all flesh shall see the salvation of God."

What this means is that my faith is an eschatological faith, not merely a means of penetrating the mystery of the divine presence, resting in Him now. Yet because my faith is eschatological it is *also* contemplative, for I am even now in the Kingdom and I can even now "see" something of the glory of the Kingdom and praise Him who is King. I would be foolish, then, if I lived blindly, putting all "seeing" off until some imagined fulfillment (for my present seeing is the beginning of a real and unimaginable fulfillment!). Thus contemplation and eschatology are one in Christian faith and in surrender to Christ. They complete each other and intensify each other. It is by contemplation and love that I can best prepare myself for the eschatological vision— and best help all the Church, and all men, to journey toward it.

*December 22, 1964, V.181–82*

# Awakened in the Holy Spirit

The union of contemplation and eschatology is clear in the gift of the Holy Spirit. In Him we are awakened to know the Father because in Him we are refashioned in the likeness of the Son. And it is in this likeness that the Spirit will bring us at last to the clear vision of the invisible Father in the Son's glory, which will also be our glory. Meanwhile, it is the Spirit who awakens in our heart the faith and hope in which we cry for the eschatological fulfillment and vision. And in this hope there is already a beginning, an earnest of the fulfillment. This is our contemplation: the realization and "experience" of the life-giving Spirit in Whom the Father is present to us through the Son, our way, truth and life. The realization that we are on the way, that because we are on the way, we are in that Truth which is the end, and by which we are already fully and eternally alive. Contemplation is the loving sense of this life and this presence and this eternity.

*December 22, 1964, V.182*

# Happy to Be Marginal

Yesterday I thought it would be snow—skies have been grey and even black for over a week. Clouds of birds gathered around the hermitage. Twenty robins or more, a dozen finches, jays, many juncos (including one I found dead on the porch), other small birds and even a couple of bluebirds—I had not seen them around in the winter. Yesterday morning about two I heard something scampering around in the house and found it was a little flying squirrel. I have no idea how he got in. I thought for a moment of keeping him and taming him, but opened the door and turned him loose. At least let the animals be free and be themselves! While they still can.

A man wrote an article in *America* magazine on the vernacular liturgy: "If the Church wants to sweep the world like the Beatles. . . ." With this kind of mentality, what can you expect? But I am afraid that is the trouble. The Church is conscious of being inferior now not only to the Communists but to four English kids with mops of hair (and I like them OK). More and more I see the importance of not mopping the world with the mops, Beatle or liturgical. I am glad to be marginal. The best thing I can do for the "world" is stay out of it—in so far as one can.

*December 14, 1966, VI.168–69*

# The Sense of a Journey Ended

After None—in the pretty pine wood of young pines by Saint Teresa's field (I still call it St. Teresa's wood)—where I have gone many times a week for four years, especially four summers, since 1957. The time has come for a kind of summing up of all this silence and sunlight and of those similar afternoons. Attached and at peace in this wood because it knows me so well now and I have no house there and nothing has ever been said or declared to indicate that I was there always. Nothing said it was "my place."

There I discovered Paraguay and for a while this wood was Paraguay (1957). I read a thing of Kierkegaard with a lovely paragraph on solitude—a bit of Henry Miller on Big Sur (in another place), much Suzuki, Vinoba Bhave. It is an oriental wood. I taught Nels Richardson (Frater Aelred) a little yoga there, walked and planned with Dom Gregorio anxiously there. There walked one afternoon after discovering some lyrics in the *I Ching*. Read *The Leopard* and Ungaretti there. Above all prayed and meditated there and will again.

St. Mary of Carmel after Vespers is tremendous: with the tall pines, the silence, the moon and stars above the pines as dark falls, the patterns of shadows, the vast valley and hills: everything speaks of a more mature and complete solitude. The pines are tall and not low. There is frankly a house, demanding not attachment but responsibility. A silence for dedication and not escape. Lit candles in the dusk. "This is my resting place forever"—the sense of a journey ended, of wandering at an end. *The first time in my life* I ever really felt I had come home and my waiting and looking were ended.

*December 26, 1960, IV.79–80*

# Idolizing the Calendar

Incomparable richness of Ananda K. Coomaraswamy! His book on Hinduism and Buddhism. I am giving it a first reading, in which I do not expect to understand and appreciate everything.

One point—already familiar—driven home more: whatever is done naturally may be either sacred or profane, according to the degree of our awareness, but whatever is done unnaturally is essentially and irrevocably profane!

One of the great problems of monastic life here, today, with machines, noise, etc., and commercialism, is that the unnatural is taken for the supernatural. No concern at all for the natural or for natural process leads to perversion and degradation of the spiritual life.

End of 1960. The tree still decorated. The tinfoil bell, the cedar wreaths, the drying pine boughs, the colored lights.

I was wondering at the beginning of morning meditation if it would be given me to see another twelve years—to come to New Year's, say, 1973. To live to be fifty-seven or nearly fifty-eight. Can such an age be possible? What foolish perspectives we get onto, by believing in our calendars. As if numbers were the great reality, the sure thing, the gods of life and death. The numbers, good old numbers, faceless, voiceless, will surely be there with nothing to say.

What is likely to happen in twelve more years? Is the final war so feared and so expected that it cannot after all happen—as if what everyone expected was by that very fact excluded?

Is this inanity of man's world finally going to work itself out to its ultimate absurdity?

*December 27 and 31, 1960, IV.80–81*

# The Hope Faith Gives Us

*(From Thomas Merton's letter to Tommie O'Callaghan*
*upon the death of her mother)*

It seems that we all have to face one sad thing after another. But let us not forget the hope our faith gives us. God is our strength and no amount of trouble should make us fail to realize it. On the contrary, trouble should help us deepen and confirm our trust. This is an old story, but as far as I am concerned, it is the one we always get back to. There is no other.

*June 28, 1968*

# A Happy Ending

Last night, after a prayer vigil in the novitiate chapel (didn't do a good job—was somewhat disorganized and distracted), I went to bed late at the hermitage. All quiet. No lights at Boone's or Newton's. Cold. Lay in bed and realized what I was: I was *happy.* Said the strange word *happiness* and realized that it was there, not as an "it" or object. It simply was. And I was that. And this morning, coming down, seeing the multitude of stars above the bare branches of the wood, I was suddenly hit, as it were, with the whole package of meaning of everything: that the immense mercy of God was upon me, that the Lord in infinite kindness had looked down on me and given me this vocation out of love, and that He had always intended this, and how foolish and trivial had been all my fears and desperation. And no matter what anyone else might do or say about it, however they might judge or evaluate it, all is irrelevant in the reality of my vocation to solitude, even though I am not a typical hermit. Quite the contrary, perhaps. It does not matter how I may or may not be classified. In the light of this simple fact of God's love and the form it has taken in the mystery of my life, classifications are ludicrous, and I have no further need to occupy my mind with them (if I ever did)—at least in this connection.

The only response is to go out from yourself with all that one is, which is nothing, and pour out that nothingness in gratitude that God is who He is. All speech is impertinent; it destroys the simplicity of that nothing before God by making it seem as if it had been "something."

*December 9, 1964, V.178*

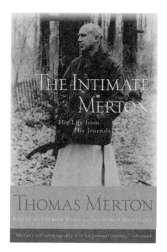

*The Intimate Merton:*
*His Life from His Journals*
ISBN: 0-06-251629-9
(Paperback)

*Dialogues with Silence:*
*Prayers and Drawings*
ISBN: 0-06-065602-6
(Hardcover)
ISBN: 0-06-065603-4
(Paperback)

*The Inner Experience:*
*Notes on Contemplation*
ISBN: 0-06-053928-3
(Hardcover)
ISBN: 0-06-059362-8
(Paperback)

*Want to receive notice*
*of events and new books*
*by Thomas Merton?*

*Sign up for Thomas*
*Merton's AuthorTracker at*
*www.authortracker.com*